THE TRAVEL GUIDE TO SOUTH AFRICA

Les de Villiers

Business Books International

The Travel Guide to South Africa
Travel
ISBN 0-916673-07-3

FOR RUTH, LAUREN AND ANDRIES

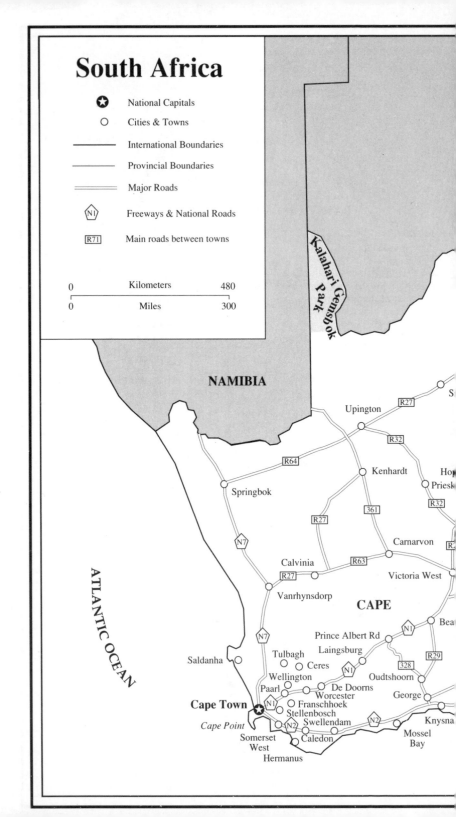

South Africa

★ National Capitals
○ Cities & Towns
—— International Boundaries
—— Provincial Boundaries
═══ Major Roads
Ⓝ1 Freeways & National Roads
R71 Main roads between towns

| 0 | Kilometers | 480 |
| 0 | Miles | 300 |

Kalahari Gemsbok Park

NAMIBIA

ATLANTIC OCEAN

Upington R27 S
R32
Springbok R64 Kenhardt Ho
Priesk
R27 361 R32
N7 Carnarvon R
Calvinia R63
R27 Victoria West
Vanrhynsdorp CAPE
N7 Prince Albert Rd N1 Bea
Tulbagh Laingsburg R29
Saldanha ○ Ceres 328
Wellington N1 Oudtshoorn
Paarl De Doorns George
N1 Worcester Knysna
Franschhoek
Cape Town Stellenbosch
Cape Point N2 Swellendam N2 Mossel
Somerset Caledon Bay
West
Hermanus

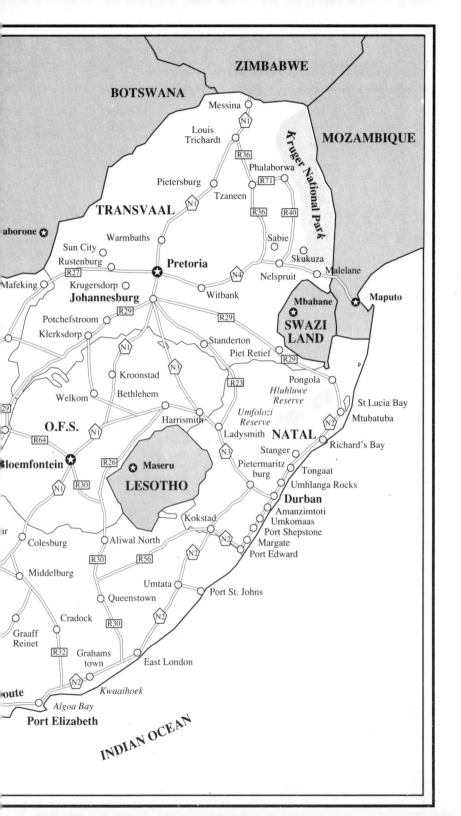

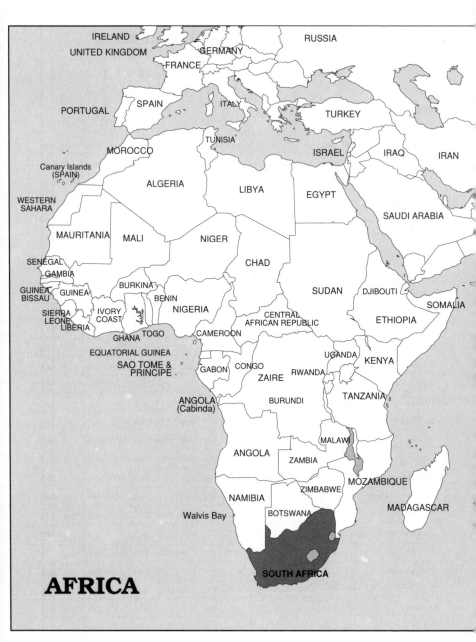

AFRICA

SOUTH AFRICA'S POSITION ON THE CONTINENT

DISTANCES IN SOUTH AFRICA

DISTANCES Kilometers 153 Miles 95	Bloemfontein		Cape Town		Durban		Johannesburg		Kimberley		Port Elizabeth		Pretoria	
Beaufort West	544	338	471	293	1192	741	950	590	504	313	501	311	1008	626
Bloemfontein	-	-	1015	631	648	403	406	252	177	110	677	421	464	288
Cape Town	1015	631	-	-	1776	1104	1421	883	975	606	790	491	1479	919
Colesberg	226	140	789	490	874	543	632	393	292	181	451	280	690	429
De Aar	346	215	774	481	994	618	752	467	305	190	520	323	810	503
Durban	648	403	1776	1104	-	-	585	364	825	513	986	613	660	410
East London	584	363	1100	684	676	420	990	615	780	485	310	193	1048	651
George	773	480	447	278	1329	826	1197	744	762	474	343	213	1237	769
Graaff-Reinet	424	263	681	423	944	587	830	516	490	304	291	181	888	552
Grahamstown	601	373	920	572	856	532	1007	626	667	414	130	81	1065	662
Harrismith	328	204	1343	835	320	199	282	175	505	314	1068	664	340	211
Johannesburg	406	252	1421	883	585	364	-	-	472	293	1083	673	58	36
Kimberley	177	110	975	606	825	513	472	293	-	-	743	462	523	325
Klerksdorp	288	179	1283	797	659	410	164	102	308	191	1009	627	222	138
Kroonstad	211	131	1226	762	551	342	195	121	339	211	888	552	253	157
Ladysmith	410	255	1425	885	238	148	364	226	587	365	1062	660	422	262
Messina	953	592	1968	1223	1149	714	547	340	1019	633	1630	1013	489	304
Nelspruit	760	472	1777	1104	712	442	358	222	830	516	1437	893	344	214
Oudtshoorn	743	462	506	314	1304	810	1190	739	703	437	402	250	1207	750
Pietermaritzburg	567	352	1695	1053	81	50	521	324	744	462	905	562	579	360
Pietersburg	742	461	1757	1092	938	583	336	209	808	502	1419	882	278	173
Port Elizabeth	677	421	790	491	986	613	1083	673	743	462	-	-	1141	709
Pretoria	464	288	1479	919	660	410	58	36	523	325	1141	709	-	-
Queenstown	377	234	1307	812	678	421	783	487	554	344	399	248	841	523
Sun City	468	291	1359	844	839	521	291	181	384	239	1145	712	299	186
Umtata	570	354	1335	830	441	274	881	547	747	464	545	339	939	583
Upington	588	365	894	556	1236	768	796	495	411	255	945	587	854	531
Welkom	153	95	1168	726	578	359	266	165	294	183	830	516	324	201

Useful travel tips to assist visitors in planning their trip, making the necessary arrangements and getting the most out of their visit to South Africa.

Safari is the primary reason for many a visit to Africa's foremost conservation nation. To get the most out of this journey into the unspoilt African veld, there are some important preparations - and choices - to be made between more than a hundred different options.

With 22,000 different kinds of wild flowering plants (one-tenth of the world's total) South Africa has been popular destination for botanists and florists from around the world for the past three centuries. Find out what you may expect to see in more than twenty major botanic gardens.

A little knowledge of South Africa's intriguing history not only makes monuments and museums come alive. Also the living acquire a new dimension as their actions and behavior are being weighed against those of past generations.

South Africa's seven major cities offer the visitor a wealth of sights and other delights. With descriptions of all important points of interest and detailed maps visitors should be able to make the most of their stay.

Rustic remnants of the past await visitors who venture beyond the city limits on one of several interesting rural routes. Points of interest range from quaint frontier towns in forest lands to oasis settlements in semi-deserts.

Dr Chris Barnard electrified the world in December 1968 when he performed the first human heart transplant at Groote Schuur Hospital in Cape Town. This momentous operation by the South African surgeon became the inspiration for others and gave new quality of life and added years to hopeless cardiac cases. For many years Dr Barnard remained in the frontline, developing new techniques and further improving man's chances for survival. He has been actively engaged in assisting South Africa's neighbors and ministering to needy patients from around the world.Today he divides his time between his Karoo farm and a new health center established near the world-famous Kruger National Park.

South African-born **Gary Player** became only the third man to have won all four major world golf titles and one of the original thirteen to be inducted in the World Golf Hall of Fame in 1974. He is still actively adding titles on the American Seniors Tour to the 150 regular tournament wins in twelve different countries since the mid-fifties. But he made his mark in the world of sports not only as a tenacious athlete but as a man of causes. His prize money when he won the US Open in 1965 went for cancer research and the promotion of golf among the youth. In South Africa he has established a school for blacks and several programs to assist underprivileged sportsmen.

Les de Villiers was born in the Karoo sheep farming region of South Africa. He lived there for forty five years before moving to the United States for business reasons. He divides his time between the United States and South Africa. He is has written extensively about business and politics. The titles include SOUTH AFRICA DRAWN IN COLOR, DOING BUSINESS WITH THE USA and DOING BUSINESS WITH SOUTHERN AFRICA. This travel book is based on many trips to the far corners of South Africa. As a consultant for American and South African companies he makes several visits every year to his mother country.

FOREWORD

South Africa has been described as a world in one country.

Having travelled more than eight million miles in pursuit of golf, I have been privileged to visit many interesting countries, but none quite as diverse as South Africa with her incomparable wildlife, rich ethnicity and majestic landscapes.

It is a kind of diversity that mesmerized a Rudyard Kipling and Arthur Conan Doyle, and more recently, a James Michener.

Visitors who follow the safari trail will soon discover why South Africa is blessed with a wider variety of wildlife than any other nation. Years ago, while others were merely preaching, South Africa was already practising conservation. My own brother Ian has been intimately involved in this important endeavor for over forty years. Together with other dedicated men and women he has played a key role in saving several threatened species, including the white rhino, which is thriving again after almost joining the dodo bird in the annals of extinct animals.

Ecotourism is a concept that will become increasingly important as more people come to realize that in saving the smallest creature, they not only serve God's universe, but also themselves. There is hardly an experience that can compare with a few days' retreat in the South African bush.

But enjoyment for the tourist in South Africa lies not only in the wilds. Within easy reach of its many game reserves are world class hotels, beach and golf resorts, and a host of other interesting pursuits. South Africa is undoubtedly the premier tourist destination in Africa.

I join all my fellow South Africans in inviting you to come and experience this microcosm at the tip of the African continent.

Welcome

Gary Player

This book is based on observing for many years the reactions of foreigners visiting South Africa - both for business or leisure.

Going to South Africa is not like visiting many other countries where visitors can remain blissfully unaware of the people and events around them while indulging in the good things of life.

Regardless of whether your purpose is to enjoy one of the many superb game reserves or experience the magnificent beaches or taste your way around the gracious Cape Dutch farmsteads of South Africa's winelands, the awareness is there that something really new and different is happening to this country almost every day.

The debate around post-apartheid South Africa is lively and open and most South Africans seem to enjoy it, notwithstanding some lingering uncertainties. The country has gone through many periods of crisis and come out of all these stronger and more viable.

This book is written in the belief that a working solution will be found. I say this because I believe in the integrity and goodwill of all South Africans, regardless of color, race or belief.

My friends, Gary Player and Chris Barnard, exemplify the very spirit that can make the new South Africa succeed - a sense of fair play and a love for the land of their birth and all its people.

I believe, as they do, that South Africa offers the traveler something very special and that it is soon destined to become one of the world's top tourist destinations. My advice is: Go soon before the big rush.

Bon Voyage.

Les de Villiers

FOREWORD

"To think that it could have happened in Africa!"

This is a response that I have often encountered during the many years of overseas travel and lecturing that followed that very first heart transplant in Cape Town in the late sixties.

Somehow otherwise informed people who have not been over here seem to have trouble in coming to terms with the fact that South Africa equals any part of the modern world when it comes to hospitals and medical services, hotels and restaurants, highways and airways and all those other things that make for comfort and safety.

Whenever I enjoy the breathtaking beauty of Cape Town from the slopes of Table Mountain, I am reminded of the words of Dag Hammarskjold when he stood here many years ago.

"This is not Africa," the former UN Secretary General exclaimed. "This is Europe." Hammarskjold spoke as a European. Many Americans have drawn similar comparisons with America.

In following the trail northwards, however, you will soon discover a healthy and unique blend of the First and Third Worlds.

If you wish to see the Africa of a Livingstone and Stanley without any hardship, South Africa is definitely the best choice.

Welcome.

Chris Barnard

SOUTH AFRICAN PROFILE

Population	39,550,00	est.1990
Urban	55%	
Annual Population Growth	2.7%	1989
Makeup		
Black	75.2%	
Whites	13.8%	
Coloreds	8.6%	
Indians (Asians)	2.6%	
Area (sq. miles/sq. km)	472,359	1,223,410
Major Urban Areas (1985)		
Johannesburg/Randburg	1,609,408	
Cape Town/Cape Peninsula	1,911,521	
East Rand	1,038,108	
Durban/Pinetown/Inanda	982,075	
Pretoria/Wonderboom/Soshanguve	822,925	
Port Elizabeth/Uitenhage	651,993	
West Rand	647,334	
Vanderbijlpark/Vereeniging/Sasolburg	540,142	
Bloemfontein	232,984	
Pietermaritzburg	192,417	
Free State Goldfields	320,319	
Kimberley	149,667	
East London/KingWilliamsTown	193,819	
GNP (US$ Millions)	$81,000	1987
Per capita income	$1,890	1987
Budget (US$ millions)	$23,300	1989
Foreign reserves (excl. gold)(US$Millions)	$1,000	1989
Gold (millions ounces)	5.5	
Inflation rate	14.7%	1989
Currency - Rand	US$0.36	Jan-91
Total trade (US$ millions)	$39,900	1989
Exports (US$ Millions)	$21,500	1989
Imports (US$ Millions)	$18,400	1989

Major Trading Partners (1985)
Exports: USA (15.1%) Japan (14.1%) UK (10.6%)
Imports: West Germany (20.1%) USA (16.7%) UK (14.6%) Japan (12.0%)

Resources & Main exports: Gold, coal, diamonds, platinum, chrome, manganese, nickel, phosphates, tin, uranium,vanadium,chemicals, machinery, steel, wool, dairy,products, grain.,tobacco, sugar, fruit, peanuts, grapes & wines

Automobiles	4,300,000
Passenger cars	3,100,000
Commercial vehicles	1,200,000

Mineral supplies
Ranking in the world

Manganese, Platinum Group, Gold, Alumino-silicates, Vanadium	1
Diamonds, Vermiculite, Coal, Uranium, Antimony	2
Zirconium min., Phosphate Rock, Fluorspar, Asbestos, Nickel	3
Titanium minerals, Zinc, Lead	4
Iron	5

TRAVEL TIPS

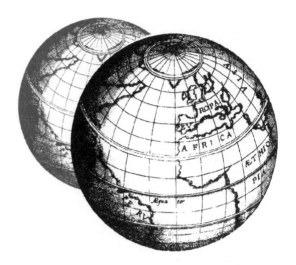

"I speak of Africa and golden joys."

This travel guide is for those who are contemplating a trip or already making arrangements to go to this continent of which Shakespeare spoke in such glittering terms in Henry IV.

This book is about the country of gold at the tip of this pear-shaped continent. South Africa is the most sophisticated country in Africa and at the same time richer in cultures and wildlife than the rest. Following in alphabetical order are tips on topics most often raised:

The following brief answers to questions regarding South Africa are supplemented with more detailed information. For further information please consult the index.

➡ **ACCOMMODATION:** There is a wide choice of hotels ranging from one to five star grading, luxury holiday apartments, beach cottages, game park chalets, guest farms and camping and caravan sites. The standard and service of graded hotels are strictly supervised by the South African Tourism Board. *(For a description and detailed listing see our chapters ON SAFARI and STAYING IN STYLE - page 179)*

➡ **AIR TRAVEL:** There are a number of international airlines providing convenient direct links to Johannesburg and in some cases Durban and Cape Town. Currently the following airlines are providing services to South Africa from major overseas departure points: Air Mauritius, Alitalia, British Airways, Cathay Pacific, China Airlines, El Al, KLM, Lufthansa, Luxavia, Qantas, Sabena, Singapore Airlines, Swissair, UTA, Varig. It is, however, **South African Airways**, the national carrier, that services these international routes most extensively with its large fleet of Boeing 747 airliners, linking up with its own network of domestic flights between major cities in South Africa. The airline is also a useful source of information and advice on travel to South Africa. *(See listing of addresses on page 234).* Although SAA dominates domestic routes services are also provided by a few additional airlines, including Comair, Flitestar, Link Airways and Magnum. On routes where no scheduled flights exist, air charters are used. For information about these charter services contact *South African Air Charters* at Lanseria Airport, near Johannesburg. *Tel. (011) 659-2770.*

➡ **ARRANGEMENTS:** There are many ways to make travel arrangements, depending on individual circumstances and preferences. Regardless of whether a traveler decides to make her or his own arrangements or leave it in the hands of a tour operator or travel agent, a phone call to the local **South African Tourism Board** office **(SATOUR)** is always a good beginning. Situated in many countries abroad, these offices do not only give sound advice but have a wide selection of brochures available. They will also provide the traveling public with a list of **tour operators** and **travel agents** with knowledge about South Africa in their area. Also **South African Airways**, the national carrier, is a useful source of information. Remember, this airline specializes in travel to South Africa. *(See KEY ADDRESSES - Page 234 for a listing of Satour and SAA offices).*

In **selecting** a travel agent or a tour operator to handle arrangements, travelers may wish to ask for references. Although most of these specialists in travel to Africa are reliable and experienced, in this trade, as in any other, the performance ranges between good, average and indifferent. Look for accreditations to recognized associations and membership of regulating bodies. The traveler may for medical or other unforeseen reasons be unable at the last minute to make a trip and discover that all or part of the tour money already paid has to be forfeited due to late cancellation. Therefore **trip cancellation insurance** is recommended.

➡ **BEST TIME TO GO:** When is the best time to visit South Africa? This one of the questions most often asked. There are many *best* times, depending on exactly what travelers want to do and in which part of the country they wish to visit. Game viewing in the Lowveld may, for example, be more rewarding during winter than in summer, when the foliage is sparse and animals more easily seen. *(See our chapter ON SAFARI - Page 27).*

Mid-summer in the subtropical Durban and Natal north and south coast areas is quite humid, so spring and fall and winter are the preferred seasons in this area. In Cape Town with its Mediterannean weather, however, winter's are usually wet and sometimes chilly so most visitors prefer the summer, spring and fall months. Summer is also the best time for wine tours and viewing the spectacular western Cape scenery. The weather in and around Johannesburg and also in the Orange Free State is pleasant throughout the year, although they both have more color in the rainy summer season. Travelers who wish to escape the should plan their visit around the school vacations. *(See HOLIDAYS in this section)*

BUS TRAVEL: There are buses serving routes in all the major cities - many of them red double-decker ones, reminiscent of London. There is also the option of bus services between cities, while several companies provide extensive tours around the country in luxury buses. The biggest, Connex, links up with Sartravel offices abroad in providing travelers complete services. *(For a listing of Connex and Sartravel numbers overseas, see KEY ADDRESSES)*

CAR & CAMPER RENTAL: Three major **car rental** firms - Avis, Budget and Imperial - are established in all the major centers and most of the other tourist spots around the country. Several have toll-free international and domestic reservations numbers. There are also a number of smaller competitors serving certain cities and regions. Some firms have **four-wheel drive vehicles** available for use in remote regions. Also available for rental from other firms are **chauffeur-driven limousines, campers** and **caravans**. The latter come with a variety of facilities and usually have their own stoves and refrigerators. Linen and kitchen utensils are optional. In all cases, except of course chauffeur-driven rentals, visitors will be asked for proof of identity (passport is sufficient) and a valid driver's license. Credit cards are accepted by most and in cases where payment is by travelers check or on a cash basis, a deposit will be required. *(For reservations and contact numbers, see page 233).*

CHILDREN: There are very few places where children are not allowed. But at most resorts, even the gambling casino's, separate entertainment and baby-sitting facilities are provided. Most beach resorts are geared towards amusement of the young. There are, however, private game lodges where children under certain age limits are not allowed to accompany game drives.

CHURCHES: Visitors will find their own denominations or a similar church in cities and other neighborhoods. South Africa is a country of many religions varying from Christianity, to Judaism, Moslem and Hindu. The black tribes also have their own traditional beliefs but their city folk belong mostly to Christian churches - some of them as part homegrown denominations - the largest being the Zion Christian Church with a membership of several million and headquarters near Pietersburg in the Transvaal.

CLIMATE: More than 40 per cent of South Africa's total land area lies in excess of 1,220 m (4,000 ft) above sea level. This influences both temperatures and rainfall in the interior. Highveld winter nights are frosty but the days bright with sun; thunderstorms bring a cool freshness in summer. With the exception of the southwest Cape Province, which has a Mediterranean-type climate (dry summers and winter rains) summer rainfall is experienced over most of the country. Winters are usually mild although snow falls on the mountain ranges of the Cape and Natal and occasionally in lower-lying areas, when a brief cold spell can be expected throughout the country. Since South Africa lies south of the Equator, the seasons are the reverse of those in the northern hemisphere: June/July is midwinter and Christmas-time falls in midsummer. The average number of sunshine hours in different parts of the country compares very favorably with the highest in the world.

Average annual hours of bright sunshine in the three capitals are: Cape Town 3,096; Pretoria 3,240; Bloemfontein 3,394. *(London has 1,480, Paris 1,740; Washington 2,200; Madrid 2,910 and Rome 2,360.)* The annual sunshine figures for other South African centres are: Johannesburg 3,175; Durban 2,413; Port Elizabeth 2,896; Kimberley 3,431; and Pietermaritzburg 2,440. At the main coastal resorts the annual average is 2,750. *(In comparison Bermuda has 2,600 and the French Riviera 2,700.)*

CREDIT CARDS: American Express, Diners Club, Visa and Mastercard are honored by most restaurants, stores, hotels, car rental firms and other points of sale and services. Proof of identity may be asked in some instances and it is therefore useful to carry a passport or other form of identification at all times.

CUSTOMS REQUIREMENTS: Personal effects are allowed into the country duty free. Visitors are also entitled to bring in R500 worth of other goods, apart from person, and duty will be levied at a flat rate of 20% on the first R1,000 over this allowance.

Limited quantities of alcoholic beverages, perfume, cigarettes and tobacco, are allowed in free of duty. Permits are required for firearms and are available at points of entry. They are valid for 180 days, and may be renewed at any South African police station.

DRIVING: Some 47 000 km of South Africa's roads are tarred and it is possible to plan an extensive tour, including most of the country's major attractions (with the exception of the game reserves), without leaving tarmac.

Driving is on the **left side** of the road and posted speed limits are strictly enforced. Basic **maps** can be obtained from car rental firms, but more extensive and detailed ones are on sale at most bookstores and some filling stations. Although **road signs** conform to international standards, there are a few unique ones. *(See symbols on page 239).* As in most other countries drunken driving is treated as a serious offense and spot-checks are undertaken on major routes.

Those who plan to undertake a long and extensive journey lasting for several weeks, may consider using the **Automobile Association** of South Africa with offices and emergency services around the country. The AA of South Africa has reciprocal arrangements with other similar organizations abroad through the *Alliance Internationale de Tourisme (AIT)* and the *Federation de l'Automobile (FIA).* Services provided by the South African Automobile Association include, apart from breakdown services and emergency assistance, advice on road travel, camping and other accommodation and tourist attractions.

It publishes a wide range of detailed maps and tour guides. For further information contact the *Automobile Association, AA House, 66 De Korte Street, Braamfontein, Johannesburg 2001. Tel. (011) 403-5700.*

DRUG STORES: Most pharmacies or drug stores stay open until 18h00 during weekdays and close at 13h00 on Saturdays. Major cities all have emergency drug stores open on a 24 hour basis. A hotel concierge or the

Yellow Pages should pinpoint these without much trouble. Visitors from especially the United States will find that several drugs available only on a prescribed basis at home, are sold over-the-counter.

➠ **DRUGS:** There are **heavy penalties** in South Africa for trading or possessing of drugs. The most commonly abused drug is *dagga*, the local version of marijuana. *Heroin* and *cocaine* form a small percentage of the drug scene and on the whole the country has a relatively low incidence of drug abuse when compared with other industrial nations.

➠ **ELECTRICITY:** Power supply is 220/240 volt 50 cycle in most parts of the country. The European type two pin plug is needed. This in turn requires another adaptor plug before it can be connected to the wall socket. These are usually available on loan at major hotels in South Africa. Be certain, however, to bring along transformers where needed. Although some stores in major cities carry them, it is not readily available. Three to five star hotels usually have 110 volt outlets for electric shavers in bathrooms and often provide hair dryers and irons.

➠ **FLORA AND FAUNA:** South Africa has a wealth of flora and fauna. Some 22 000 species of flowering plants (of which 730 are classed as trees) are indigenous to the country, and about 900 species of birds, representing 22 out of the world's 27 living orders, are found here. The aboriginal animals range from elephants to tiny shrews and include many carnivores as well as a large number and diversity of antelopes and other herbivores. Apart from the 17 major national parks (with Kruger Park as the largest) there close

to 200 other proclaimed wildlife sanctuaries, provincial parks and private game lodges.

➠ **GAMBLING:** Although horse racing is the popular past-time of the wealthy and the wishful, gambling casinos are not allowed by law. Neither are any games of chance for money or lotteries. Gambling flourishes, however, in the homelands which are expected to be rejoining South Africa in its new form. In the meantime visitors in search of gambling have easy access to these sophisticated casino resorts near cities such as Pretoria, Johannesburg, Durban and Port Elizabeth. These resorts offer not only gambling but a whole range of other recreation and entertainment worthy of the best in Las Vegas. *(See also RESORTS AND SPORTS - Page 191 & STAYING IN STYLE - Page 179).*

➠ **GETTING ALONG:** South Africa is a multi-cultured country and visitors will encounter many different languages. As one of the official languages **English** is, however, understood and spoken in most parts - except the furthest outposts or some rural tribal regions. Dutch and Flemish visitors will find the second official language, **Afrikaans**, familiar to their own.

Other European tongues spoken by small white minorities are **Dutch, German, Portuguese, French, Italian** and **Greek**. Among whites, Afrikaans is the first language for about sixty percent and English for forty percent. Most Afrikaners speak English fluently and a large percentage of the English-speaking understand Afrikaans. Coloreds usually speak Afrikaans at home, but are bilingual as well. Many blacks speak their own mother tongue and English as well as Afrikaans.

In EMERGENCY dial 10111

Although Afrikaans and English are the official languages, **Zulu** and **Xhosa** are widely used among the black peoples of South Africa. These are both Nguni languages. Blacks in South Africa belong to four major linguistic groupings, each speaking a variety of interrelated languages and dialects. Apart from the Nguni there are the **Sotho, Venda** and **Tsonga** groupings. The Asian or East **Indian** communities speak English, **Gujarati, Urdu, Tamil, Hindi** and **Telegu**. On the mines and in some industries a *lingua franca* called **Fanagalo** is used between different black tribes and the whites. Consisting of Zulu, English and Afrikaans, it has a limited vocabulary and simple grammar. Of the original Khoisan languages only San or **Bushmen** is still spoken in the Kalahari desert, while traces of Khoi Khoin or Hottentot are only to be found in the click-sounds of the Xhosa tongue. *(See the chapter HISTORIC TRAILS and the sampling of phrases on this page).*

➡ **HANDICAPPED TRAVELERS:** There are special facilities for the physically handicapped in most first-class South African hotels, resorts, national game parks and lodges, restaurants and places of entertainment. (Kruger National Park has built specially designed chalets at Skukuza rest-camp for the exclusive use of the handicapped.). Reserved parking and other special facilities for the handicapped are identified in literature and on site with the internationally recognized symbol.

Some car rental firms have cars specially fitted with hand controls, while air carriers offer aid to handicapped passengers at airports. (South African Airways has been rated among the top performers internationally in catering to the needs of physically and other handicapped passengers). Wheelchair and other equipment for the disabled can be rented in the major cities. In several botanical gardens and zoos there are special smell and touch tours to accommodate to the blind.

➡ **HEALTH REQUIREMENTS:** Visitors who come from or pass through a **yellow fever** zone on their way to South Africa should produce a valid International Certificate of Vaccination on their arrival. Passengers whose aircraft land for refuelling in or travel in transit through an airport in a yellow fever zone do not need a vaccination certificate. **Cholera** and **smallpox** vaccination certificates are **not** required. Visitors are not screened for **Aids** at present. Travellers who intend to visit the Transvaal Lowveld or northern Natal and Zululand, where most of the National Parks and private game lodges are situated, are urged to begin a course of anti-**malaria** tablets before starting out. These are sold over the counter at pharmacies (drug stores) in South Africa and some other countries and by doctors' prescription in others.

➡ **HIKING: This** form of recreation has become very popular with South

---

A FEW PHRASES AND WORDS

English	Afrikaans
Good morning	Goeie more
Good afternoon	Goeie middag
Good evening	Goeienaand
Yes	Ja
Thank you	Dankie
No	Nee
No thank you	Nee dankie
Goodbye	Totsiens
My name is....	My naam is
What is your name?	Wat is jou naam?
Where is a garage?	Waar is die naaste garage?
...the nearest hotel?	Waar is die naaste hotel?
...the nearest doctor?	Waar is die naaste dokter?
...the nearest telephone?	Waar is die naaste telefoon
...the nearest hospital?	Waar is die naaste hospitaa
My car has broken down	My motorkar het gaan staa
Show me the way to.....	Kan u my die pad beduie n
Is this the right way to.....	Is dit die regte pad na.....
I am sick	Ek is siek
My wife is sick	My vrou is siek
My child is sick	My kind is siek
This person is sick	Hierdie persoon is siek

Africans and increasing numbers of overseas visitors. With its majestic mountains, rich in fauna and flora, and conducive weather, South Africa lends itself to **hiking.** In recent years conservation and tourism authorities have joined together to design a network of trails called the **National Hiking Way,** comprising main, supplementary and connecting routes. The major regions included are the mountains and coastlines of the Cape and Natal, and the Eastern Transvaal escarpment. Trails vary in length from 5 km to some 100 km and in degree of difficulty from mild to strenuous. Trails are equipped with overnight huts, cooking and washing facilities. At a nominal fee full information and detailed maps of the trails can be purchased from the *National Hiking Highway Board, Private Bag X447, Pretoria 0001. Tel, (012) 310-3911.*

Mountaineering has a small but very active group that assists visitors interested in challenging some of the steep mountain slopes. Often combined with hiking, it is a non-competitive sport in South Africa. The most popular areas for climbing are peaks such as Montaux-Sources in the Drakensberg range, the mountains of the Western Cape, including famous Table Mountain, and the Magaliesberg range in the Transvaal. Equipment is available for sale but not for rental at specialized stores. For information contact *The Honorary Secretary, the Mountain Club of South Africa, 97 Hatfield Street, Gardens, Cape Town 8001. Tel. (021) 45-3412.*

➡ **HOLIDAYS:** The major **official holidays** are New Year's Day; Good Friday; Family Day (I April); Founders' Day (6 April); Workers' Day (I May); Ascension Day; Republic Day (31 May); Kruger Day (10 October); Day of the Covenant (16 December); Christmas Day (25 December) and the Day of Goodwill (26 December). In the Western Cape 2 January (Boxing Day) is celebrated, while Soweto Day (16 June) is commemorated by many South Africans. Jewish, Islamic and Hindu communities observe also their own holy days.

Zulu	Xhosa
Sakubona	Molo
Sakubona	Molo
Sakubona	Molo
Yebo	Ewe
Niyabonga	Enkosi
Hayi	Hayi
Hayi ngiyabonga	Hayi enkosi
Hamba kahle	Hamba kahuhle
Igama lam ngu....	Igama lam ngu....
Igama lakho ngubani?	Ungubani igama lakho?
Likuphi igaraji elikufuphi?	Iphi igaraji ekufuphi apha?
Likuphi ihotele elikufuphi?	Iphi ihoteli ekufuphi apha?
Ukuphi efoni okufuphi?	Uphi ugqirha okufuphi apha?
Ukuphi udokotela okufuphi?	Iphi ifoni ekufuphi alpha?
Sikuphi isibbhedlela esikufufphi?	Siphi isibhedlele esikufuphi apha?
Imoto yami yonakele	Imoto yam yaphukile
Ungangibonisa umgaco oya e....	Ungandikhombisa indlela eya e....
Ingaba ngumwaco ochanekile lo oya e....	Ingaba yindlela echanekileyo la eya e....
Ngiyafa	Ndiyagula
Umkami uyafa	Inkosikazi yam iyagula
Ingane yami iyafa	Umntwana wam uyagula
Lo muntu uyafa	Lo mntu uyagula

Although **school vacations** vary between the four provinces, most observe reasonably extensive holiday periods from mid-December to mid-January and from mid-June to mid-July. They also have ten day to two week long vacations around Easter and during September.

► LIQUOR: In most cases **bars** stay open from 10h00 and close at 23h00 on weekdays and Saturdays. Normally alcoholic beverages are only served with meals on Sundays. City **nightclubs** remain open until 02h00 or later on weekdays. Deluxe hotels offer alcoholic beverages on a 24-hour room service basis. **Liquor stores** do business from 08h00 to 18h00 on weekdays and Saturdays until 13h00. Some **grocery stores and supermarkets** offer beer and wine (not spirits) during licensing hours.

Restaurants fall into three categories: fully licensed, licensed for wine and beer (malt), or unlicensed. The last category includes some of the best restaurants in the country and allow patrons bring their own alcoholic beverages. This gives patrons an opportunity to bring their favorite wine. *(See the chapter WINE COUNTRY for buying tips).*

► MALARIA: Although this disease is very much under control in South Africa, visitors to some of the game regions, notably the Transvaal Lowveld and northern Natal, are advised to take a course of malaria pills on a prophylactic basis, starting a week before the actual visit. While these pills are obtained on a prescribed basis only in some countries, they can be purchased over-the-counter at drug stores in South Africa.

► MEDICAL SERVICES: One of the areas where South Africa stands out from the rest on the continent (and competes with the most sophisticated in the world) is in medical services. Remember this is where Dr Christiaan Barnard performed the world's first heart transplant in 1968. The possibility of contracting Aids is about what one could expect in developed countries such as the United States, Britain, Germany or Japan. Highly unlikely but as we have seen elsewhere in the developed world, not impossible. The doctor, hospital and ambulance per capita ratio is comfortable and reassuring. Foreign visitors are advised to determine beforehand to what extent their own medical insurance will cover emergencies while in South Africa. *(See also MALARIA in this section)*

► METRIC SYSTEM: Expect to see everything measured, weighed and expressed in metric terms. *(For those who do not travel conversion calculators, a conversion table is provided on page 238).*

► MONEY MATTERS: The South African **currency** is based on the Rand (R), consisting of 100 cents (c). Coins are in denominations of 1c, 2c, 5c, 10c, 20c, 50c, R1 and R2. The R2 coin is much smaller than the 50c and R1 pieces, but square-round to distinguish it from the 20 cent piece, which is similar in size. Bank notes are in denominations of R5, R10, R20 and R50. There is no limit on amount of **foreign currency** that travelers may bring into the country. They are, however, limited to R500 in South African currency. Foreign currency can be **converted** into rands at banks, certain hotels and other bureaus such as Thomas Cook and American Express. There are facilities at Jan Smuts Airport and other major ports of entry to exchange currency on arrival and departure.

South African **banks** follow the same practices as their counterparts in Europe, America and the Far East. Apart from local banking groups, a number of foreign banks are also represented. **Banking hours** in the major cities and towns are usually from 09h00 to 15h30 on weekdays and from 08h30 or 09h00 to 11h00 on Saturdays. Most hotels, restaurants, stores and other places of business accept one or more of the major **credit cards**. In some instances travellers may be required to show proof of identity in the form of a passport or driver's license.

➠ **NIGHT LIFE:** Although some of the gambling resorts succeed in duplicating (and sometimes surpassing) Las Vegas glitz and glamor of their spectaculars, night life in South Africa is no throbbing affair. There are, however, some places with local hit music groups which may be of interest and a few nightclubs where the local socialites like to be seen. Theater in most cities is alive and well and worth considering. As in every other city, the best up-to-date informants are hotel concierges or the entertainment pages of the local press.

➠ **PACKING:** Usually informal, casual dress is sufficient, with elegant or smart casual wear for occasions where tie and jacket are required at restaurants, nightclubs or concerts. For the summer months from October to April lightweight clothing is sufficient, but keep in mind that even hot areas such as the Lowveld where the game parks are situated, may experience chilly nights in summer and require at least a sweater or jacket. Most of the country, with the exception of the Western Cape region, has rains in summer. A compact umbrella or raincoat is useful. During the winter months warm clothing is needed, even indoors especially in some public places where central heating often seems to be turned down low or absent.

➠ **PASSPORTS & VISAS:** Foreigners need valid passports and, in most cases, visas to gain entry to South Africa.

Holiday travellers from the United Kingdom, Ireland, Germany and Lichtenstein, and neighboring Lesotho, Swaziland and Botswana, are exempt from the visa requirements as long as their visit does not exceed 14 days. Visas are obtained free of charge from South African diplomatic and consular offices abroad and in countries where there is no South African diplomatic presence, from the nearest overseas mission or by writing to the *Director General of Home Affairs, Private Bag X114, Pretoria 0001 (Telex: 321 353 SA)* directly.

Applicants are required to fill out a form and submit it together with their passport, either in person or by secure mail. Issuance of a visa can take time and travellers are advised to obtain this essential travel document as soon as they have made their decision to visit South Africa. Depending on circumstances, diplomatic missions will handle applications on an emergency basis.

Transit visas are issued to travellers who pass through South Africa on their way to or from a neighboring country. Applicants for these transit visas must produce a return ticket and a visa or other written authority from the country of destination. *(For the nearest South African diplomatic missions see KEY ADDRESSES - Page 233).*

➠ **PETS:** There are a few hotels that would permit guests to bring their dogs or cats (or other pets) along and some even provide kennels. Assume, however, that pets are prohibited at most establishments and definitely not allowed at game parks.

➠ **PHOTOGRAPHY:** Film is readily available in most centers and at the game parks. In city stores the range in make and speed and size is as wide as any photographer may require. Some visitors, however, still prefer to bring their own supply. One hour development is offered in most cities and some touristic towns. Although custom photographic batteries may be in supply at specialized camera stores, it is prudent to carry a spare. Cameras and photographic equipment are imported and steeply priced.

➡ **RESTAURANTS:** South Africa is probably one of the world's most desirable regions as far as food and wine are concerned. Hundreds of good to outstanding restaurants around the country provide food fare that varies from the interesting traditional dishes to genuine French, Continental, Middle Eastern and Far Eastern. Good local wines are plentiful and easy to obtain at liquor stores and estates. *(See the chapters DINING AND WINING, - Page 213 for a detailed listing, and WINE COUNTRY - Page 153)*

➡ **SEA TRAVEL:** A few shipping lines offer passenger services, often on cargo ships, from Europe to South Africa. Expect to pay fares equal to staying in a first class hotel for several weeks.

➡ **SECURITY:** Seasoned travelers know the potential pitfalls when leaving valuables unattended or strolling down dark and lonely alleys in cities anywhere in the world. Unfortunately petty thievery and more serious crime is also a factor in South Africa. Take the same precautions as you would in any major city.

Here are a few universal rules:

Don't walk alone in apparently deserted areas, especially in and around the cities. It is preferable and usually more enjoyable to walk with company or in groups.
Don't carry large sums of cash in your purse or pocket..
Be aware of the possibility of pick-pockets and bag snatchers in crowded areas.

Don't leave valuables in a hotel room. Most of them offer safety deposit box services.
Make photocopies of the first few pages of your passport, air ticket and other important travel documents. These should obviously be in safekeeping separate from the originals and will helps towards expediting replacement in case of loss or theft.
Be certain that you have adequate insurance cover.

➡ **SHOPPING:** Shopping in South Africa's major malls may leave the feeling of never having left home. They're sophisticated and well stocked. Expect, however, to pay more for items such as appliances, photographic equipment, perfumes, books and imported items than in most other developed countries.

Those looking for worthwhile **mementoes** or local wares to take home, will find curio stores in the malls and major hotels as well as some of the game parks. Apart from tribal carvings, beadwork, leather items from ostrich and other exotic skins, ivory jewelry and carvings are available. (South Africa's conservation authorities maintain strict control over the culling of its overpopulated elephant regions and money from ivory sales is usually plowed back into conservation).

South African **art** is sold by a number of galleries in major city centers and a budding entertainment industry feeds interesting recordings of local hits in tape and CD form into the regular **music** stores. Visitors who have tasted South African **wines** in restaurants, or went on a wine tasting tour in the Cape, may decide to purchase a few bottles for export - or arrange to have some delivered at their home address. *(See the chapter WINE COUNTRY and the listing of addresses on page 233)*

STAYING INFORMED: All cities have local daily **newspapers** published in English and Afrikaans. Although the focus is largely on local news and foreign happenings of specific importance to South Africa, some papers devote extensive space to international news in general. The mass circulation Sunday newspapers tend to be more sensational than purely informative. Leading hotels and magazine and book stores also carry leading papers from abroad (sold at a premium and dated by a day or more), as well as a full range of international **magazines. South** Africa offers its own wide range of magazines - varying from upmarket to lowbrow, financial to female, and political to polemical. The daily political debate that has always been part of South Africa, makes for interesting reading - and can be as good an education as any to understanding the complexities of modern-day South Africa.

Radio and television operated by the semi-government South African Broadcasting Service offer programs in English, Afrikaans, Zulu, Xhosa, Sesotho, Setswana, Tsonga, and Venda. Private radio is beamed in from neighboring territories and M-Net, operated by a consortium of newspapers provide an additional pay TV channel. Its variety of entertainment programs, sport, and feature films adds to the choices of channels available at most hotels. While the SABC telecasts the American Cable News Network (CNN) service at regular times, some hotels subscribe to this news network on a full-time basis.

TAXIS: Taxicabs are available at major hotels and a few other strategic points in the cities. They normally don't cruise for pick-ups and will only be available by chance after dropping off passengers and returning to their taxi rank. Fees are by meter and tipping is about ten percent. In the center of Johannesburg visitors will see minibuses moving along the streets picking up and dropping passengers along the way. These mini-buses are part of a thriving black-owned business that also maintains links with Soweto and other townships near Johannesburg. *(See also BUS SERVICES in this section).*

TELEPHONES & FAXES: Most countries can be dialed directly from South Africa which has a fully automated telephone system in most parts - except a few remote rural regions. All major hotels have fax machines at the disposal of their guests, as well as telex services. Telephone directories will list all the international dialing codes. Both local and long-distance calls are metered on a time basis and every second counts in terms of cost.

Also keep in mind that as elsewhere hotels levy a charge on every call. Should visitors wish to have their relatives at home call them they should keep in mind that regardless of where the call originates from the zero (0) in front of the city code, which is used domestically, has to be dropped. For example, in dialing Johannesburg from overseas the caller should use South Africa's country code 27 + 11 (instead of 011) + the number of the hotel.

TIPPING: Tips are normally not included. At restaurants between 10-15% is adequate. Hotel, airport and railway porters are normally given R2. At game lodges it is customary to contribute to a communal tip for the game rangers and other staff involved in providing hospitality and services. In this, as in any other cases, the ultimate yardstick is good service.

TRAIN TRAVEL: Although there are suburban train services and the possibility of convenient regular long-distance travel by train, the **Blue Train** usually comes to mind first when foreigners think in terms of trains in South Africa. This luxury train offers a full overnight service and accommodations ranging from luxury suites (Type A) to standard (Type D) Lunch, dinner and breakfast are included in the fare. Amenities include baths, showers, a lounge, bar, dining room and all the comforts that go with five star treatment. The Blue Train starts its journey from either Cape Town or Pretoria and makes a major stop in Johannesburg. It is rated among the top few in the world by connoisseurs and usually requires reservations months ahead. In several countries overseas *Sartravel offices handle reservations and in other cases bookings are made by contacting the Johannesburg offices of Spoornet - Tel. (011) 773-7640. Fax. (011) 773-7643.*

Spoornet which owns and operates the Blue Train, also offers somewhat less luxurious and slower name train services between Johannesburg and several other points: **Trans-Karoo** to Cape Town; **Trans-Natal** to Durban; **Algoa** to Port Elizabeth; **Amatola** to East London; **Komati** to Komatipoort (near Kruger National Park); and the **Bosvelder** (Bushvelder) to Louis Trichardt. These trains have dining saloons and operate catering trolleys; offer sleeping berths in first and second class two passenger coupes and six passenger compartments.

Despite the advent of diesel and electricity, **steam train** buffs will find in South Africa quite a few remaining steam locomotives operating commercially. Spoornet offers custom steam train tours around the country. *For detail contact the nearest Sartravel office or Spoornet in Johannesburg.*

For short runs there are narrow gauge trains in the Southern and Eastern Cape and Natal. The Class 24 **Outeniqua Choo-Tjoe** steams from George to Knysna and back every day. The journey starts at eight in the morning and returns to George at about five in the afternoon and leaves time for a quick lunch at Knysna. It is actually a working freight train with passenger coaches. The **Dias Express** in Port Elizabeth offers a short journey along the beach and the **Apple Express** ventures from this resort city into the spectacular Long Kloof area, crossing the 125 m high bridge Van Stadens River Gorge. (This is the world's highest narrow gauge bridge). The **Banana Express** operates along the South Coast of Natal. In all these cases tickets can be purchased at the point of departure or any other railroad station around the country.

The independent **Rovos Rail** offers unique four day steam train safaris through the Eastern Transvaal in meticulously restored pre-1950 coaches. Tours include a 24-hour stay at one of the private game lodges in the area, guided tours by luxury bus at stops, all meals, accommodation, liquor and insurance. There is also the opportunity to travel one way by train and return by road or air. Rovos also operates the old Edwardian-style restored Victoria Hotel near the Pretoria station from where its tours depart. *Reservations and information: Rovos Rail, Box 2837, Pretoria 0001. Tel. (012) 323-6052. Fax. (012) 323-0843.*

▶ TRIP CANCELLATION INSURANCE: Most reputable travel agencies offer such insurance at standard rates. This protects the traveler against heavy penalties by way of lost deposits in the case of last-minute cancellations in the event of sickness or other emergency. It may also cover emergency cancellation after the trip actually started.

▶ WATER Throughout South Africa at hotels, inns, lodges and other public places faucet or tap water is safe. Be careful, however, about dipping into or drinking water at pools and slow moving streams in some of the outlying areas, as this may contain organisms, including *bilharzia*.

ON SAFARI

We are going on safari.

This is how most first time visitors describe their impending visit to Africa. Despite all its other attractions, tracking wildlife in their natural habitat is still the main drawcard for visitors to South Africa.

Safari means journey in Kiswahili. A journey can take many forms. In this section we discuss the more than one hundred options open to visitors who wish to go on safari to South Africa - Africa's foremost conservation nation.

Safari conjures up visions of people in khaki and pith helmets snaking with a whole army of scantily clad natives through the lion-ridden jungles and crocodile-infested rivers. These are images created by Livingstone, Stanley, Teddy Roosevelt, and more recently Hemingway and Ruark. It is one perpetuated by the dream merchants of Hollywood in films ranging from *African Queen* to *Out of Africa*.

Although those who insist on having hardship with their game viewing may do so by opting for long hikes (under supervision) today's safari's are pleasant, relaxing experiences, designed to be enjoyed by young and old alike, both the fit and infirm.

Well-managed, conservation-conscious national and private game parks in South Africa provide visitors with the opportunity to view wildlife on hazard and hassle-free drives and walks. Game viewing is as good as it is ever going to be in South Africa, where conservation has been a science long before it became a slogan elsewhere.

South Africa offers Africa's widest variety of animals. Mammals alone number close to three hundred species, ranging from the tiny pygmy shrew to the big friendly giant, the elephant. It has more than 800 bird species - one tenth of the world's total.

Conservation

Conservation is in the hands of both governmental and private institutions. Private organizations such as the Southern African Nature Foundation, the Endangered Wildlife Trust, the Rhino Foundation and the International Wilderness Leadership Foundation, as well as several statutory bodies assist Mother Nature and her creatures to thrive at the tip of the African continent. Personalities such as Ian Player, Anthony Hall, John Ledger and Clive Walker have been recognized around the world for their invaluable contribution to wildlife preservation.

The national carrier, South African Airways, established the Heritage Foundation to promote genuine ecotourism by raising money for various conservation projects. The airline itself pledged a portion of its earnings on every overseas ticket to conservation and has donated hundreds of thousands of dollars to conservation over the past few years.

Early Days

Before Jan Van Riebeeck and the first white settlers arrived, the native Hottentot and Bushmen lived in harmony with nature - hunting only

On Safari (Drawing by E Heyn)

when they needed food. With their primitive bows and arrows and throwing spears, they were in any event hardly a threat to any of the species.

In the mid-seventeenth century the Dutch arrived with their guns. In the beginning the rhinoceros with its armor-like skin seemed almost impervious to these newcomers with their flint-lock guns. In 1657 Commander van Riebeeck records in his diary the grotesque story of a rhinoceros being killed after it got stuck in the mud.

"It took more than a hundred shots before he was killed," Van Riebeeck quotes a messenger as saying. *"Many bullets bounded off his body so that we hewed out a piece of his side with axes, and then shot between the ribs and the entrails, and killed him."*

But some antelope were less fortunate. The very first animal that succumbed and disappeared from the face of South Africa as the settlers moved northwards in search of new grazing, was the *blaauwbok* or blue buck.

Another graceful antelope, die *bontebok*, was saved in the nick of time by a handful of thoughtful farmers who held a few specimens in captivity and eventually helped the authorities to breed them back into large numbers in the Bontebok National Park.

ZEBRA TO ZERO

It was, however, the zebra that became the target for the most senseless carnage in the history of South Africa. The last animal on the alphabet, the zebra became one of the first to fall prey as a wave of European settlers progressed north, gun in hand. These early cattle farmers viewed the zebra as a drain on valuable grazing land. They also found a few uses for its skin. The meat was not very tasty but could be fed to farm workers and slaves.

Described more than two thousand years ago by Roman historian Dio Cassius as *"horses of the sun, resembling tigers"*, zebras were encountered in several colorings and shapes and in very large numbers when the Cape was settled.

Travelling around the South African interior in 1811 English naturalist William Burchell encountered large herds of these striped sun horses.

"I could compare it to nothing but to the din of a tremendous charge of cavalry, or to the rushing of a mighty tempest," wrote Burchell. *"I could not estimate the accumulated number at less than fifteen thousand, a great extent of the country being actually chequered black and white with their congregated masses."*

Before the end of that century, the plains fell silent. The last living quagga had died in an Amsterdam zoo. This zebra species was called *quahkah* by the Hottentot tribes. The word imitated its bark-like neighing and was changed to *quagga* by the Dutch. The quagga had stripes down from his head to its shoulders and the rest of its body was light brown. Today *Equus Quagga Quagga* is to be seen only in old etchings.

Extinct Quagga - 1800 etching

29

Other zebra family members narrowly escaped the same fate. Burchell's zebra (so named after the naturalist) found refuge in the north, while the Cape Mountain zebra dwindled down to a few on a farm before they were nurtured back to bigger herds in the Cape Mountain Zebra Park.

Kruger Millions

Until this day there is much speculation in South Africa about the so-called Kruger Millions. Supposedly at the turn of the century, the Boers buried millions of gold coins at a secret spot as the British troops advanced towards Pretoria. If there is, however, a real treasure that Oom Paul Kruger, the President of the old Transvaal Republic, left, it is undoubtedly the Kruger National Park.

Over strenuous objections from his constituents, Paul Kruger set aside millions of acres for wildlife protection. These Transvaal farmers found it difficult to accept that so much in good grazing land should "go waste." But Kruger persisted and today this park named after him ranks as one of the world's premier conservation areas.

Male lion (Drawing by Lydekker)

Game reserves

Following Kruger's lead numerous other national parks and a growing number of private game reserves and lodges sprung up around South Africa.

Visitors have a choice between more than a hundred, depending on the time at their disposal, their budgets and their preferences. Some of these areas are small and compact, others large and complex, some offer free day-trips, most of them reasonably priced, and a few are quite expensive and exclusive.

Where to Go

For those who wish to see a good cross section of African wildlife, including the so-called Big Five (buffalo, elephant, lion, leopard and rhinoceros), Kruger National Park and the adjoining private game lodges offer the best opportunities.

Visitors who wish to have the experience without spending big bucks usually opt for Kruger National Park, while others who do not mind dipping a little deeper into their pockets, tend to go to one of a number of private game parks.

There are tours where operators combine overnighting in Skukuza, one of the Kruger Park's major rest camps, with a day in one of the nearby private game parks. This is a convenient compromise for tourists on a budget who also wish to experience a private game park. Tourists without any monetary restraints have the option of staying in a secluded mountain lodge and shuttling by helicopter to one of the private game parks.

The difference

So what is the difference between Kruger National Park and the private game parks?

Kruger Park offers more wildlife in a larger area than any of the smaller private game parks. Attached like a kernel to the bean-shaped Kruger Park, the private game areas share some wildlife between themselves and to a certain extent with the national park. Most of the private game lodges have traverse arrangements among themselves, leaving their borders open for free movement of animals.

The rule of thumb is that visitors to the private lodges are bound to see more animals in a shorter time than they would in the much larger Kruger Park, even though the latter outstrips the rest many times over in animal population. The rates are also higher.

In these private game reserves, experienced game rangers take visitors off the beaten track in open landrover vehicles, tracking animals. In Kruger visitors also have the option of four wheel drive excursions and interesting hiking trails, but normally trips are undertaken in closed vehicles on clearly defined routes. Thoughtful rangers in Kruger Park do, however, advise self-drive tourists of worthwhile sightings to help them see as much as possible.

CROSSED FINGERS

Sometimes, however, crossed fingers seem to work better than the rule of thumb as visitors to Kruger encounter a larger variety of animals in bigger numbers than others who paid more to go to private reserves. These are not zoos and although rangers have a fair indication of the migration and general location of the animals, chance plays a role.

At both Kruger and the private game parks, water holes at the right time of day usually present good opportunities to see a variety of animals - and if you're very lucky, a kill by lions or leopards.

He was known as the lion of the Transvaal. Paul Kruger was a fearless Boer leader who challenged

President Paul Kruger

the full might of the British Empire at the turn of the century.

His name is immortalized in many ways, ranging from a town called Krugersdorp to gold coins, named Krugerrands. But perhaps his greatest legacy is the Kruger National Park. As an enthusiastic but discriminate hunter in his younger days, Kruger decided in the 1890s to set aside millions of acres of Transvaal territory for wildlife preservation. This was an act that cost him much support among his farmer constituents who saw this as senseless waste of good grazing land.

Kruger simply called this area, Sabie Game Reserve, after the river running through it.

Twenty years later a British soldier who fought against Kruger and was placed in charge of the reserve after the Anglo-Boer War, Colonel Stevenson-Hamilton, insisted that it be renamed Kruger National Park in honor of the visionary Transvaal President who saved so many species from extinction.

Col. Stevenson-Hamilton

Nature Conservation brings opposites together. President Paul Kruger of the Transvaal Republic could never have imagined that the enormous area that he set aside for wildlife conservation in 1898, would become a compassionate obsession of a member of the British enemy forces.

In 1902, immediately after the Anglo-Boer War, the interim British government in the Transvaal assigned Col. James Stevenson-Hamilton to the task of developing the Sabie Game Reserve, which was renamed Kruger National Park.

For close to a half century, Stevenson-Hamilton worked full-time to consolidate and safeguard Africa's first and foremost game sanctuary. The officer was definitely not a gentleman when it came to fighting critics, intruders and poachers.

Skukuza, the main camp in Kruger, is a tribute to this pioneer in African conservation. Skukuza was the name given to Stevenson-Hamilton by the local Shangaan tribesmen who served under him as game trackers and poacher catchers. It means:*" The man who turns everything upside down."*

Accommodations at both Kruger and the private game parks are comfortable, with the latter offering additional frills. Some private game lodges are quite luxurious. Meals at the private game parks are more elaborate and some offer tribal dances and other entertainment in open-air bomas.

Meat dishes include venison from animals that are culled from time to time for ecological reasons, ranging from impala cutlets, to kudu steak and warthog spare ribs.

Stores at Kruger offer a complete range of meats and groceries to self-drive travelers who wish to cook their own at the amenities provided in various rest camps.

BIG FIVE

A few years ago, hunters got together and picked Africa's five 'most dangerous animals'.

This is how they rate the Big Five: (1) Buffalo, (2) Lion, (3) Elephant, (4) Leopard, and (5) Rhino.

Tour operators have seized on this idea to lure tourists to South and East Africa. In advertisements and tourist literature foreigners are invited to come and see so-called Big Five.

The success of a safari is unfortunately often measured in terms of how many of the Big Five were sighted.

AFRICAN BUSH

Fortunately, most visitors realize, once they step into African bush, that going on safari means much more than these five species.

It is a world of sights and sounds and smells that removes the visitors in body and spirit from the humdrum of modern existence and renews the spirit.

The setting sun turns the water of the Okavango
Swamps into rippling gold as a giant moves slowly in the
steady evening breeze. Gandaya, The Mighty One.

It is the poacher's dream to capture him. Many have
tried. Many have failed.

They say an elephant's memory is as long as the path
of life itself. Gandaya remembers. Spears. Traps. Rifles.

How would it be then, if what Gandaya remem-
bered of humans were those who helped his herd.

Not those who came to destroy it.

LINDSAY SMITHERS-FCB 4861

LIKE GANDAYA
WE NEVER FORGET

At South African Airways, we never forget that the wildlife of the world is the heritage of our children. That's why every time you fly to or from Southern Africa with us, South African Airways' African Wildlife Heritage Trust will benefit directly.

We never forget that you have a choice of airlines and that though readers of the UK's prestigious Executive Travel magazine voted us Best Airline to Africa for the third year running, we should not rest on our laurels.

That is why we keep striving for quality. And perfection.

Cape Peninsula.
Game viewing at Sabi Sabi

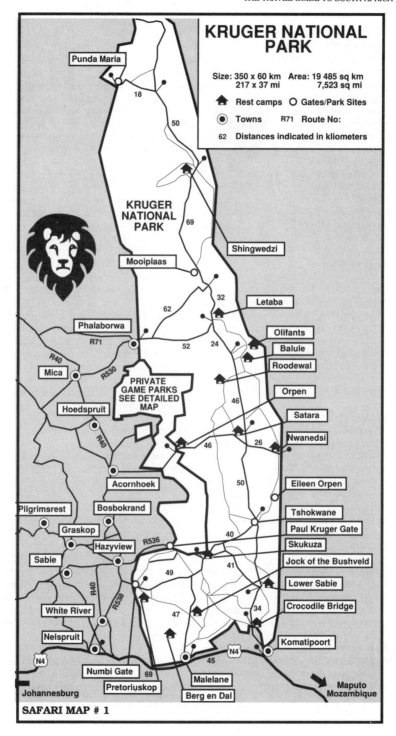

KRUGER NATIONAL PARK

Size: 350 x 60 km   Area: 19 485 sq km
217 x 37 mi   7,523 sq mi

🏠 Rest camps   O Gates/Park Sites

◉ Towns   R71 Route No:

62 Distances indicated in kliometers

Punda Maria

18

50

KRUGER NATIONAL PARK

69

Shingwedzi

Mooiplaas

32

Letaba

62

Phalaborwa

R71

52   24

Olifants

Balule

Roodewal

R40

R530

Mica

PRIVATE GAME PARKS SEE DETAILED MAP

Orpen

46

Satara

Hoedspruit

Nwanedsi

R40

46   26

Acornhoek

50

Eileen Orpen

Pilgrimsrest

Bosbokrand

Tshokwane

Graskop

R536

40

Paul Kruger Gate

Hazyview

Skukuza

Sabie

49   41

Jock of the Bushveld

R40

R538

Lower Sabie

White River

47   34

Crocodile Bridge

Nelspruit

Komatipoort

N4

N4

Numbi Gate   69   45

Maputo
Mozambique

Johannesburg

Pretoriuskop

Malelane

Berg en Dal

SAFARI MAP # 1

Watching a dung-beetle rolling a dung-ball many times its size to a safe place where it will be buried and serve to feed its larvae under-ground, can be as in-triguing as sitting around a water hole watching the large ones. And the aero-batics of a lilac-breasted roller in courtship or trying to distract an in-

Dung Beetle

truder from finding its nest, is no less an experience than being charged by a protective mother elephant. And much more colorful.

WHAT TO WEAR

There is no need to rush to the nearest store and buy special safari clothes. There are a number of South African stores with specialized safari dress (called *Bush Casuals*) and a variety of interesting headdress, ranging from pith helmets to floppy hats. Most game reserves and lodges offer a selection of clothes, imprinted with their names.

Sharply contrasting bright colors are supposed to scare away animals, but nobody prescribes a dress code or colors. Sticking to browns, greens and autumn colors will, however, place you in greater harmony with nature and your fellow safari-goers. Comfortable boots or high-tops and long pants or socks are advisable, especially for hikes.

WEATHER

Kruger and the private game parks are all situated in the Lowveld - a savan-nah type region with hot summers and mild winters, nights are chilly in sum-mer and cold in winter. Take a sweater along for evening drives and heavier clothing during the winter months from May to September. Those with sensi-tive skins should bring long-sleeved garb to prevent sun-burn.

SMELLS

Smoking or strong perfumes are claimed to deter shy smell-sensitive animals from showing themselves. Wearing the same clothes for several days, the experts say, is the best way to camouflage your presence to smell-conscious wildlife. (This may, however, scare away your fellow travelers).

WHEN TO GO

Some visitors prefer the dry winter months when the underbrush turns sparse and animals can be spotted more easily. Others swear by summers when animals contrast more sharply against green. Most game areas offer special rates not on a basis of seasons but to fill proven slack periods.

Kruger National Park, a favorite for South African tourists and their fami-lies, tend to be quite full during the school holidays. At the same time there are private game parks that would cut their rates by as much as fifty percent during short elbow periods between peak seasons.

VIEWING TIMES

The best time to view animals is at dawn or dusk - and for nocturnal crea-tures, of course, at night.

Most animals seek out the shadows of the underbrush and trees during the heat of the day.

Expect to be woken up at the crack of dawn, to spend the middle of the day around the pool at a rest camp, relax-ing and talking about the sights and experiences of the morning, and again leaving for a game drive in the late afternoon.

In the private game parks and in some of the Kruger Park lodges night drives are arranged before dinner.

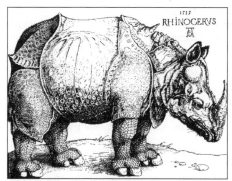

In 1515 Albrecht Durer developed this woodcut from a sketch and description sent to him from Spain. He never saw a rhinocerus.

PHOTOGRAPHY

For tourists who are interested in snapshots for the family album, the regular point-and-shoot camera will suffice. Serious photographers will need something more substantial.

A zoom or long telephoto lens of up to 500 mm is needed for good pictures, even in the private game parks where game rangers are bound to bring visitors on safari closer to the animals. For night-time photography a flash is needed and for spectacular sunsets and scenery, a wide-angle lens. All types and makes of film are readily available in South Africa. The game parks also keep a good supply on hand. Be sure, however, to take along a spare battery for cameras requiring any, as these may not be stocked.

Often game rangers are also experienced wild-life photographers. Good advice can often be obtained from them on exposures and timing. Rangers know the habits of animals and will steer their guests towards good action pictures instead of deadpan photographs.

Although not essential, binoculars are certainly useful, especially for bird-watching. Rangers usually take along a pair of binoculars for the convenience of their guests, but many visitors prefer to take their own instead of scrambling for a loaner when exciting things start to happen.

CHILDREN

While there are no age restrictions in Kruger National Park or the other national parks, individual private game lodges have their own rules. In most cases children of all ages are accepted in the camps, but not allowed to accompany game drives under a certain age, unless a family occupies a whole vehicle by themselves. In some lodges separate dining arrangements are made and in most of them baby sitting facilities are provided.

ARRANGEMENTS

Some may already have made their arrangements before they purchased (or borrowed) our travel guide, and

Burchell's Rhinocerus as seen by Lydekker

THE RHINOCERUS

Rhinocerus, your hide looks all undone,
You do not take my fancy in the least;
You have a horn where other brutes have none:
Rhinocerus, you are an ugly beast.

Hilaire Belloc

FEMALE

MALE

HOLDING BRANCH

PROFILE

PLUCKING GRASS

Elephant trunk as depicted in Greenwood's Wild Sports (1864)

may therefore disregard this advice unless they wish to read it for future reference. In making arrangements for a safari to South Africa there are several choices:

Tour Companies: Most first-time (and many repeat visitors) utilize the services of a tour operator in their respective countries who specialize in safaris to South Africa. As with any industry, these tour companies vary from the magnificent to the indifferent (and on rare occasions, the incompetent). Most of these companies produce very attractive brochures - so don't judge them by their publicity alone. Ask around and get references if possible, of discerning people who have used specific operators in the past.

(Although they will not select or guarantee an operator for you, Satour and SA Airways are useful sources of information. See our chapter KEY CONTACTS).

Travel Agents: Although most tour companies would not turn away direct enquiries from prospective clients, travellers usually work with them through their neighborhood travel agency. It does not cost any additional money to do so as these agencies rely on a commission from the tour companies.

Direct Bookings: For travelers who prefer to make their own arrangements, there is the convenience of direct booking facilities. All leading private game lodges and national game parks maintain reservations offices in Johannesburg and some of the other city centers.

Read the fine print. Many a disappointment and misunderstanding may be prevented by being certain beforehand what exactly a travel agent, tour operator or game reserve offers - and the late cancellation penalties levied. Travel insurance is strongly recommended. *(See our chapter TRAVEL TIPS).*

BAGGAGE

The first rule to remember when packing for safari is to stay on the light side. Its a good idea to take along a separate overnight bag as bus tour operators, and regular and charter air services, normally limit luggage.

It is customary to take the smaller overnight bag and to leave heavier and bulkier baggage back in city hotels for safekeeping. The airlines operating into the game reserves will also store excess baggage at the various airports. Here are a few suggestions on **what to pack** for safari:

✔ Safari-type clothing, adaptable to hot and cold conditions
✔ Boots or high-tops (especially for hiking in the bush)
✔ Camera with long lens (optional)
✔ Binoculars (optional)
✔ Sun-bloc or suntan lotion.
✔ Malaria pills (take the first two a week before entering the parks)
✔ Insect repellant
✔ Sunglasses (optional)
✔ Smaller travel bag for safari portion of trip.

CAUTION

In contrast with certain other safari regions in Africa, where danger lurks in everything from the drinking water to raw fruit, very few words of caution are required in South Africa. Drinking water is safe and the food very edible, enjoyable and digestible.

The bonhomie of a *braaivleis* (barbecue) around a campfire in an open-air boma is as memorable as any animal sighting and seasoned safari-goers return as much for this experience as they do for the animals.

MALARIA

Malaria, although well contained, is, however, still a potential problem in the Lowveld region (where Kruger National Park and most of the private game parks are situated).

It is therefore recommended that visitors start a prophylactic course of antimalarial tablets at least a week before entering. This regular intake of a few pills per week is continued for a few weeks after completion of the trip.

These tablets can be obtained on prescription from your physician or from medical departments. *In South African malaria tablets are sold over the counter at pharmacies and drug stores.*

There is no vaccination or immunization against **bilharzia**, a disease caused by water-borne microscopic organisms which penetrate the skin. Although largely eradicated, bilharzia is still a possibility in still water in remote areas of the Transvaal and Natal.

Do not take a dip or a drink at a water holes or quiet streams in these regions - unless your host declares it safe. *Drinking, bathing and running water at game lodges are unaffected and completely safe.*

GAME RESERVES

TRANSVAAL REGION

The Transvaal region outstrips the rest of the country in game reserves, both as far as number and size are concerned. There are more than 50 registered game reserves and lodges, some close to Pretoria and Johannesburg.

The savannah type Lowveld region about five hours drive or an hour and a half by air from Johannesburg, is however, the prime stomping grounds for serious safari-goers. This is where the famous Kruger National Park and a number of privately owned and managed game lodges are situated. It is not only South Africa, but Africa's premier wildlife preserve.

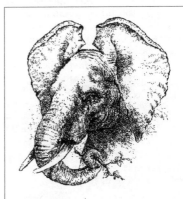

"This creature is saide to live 150 yeeres; he is of gentle disposition; and relying upon his great strength, he hurteth none but such as do him inure; only he will in a sporting manner gently heave up with his snowte such persons as he meeteth."

Leo Africanus (1494-1552) - The History and Description of Africa and of the Notable Things Therein Contained - Published in English 1600.

KRUGER NATIONAL PARK

SAFARI MAPS 1, 2 & 3
PAGES 33, 41 7 45
National Parks Board. P O Box 787,
Pretoria 0001.Reservations: (012) 44-
1191 Cape Town: (021) 24-3120

Established at the turn of the century at the insistence of President Paul Kruger as the Sabie Game Reserve and since renamed Kruger National Park (KNP), this is recognized as one of the top national parks in the world.

The southern region consists of mixed vegetation and terrain, the central portion of rolling grassy plains and *mopane veld* and the northern region of sandy plains and lush riverine forests.

The park supports more species of wildlife than any other game sanctuary: It is natural habitat for 137 mammal species, 493 bird species, 112 reptile species and 49 different types of freshwater fish. With 15 types of eagles, the park also has the highest density of birds of prey in the world.

La Giraffe - 18th Century French engraving

Kruger Park employs a permanent staff of 1500 people as game rangers, scientists, technicians and managers. With an area of close to 5 million acres it is roughly the size of Wales.

SKUKUZA

Eight entrance gates provide access for visitors by car and bus while the airport at Skukuza rest camp has several daily scheduled flights to and from Durban, Johannesburg, Nelspruit and Phalaborwa. Luxury coach tours into the park are available on a regular basis from Durban, Johannesburg and Nelspruit.

TRAILS

Six guided wilderness hiking trails are offered: *The Wolhuter Trail* (named after a famous game ranger) in the southern section of the park offers the opportunity to observe on foot rare mammal species such as roan, sable, reedbuck, oribi and white rhino. Further south, *The Bushman Trail,* covers an area with wildlife and Bushman rock art.

On the *Olifants Trail*, in the central district of the park, close encounters with zebra, wildebeest, buffalo, elephant, crocodile and hippo, are likely. The *Nyalaland Trail* covering the northern region, is intended for bird-watchers. *The Metsi Trail*, northeast of Skukuza Rest Camp, offers a large diversity of mammals, and the *Sweni Trail*, east of Satara Rest Camp, goes through an area known for its lions. The trails are flexible and do not follow set routes. Distances vary according to circumstances and huts are provided at all base camps.

GAME DRIVES

Trained rangers are available to take groups out in four-wheel drive vehicles, while visitors on self-drive excursions should experience no difficulty. Good maps are available at all entrance gates and camps, and the roads are well signposted.

ACCOMMODATION

Accommodation is provided in 19 rest camps, ranging from fully equipped guest cottages to huts with kitchenettes and a shower or bath. The luxury Rembrandt Lodge at Skukuza accommodates 20 people Camping sites are also available for those with caravans or recreational vehicles. Chalets in the larger camps are designed to meet the needs of the handicapped.

FACILITIES

All of the main camps have restaurants and shops with fresh provisions, canned foods and curios. There are picnic spots, filling stations, vehicle workshops, conservation-related film shows, information centers, conference facilities and post offices. Cars are available for rental at Skukuza.

PRIVATE RESERVES
SAFARI MAPS 2 & 3, PAGES 41 & 45

There are three major private game reserves bordering Kruger National Park. Sabi-Sand and Timbavati have been established tourist havens for many years, while Manyeleti has been opened for tourism more recently. Each of these reserves offer a choice of several private game lodges.

The **Sabi-Sand Private Nature Reserve** adjoins the southwestern part of Kruger National Park and is within easy driving distance of Skukuza Airport. It covers 120,000 acres and encompasses the *Sabi Sabi Private Game Lodges, Rattray Reserves* with its three camps, *MalaMala, Harry's Huts* and *Kirk-mans*, as well as *Inyati* and *Londolozi.*

Although all these lodges are within easy driving distance from Skukuza, some still maintain their own private airstrips for the sake of those who wish to use direct charter services instead of scheduled air links. (Visitors will see thornbushes draped around the wheels of these charter planes on the airstrip to discourage hyenas from chewing through the tires!)

Immediately north of Sabi Sand is **Manyeleti Game Reserve** which is in the process of being developed. It currently offers lodging at camps such as *Khoka Moya* and *Honey Guide.*

Furthest north is **Timbavati Private Game Reserve** which covers approximately 150,000 acres. It is the home of the famous white lions and accommodates tourists at the *Motswari, M'bali, Ngala* and *Tanda Tula* game lodges. These lodges are all about an hour's drive from Phalaborwa Airport. Some, however, have their own airstrip for direct charter services.

LUXURY

These private lodges all offer special luxuries and a great degree of pampering. Both in accommodations and services, however, these lodges try to blend with their bushveld surroundings both in buildings and life-style.

Bosbok - Early French Engraving

And for those who complain about too much luxury and refinement, MalaMala owner and private game lodge pioneer Michael Rattray has a short answer: *"To love an animal, one should not be required to live like one."*

TYPICAL TREATMENT

Typical of the treatment and accommodations that visitors can expect at these private game lodges is:

To be met on arrival at Phalaborwa or Skukuza Airports and taken to the lodge by car or minibus. Those who travel by car will find the last few miles of road untarred and game crossing without warning.

Accommodations at most of these lodges are air-conditioned and facilities usually include swimming pools and *bomas*, (walled enclosures, made of reed or thorn bush, where guests dine in the open air around a camp fire). Lodges are usually licensed and operate *bushveld bars* and lounges and stock good wines.

Day and night game viewing is conducted in open four-wheel drive vehicles and walking safaris are offered under the guidance of experienced rangers and trackers.

How cheerfully he seems to grin
How neatly spreads his claws,
And welcomes little fishes in
With gently smiling jaws!

Lewis Caroll
Alice's Adventures in Wonderland

Meals are mostly *braais* or barbecues in the *bomas* and include venison ranging from impala to kudu and warthog are often included. These are animals culled for ecological reasons to prevent over-grazing. (Visiting a private game lodge is as much a gourmet as a viewing experience).

Curio shops stock, apart from interesting artifacts, necessities such as sunblock, film, toothpaste and shaving cream. Most have safari clothes and hats displaying the lodge's emblem and name.

With few exceptions, telephone and telefax communications are good and direct dialling overseas possible.

Every few guests are assigned a whole complement of staff, including a game ranger and housekeeper. The staff guest ratio is pretty high, ensuring constant and efficient personalized service.

TYPICAL DAY

The day usually starts at the crack of dawn when visitors are woken up with coffee and *biskuit* (rusks) and taken on an early morning game drive. Later in the morning guests return to the camp where they are served a sumptuous breakfast, spend a leisurely time around the pool or go on nature hikes, guided by expert rangers. Lunch and refreshments are followed by a late afternoon game drive and cocktails in the bush while trying to spot nocturnal animals, before returning to camp for a *braai* (barbecue) in the *boma*. Sometimes local tribes will perform ceremonial dances in the boma and on occasion visiting artists will give open-air concerts on guitar, flute or other instruments.

WHAT IS INCLUDED?

Rates normally include all meals, accommodation, game drives, the services of qualified game rangers and trackers, teas, coffees and snacks, and transfers to and from the nearest airport. Bar and curio store purchases and government and airport taxes are excluded from these quoted tariffs.

GAME

All of these private lodges bordering the Kruger National Park, fall within so-called 'Big Five' country. Similar game, bird, reptile and insect species occur as those found in the Kruger National Park, although somewhat less in number and variety. There are few fences between the private reserves.

SAFARI MAP # 2

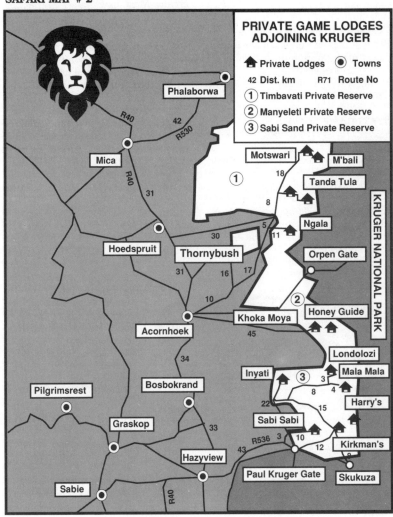

PRIVATE GAME LODGES
ADJOINING KRUGER

🏠 Private Lodges   ◉ Towns
42 **Dist. km**   R71 **Route No**
① Timbavati Private Reserve
② Manyeleti Private Reserve
③ Sabi Sand Private Reserve

Phalaborwa

R40   42   R530

Mica

R40   31

Motswari   M'bali
①   18
Tanda Tula
8

Hoedspruit   30   5   Ngala
11

Thornybush   Orpen Gate
31   16   17

10

Acornhoek   Khoka Moya   ②   Honey Guide
45

34

Londolozi

Pilgrimsrest   Bosbokrand   Inyati   ③   3   Mala Mala
8   4

Graskop   33   22   15   Harry's

Sabi Sabi

R536   3   10   Kirkman's
43   12

Hazyview   Paul Kruger Gate   Skukuza

Sabie   R40

KRUGER NATIONAL PARK

GETTING THERE

Most private lodges in the eastern Transvaal are within easy motoring distance of Johannesburg, while Comair operates daily flights from Jan Smuts Airport to Skukuza (Kruger) and Phalaborwa. Magnum Airlines and Comair operate schedules from Johannesburg and Durban to Nelspruit. Most of these reserves also have their own landing strips and some provide scheduled services.

Following, in alphabetical order, are the most popular lodges in the region. Expect to pay a premium for elaborate service and special attention. These private reserves all try to make the safari experience an outstanding one:

INYATI GAME LODGE
Reservations: P O Box 38838, Booysens 2016. Tel: (011) 493-0755 Fax: (011) 493-0837. On the banks of the Sand River in the Sabi Sand Private Nature Reserve. *Accommodation* : Maximum of 18 in thatched air-conditioned en-suite chalets. *Facilities:* Conference facilities. Pangola overlooking river. Boma, swimming pool, bar and lounge. *Closest airport:* Skukuza.

"I'll take spots, then," said the Leopard, "but don't make 'em too vulgar-big. I wouldn't look like Giraffe - not for ever so."

Rudyard Kipling
'How the Leopard Got His Spots'

2. KHOKA MOYA/HONEY GUIDE
Reservations: Safariplan P O Box 4245 Randburg 2125.Tel: (011) 886-1810. Fax: (011) 886-1815. In Manyeleti reserve. *Accommodation:* Khoka Moya has 4 double en-suite cabins, while Honey Guide accommodates maximum of 12 in 6 large East African tents. *Facilities:* Khoka Moya has dining room, lounge and bar. *Closest Airport: Phalaborwa.*

3. LONDOLOZI GAME RESERVE
Reservations: Box 1211, Sunninghill Park 2157. Tel: (011) 803-8421. Fax: (011) 803-1810. Along the Sabi River. Has been run by the Varty family for sixty years, who are prominent in conservation circles. *Accommodation: Tree Camp* has double accommodation with en-suite facilities for four couples in chalets overlooking river. The *Bush Camp* accommodates 4 couples in individual rock cabins and the *Main Camp* accommodates 12 couples in en-suite chalets. *Facilities* include a bar, lounges, balconies overlooking the river, swimming pool, a boma and a curio shop. Airport: Skukuza.

MALAMALA
Reservations: Box 2575, Randburg 2125.Tel: (011) 789-2677. Fax:(011) 886-4382. Although Mala Mala is one of several lodges operated by Rattray Reserves, it has become the collective name for three game lodges operated by the group in the Sabi Sand area. *Accommodation & Facilities: MalaMala Camp* accommodates 50 guests in air-conditioned huts with 'his' and 'her' bathrooms, 24-hour room service and same-day laundry service. There are conference facilities, a well-appointed bar and lounges.At *Harry's* accommodation is provided for 16 in Ndebele-style bungalows. *Kirkman's Kamp*

accommodates a maximum of 20 guests in semi-detached cottages with en-suite bathrooms and verandahs overlooking the river. A converted historic homestead decorated in 1920's fashion serves as a lounge and dining room. Airport: Skukuza. Also direct charter services to an airstrip at Mala Mala.

MOTSWARI/M'BALI
Reservations: Box 76037, Wendywood 2144. Tel: (011)-802-1002. Both Motswari and neighboring M'bali are situated in the Timbavati Reserve. *Accommodation: Motswari* has 11 en-suite *rondavels* (chalets) for a maximum of 22 guests. *M'bali*, 9 km away, has space for 14 in 7 Hemingway-style *habitents* perched high above the ground on wooden platforms overlooking a dam on the Sharalumi River. *Facilities:* Both camps have a swimming pool and Motswari has conference facilities. *Closest Airport:* Phalaborwa..

NGALA GAME LODGE
Reservations: Box 4068 Rivonia 2128. Tel: (011) 803-7400 Fax: (011) 803-7411. In the Timbavati Private Game Reserve. Ngala means lion in the local tribal language. *Accommodation:* Ngala has 22 twin-bedded rooms with air-conditioning and en-suite bathrooms. Also provides 'sleep-out' *bomas* where guests can overnight under the stars (weather permitting). *Facilities:* Bar, lounge, swimming pool, curio shop and conference facilities. *Closest Airport:* Phalaborwa. Also has own airstrip.

SABI SABI PRIVATE RESERVE
Reservations: Box 52665 Saxonwold 2132. Tel: (011) 880-4840 Fax: (011) 447-2019. As one of the very first of its kind, Sabi Sabi contributed largely to the popularity of "private" game viewing. Situated in the Sabi Sand region bordering the Kruger Park. Has access to all of South Africa's large and most of the smaller mammals. Close to 350 bird species. Sabi Sabi is included at

Kingfisher

special reduced rates in tour packages that also include Kruger National Park. *Accommodation:* Sabi Sabi operates two camps. *Bush Lodge* comprises 25 and the *River Lodge* 20 twin-bedded en-suite thatched chalets. *Facilities:* Sabi Sabi has conference facilities, bar and lounges and a tree house overlooking the perennial Sabi River. Has a swimming pool and curio shop. *Airport:* Short drive from Kruger Park's Skukuza Airport with scheduled air links to and from Johannesburg and Durban.

TANDA TULA GAME LODGE
Reservations: Box 32, Constantia 7848. Toll free (0800) 220055 Fax: (021) 794-7605. In the Timbavati Game Reserve. *Accommodation:* En-suite air-conditioned rondavels for total of sixteen guests. *Facilities:* Bar, lounge and wine cellar, boma and swimming pool. *Airport:* Phalaborwa. Own airstrip.

THORNYBUSH GAME LODGE
Reservations: Box 798, Northlands 2116. Tel. (011) 883-7918. Fax. (011) 883-8201. Adjacent to Timbavati Game Reserve. *Accommodation:* Air-conditioned thatched rooms for a total of 16. *Facilities:* Conference room, bar, lounge, swimming pool and boma. *Airport:* Phalaborwa. Also own airstrip.

OTHER TRANSVAAL RESERVES
SAFARI MAP # 3 - OPPOSITE PAGE

For those visitors who wish to go beyond the better known reserves in the Transvaal, there are a variety of other options.

Eland Bull

Some of these offer day visits at a nominal or no cost, while others have accommodation ranging from camping sites to first class cabins and chalets. There are also worthwhile zoos and bird sanctuaries in and around Johannesburg and Pretoria. *(See the chapter CITY SIGHTS).*

Following, in alphabetical order, are a number of other reputable game lodges, provincial parks and game farms offering opportunities to safari-seeking tourists.

ABE BAILEY NATURE RESERVE
Box 13, Carletonville 2908. Tel. (01491)
2908. 8 km north of Carletonville, with zebra, red hartebeest, springbok, blesbok and steenbok, waterfowl and raptors. Camping.

BADPLAAS NATURE RESERVE
Box 15, Badplaas 1190. Tel. (01344)
41020. Near Carolina. Species include springbok, wildebeest, blesbok and eland. Accommodation in chalets and rondavels. Camping. Stores.

BARBERSPAN NATURE RESERVE
Barberspan 2765. Tel. (01443) 1202.
16 km north-east of Delareyville.

Transvaal's largest waterfowl sanctuary and world famous for ornithological research. More than 350 species recorded. Also mammals. Camping.

BEN ALBERTS NATURE RESERVE
Box 50, Thabazimbi 0380. Tel. (01537)
2-1509. 7 km from Thabazimbi. Game includes rhino, giraffe, eland, waterbuck and kudu. No accommodation.

BEN LAVIN NATURE RESERVE
Box 782, Louis Trichardt 0920. Tel.
(01551) 3834. Some 12 km from town. Noted for rare species and bird life. Accommodation in self-contained units.

BLOEMHOF DAM NATURE RESERVE
Private Bag X7, Bloemhof 2660. Tel.
(018022) 1122. On north shore of Bloemhof Dam. Supports black wildebeest, springbok, blesbok, gemsbok, eland, white rhino and ostrich. Fishing.No accommodation.

BLYDERIVIERSPOORT RESERVE
Box 281, Hoedspruit 1380. Tel. (0020) Ask for Blydedam 1 or 2. Near Klaserie. Offers rich bird life, including a breeding colony of rare bald ibis. Accommodation and camping. Facilities include restaurants, swimming pool, and horse riding.

BOSKOP DAM NATURE RESERVE
Box 24, Boskop 2528. Tel. (0148) 22430.
20 km north-east of Potchefstroom. Attracts a diversity of birds. Mammals include eland, red hartebeest, zebra and blesbok. Camping.

BRONKHORSTSPRUIT RESERVE
Box 583, Bronkhorstspruit 1020. Tel.
(01212) 21621. Black wildebeest, blesbok and variety of water birds on dam.Camping. Fishing. Watersports.

DE WILDT CHEETAH STATION
Administered by the National Zoological Gardens of South Africa (Tel.012-3265). Breeding farm 25 km west of Pretoria, specializing in cheetah.Several

PARKS AND GAME & NATURE RESERVES - TRANSVAAL

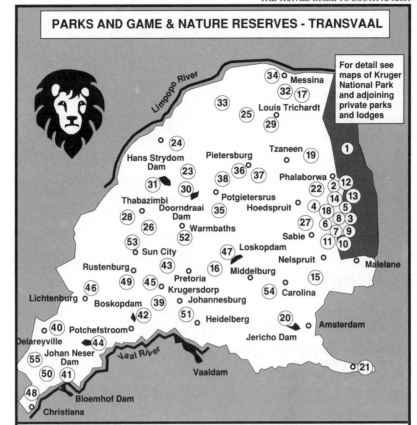

For detail see maps of Kruger National Park and adjoining private parks and lodges

SAFARI MAP # 3

1 Kruger National Park
2 Timbavati
3 Sabi-Sand Private Reserve
4 Matumi Game Lodge
5 Khoka Moya/Honey Guide
6 Inyati
7 Londolozi Game Lodge
8 Mala Mala
9 Harry's Huts
10 Kirkman's Kamp
11 Sabi Sabi Game Lodge
12 Motswari/M'bali Lodges
13 Ngala Game Lodge
14 Tanda Tula Game Lodge
15 Badplaas Nature Reserve
16 Bronkhorstspruit Reserve
17 Entabeni State Forest
18 Blyderivierspoort Reserve
19 Hans Merensky Reserve
20 Jericho Dam Nature Reserve
21 Pongola Nature Reserve
22 Klaserie Private Reserve
23 Emaweni Game Lodge
24 Lapalala Wilderness
25 Leshabi Wilderness
26 Mabula Lodge
27 Mount Sheba Reserve
28 Ben Alberts Nature Reserve
29 Ben Lavin Nature Reserve
30 Doorndraai Dam Reserve
31 Hans Strydom Dam Reserve
32 Honnet Nature Reserve
33 Lanjan Nature Reserve
34 Messina Nature Reserve
35 Nylsvley Nature Reserve
36 Percy Fyfe Nature Reserve
37 Pietersburg Nature Reserve
38 Potgietersrus Nature Reserve
39 Abe Bailey Nature Reserve
40 Barberspan Nature Reserve
41 Bloemhof Dam Reserve
42 Boskop Dam Nature Reserve
43 De Wildt Cheetha Farm
44 Faan Meinjties Reserve
45 Krugersdorp Game Reserve
46 Lichtenburg Nature Reserve
47 Loskop Dam Game Reserve
48 Rob Ferreira Game Reserve
49 Rustenburg Nature Reserve
50 S A Lombard Nature Reserve
51 Suikerboschrand Reserve
52 Warmbaths Nature Reserve
53 Pilanesburg Private Reserve
54 Nooitgedacht Nature Reserve
55 Lindbergh Lodge

specimens of rare King Cheetah. De Wildt is Open Saturdays. Reservations essential. No accommodation.

DOORNDRAAI DAM RESERVE
*Box 983, Potgietersrus 0600. Tel. (015423) 629.*Some 45 km south-west of Potgietersrus. Has kudu, reedbuck, leopard, sable, roan and tsessebe. Fishing. Camping.

ENTABENI STATE FOREST
Private Bag 2413, Louis Trichardt 0920. Tel. (01551) 2201. Three reserves - Entabeni, Ratombo and Matiwa - on slopes of Soutpansberg east of Louis Trichardt. Bushbuck, red duiker, samango monkeys, mongoose, leopard and caracal as well as crowned eagle and other raptors. Hiking trails. No accommodation.

FAAN MEINTJIES RESERVE
Box 99, Klerksdorp 2570. Tel. (018) 23635. About 14 km north of town wildlife and close to Johannesburg. Herds of buffalo, giraffe, and zebra, several antelope species, and white rhino. No accommodation.

HANS MERENSKY RESERVE
Private Bag X502, Letsitele 0885. Tel. (015238) 633. Some 70 km east of Tzaneen. Sable antelope, roan, zebra and prolific bird life. Close to Chris

Gemsbok

Barnard Health Center and mineral spa. Nature trails, swimming, horse riding and tennis. Accommodation. *(For further detail about the newly opened Barnard Health Center see SPAS in our chapter on RESORTS AND SPORTS).*

HANS STRYDOM DAM RESERVE
Box 473, Ellisras 0555. Tel. (01536) 33384. About 64 km south of Ellisras. Antelope include rare roan antelope. Fishing. No accommodation.

HONNET NATURE RESERVE
Box 4, Tshipise 0901. Tel. (015539) 624. Near Thsipise. Inhabited by giraffe, kudu, waterbuck, nyala, sable and tsessebe. Riding trails along the 10 km Baobab Trail. Accommodation at mineral spa. Camping.

JERICHO DAM RESERVE
Box 74, Amsterdam 2375. Tel. (01342) 307. About 20 km north-west of Amsterdam. Oribi, steenbok, duiker and bird life. Renowned for black bass fishing. No accommodation.

KLASERIE PRIVATE RESERVE
Box 645, Bedfordview 2008. Tel. (011) 53-1814. South of Phalaborwa. Elephant, giraffe, kudu, buffalo and impala. Transport from Johannesburg. Tented camps.

KRUGERSDORP GAME RESERVE
Box 94, Krugersdorp 1740. Tel. (011) 660-1076. Forty minutes' by car west of Johannesburg. Giraffe, white rhino, eland, blue wildebeest, kudu, sable, roan antelope and buffalo.There is also a 400 acre lion enclosure. Accommodation in chalets and rondavels. Caravan park.

LICHTENBURG NATURE RESERVE
Box 716, Lichtenburg 2740. Tel. (01441) 22818. Administered by the National Zoological Gardens. North of Lichtenburg. Sanctuary for some 40 mammal species. Thousands of waterfowl at dam. No accommodation.

LOSKOP DAM GAME RESERVE

Private Bag X1525, Middelburg 1050. Tel. (01202) 3075. Some 53 km north of Middelburg. Wildlife includes white rhino, giraffe, zebra, buffalo, kudu and over 200 bird species. Fishing.Camping. Accommodation in adjoining resort.

LANGJAN NATURE RESERVE

Box 15, Vivo 0924. Tel. (0155562) 1211. Situated 94 km north of Pietersburg.Inhabited by giraffe, zebra, gemsbok, eland, kudu and impala. Abundant bird life. Accommodation in thatched roof huts.

LAPALALA WILDERNESS

Box 577, Bedfordview 2008. Tel. (011) 53-1814. In the Waterberg Mountains, some 125 km north-west of Nylstroom. White rhino, sable and roan, as well as diversity of birds. Canoeing and fishing. Guided wilderness trails.Self-contained chalets and camping.

LESHEBA WILDERNESS

Box 13, Mara 0934. Tel. (015562) Ask for 3004. Halfway between Louis Trichardt and Vivo. High cliffs, deep gorges and weathered rocks inhabited by leopard, white rhino, eland, giraffe, zebra, klipspringer and smaller mammals. Hundreds of bird species include colony of Cape vultures. Two self-catering camps.

LINDBERGH LODGE

Private Bag X1010, Wolmaransstad 2630.Tel: (01811) 22041 Fax: (01811) 22048. Private Lindbergh Lodge is situated about 3 hours by car west of Johannesburg on plains reminiscent of Serengeti in East Africa. Variety of antelope and other indigenous animals viewed from open four-wheel drive vehicles or by balloon. Several strategically placed hides from where guests view animals over cocktails at dusk.Upmarket accommodations for a small number of guests in a historic homestead.Airstrip. Boma, tennis and swimming pool.

MABULA LODGE

*Box 651944, Benmore 2010. Tel. (011) 883-7140.*North-west of Warmbaths at the foot of the Waterberg mountains, about 2 hour drive from Johannesburg. Wildlife include "Big Five" and 250 bird species. Walks and game drives in open vehicles. Fully licensed accommodations and all meals are provided. Swimming pool, tennis courts and golf nearby.

African Shrike

MESSINA NATURE RESERVE

*Box 78, Messina 0090. Tel. (01553) 3235.*Outskirts of Messina. The reserve has several large species and noted for giant baobab trees. Independent game drives along two trails. No accommodation.

MOUNT SHEBA RESERVE

Box 100, Pilgrim's Rest 1290. Tel. (0131532) Ask for 17. Some 12 km from Pilgrim's Rest. Indigenous forest with red duiker, bushbuck, samango money and bird life. Accommodation at Mount Sheba Hotel.

NOOITGEDACHT DAM RESERVE

*Box 327, Carolina 1185. Tel. (01344) 32603.*Near town. Large flocks of Egyptian geese, spurwing and blue cranes. Fishing. Camping.

NYLSVLEY NATURE RESERVE

Box 508, Naboomspruit 0560. Tel. (01534) 31074. Some 20 km south of Naboomspruit. Primarily a birdwatcher's paradise with 400 species. Other wildlife includes kudu, impala, roan antelope and tsessebe. No accommodation.

PERCY FYFE NATURE RESERVE
Box 217, Pietersburg 0700. Tel. (01541)
5678. Some 26 km north-east of
Potgietersrus. Breeds tsessebe, roan
and sable. Rich bird life. Basic accommodation for groups.

PIETERSBURG NATURE RESERVE
Box 111, Pietersburg 0700. Tel. (01521)
93-1114. Five km south of Pietersburg.
Wildlife includes rhino, zebra and gemsbok. Accommodation in chalets.

PILANESBERG PRIVATE RESERVE
Box 1201, Mogwase 0302. Tel. (014652)
2405.Private reserve adjoins South
Africa's premier gambling resort, Sun
City. Game reserve created around
Pilanesberg mountain. Through Operation Genesis stocked with full range
of mammals, predators and birds. Accommodation in *Tshukudu, Manyane,*
Mankwe, Kololo, Metswedi and *Bosele*
rest camps, varying in degrees of luxury
from tents to chalets. Restaurants.
Swimming pools. Stores.

PONGOLA NATURE RESERVE
Box 29, Golela 3990. Tel. (03843) 51012.
In narrow corridor between Swaziland
and Natal. Reedbuck, bushbuck, grey

Kudu bull and cow

and red duiker, suni and impala. Rare
reptiles and birds.No accommodation.

POTGIETERSRUS RESERVE
Box 170, Potgietersrus 0600. Tel.
*(01541) 4314.*Breeding center administered by the National Zoological Gardens at northern outskirts of Potgietersrus. Specializes in rare species such as
tsessebe and pygmy hippopotamus.
There are numerous birds. No accommodation.

ROB FERREIRA GAME RESERVE
Box 19, Christiana 2680. Tel. (0534)
*2244.*North-east of Christiana. White
rhino, impala, zebra, black wildebeest,
red hartebeest and gemsbok. Accommodation in self-contained chalets.
Caravan park.

RUSTENBURG NATURE RESERVE
Box 511, Rustenburg 0300. Tel. (01421)
31050. Some 95 km from Johannesburg. Wildlife includes oribi, eland,
sable, kudu, zebra and 256 bird species. Two hour and two day walking
trails.

S A LOMBARD NATURE RESERVE
Box 174, Bloemhof 2660. Tel. (018022)
4203. Near Bloemhof. Known for bird-
life. Large dam on the reserve attracts
waterfowl. More than 250 bird species
have been recorded. No accommodation.

SUIKERBOSCHRAND RESERVE
Private Bag H616, Heidelberg 2400.
Tel. (0151) 2181. Near Heidelberg. Habi-
tat for duiker, rhebok, baboon, zebra,
kudu and more than 200 bird species.
Three trails range from 4 to 66 km.
Caravan park.

WARMBATHS NATURE RESERVE
P O Box 75, Warmbaths 0480. Tel.
(015331) 2200. Reserve adjoins
Warmbaths hot springs. Red harte-
beest, Burchell's zebra and impala.
Accommodation at the mineral spa.
Caravan camping.

NATAL REGION

SAFARI MAP #4 - PAGE 51

Natal, the smallest of South Africa's four provinces, competes with the Transvaal when it comes to game reserves - both in number and variety.

Most of these nature reserves are in the vicinity of the Drakensberg mountains and Lake St. Lucia in northern Natal and Zululand. Not only the well-known Hluhluwe (pronounced looloowe), but most other reserves in the province are under control of the *Natal Parks Board, P O Box 662, Pietermaritzburg 3200. Tel. (03311) 47-1961.*

ACCOMMODATION

Accommodation vary and in many cases visitors are required to bring their own food and beverages. Cooks are available at bungalows, cottages, lodges, huts and rest huts.In most instances advance reservations are essential. There are also a few private lodges, where a little extra luxury is offered. (Anti-malaria medication should be taken when visiting the Natal north coast, northern Natal and Zululand).

GETTING THERE

There are daily flights from Johannesburg to Richards Bay the only commercial airport in Zululand. Several private reserves will meet their guests at this airport. Rental cars are also available at this airport. Durban is the best starting point for game reserves in the midland or the Drakensberg regions.

The city has scheduled air links from all other cities in the country and also a few international flights. Several bus tour companies combine visits to Kruger National Park and the Lowveld with stopovers at Hluhluwe or other game reserves in Natal.

Following is an alphabetical listing of the game public and private reserves in the Natal region:

BAYA CAMP

Kwazulu Bureau of Natural Resources, Private Bag X23, Ulundi 3838. On the shore of Lake Sibaya, the largest natural freshwater lake in South Africa, with a surface area of 77 sq km and an average depth of 13 m. Two hides for bird-watchers.Fishing. Rental boats with a coxswain are available for hire. Huts and swimming pool. No camping.

CAPE VIDAL STATE FOREST

Private Bag, St Lucia Estuary 3936. Tel. (03592) 1104. About 32 km north of St Lucia Estuary. Forested dunes along the lake (up to 150 m) are among the world's highest. Variety of tropical plants and animal life including red duiker, bushbuck, bushpig, vervet and samango monkey. Abundant bird life. Hiking Trails include the 3-day Mziki linking St Lucia with Cape Vidal. Game fishing. Log cabins. Camping.

COLEFORD NATURE RESERVE

Natal Parks Board, P O Box 662, Pietermaritzburg 3200. Tel. (03311) 47-1961. Some 27 km south of Underberg along the Ingwangwana River. Wildlife includes wildebeest, blesbok, oribi and other antelope. Wattled cranes and wetland bird species. Rainbow trout fishing. Tackle for rental and permits obtainable from the Camp Superintendent. Huts, bungalows, cottages. Horseriding, tennis and croquet.

Flamingo

Bateleur Eagle

Self-guided nature trails and boat tours of the lake. Fishing. Equipped huts at Charters Creek, Fanies Island and Dugandlovu. Caravan camping.

GIANT'S CASTLE RESERVE
Box 288, Estcourt 3310. Tel. (03631) 24435. About 70 km southwest of Estcourt. Rugged area of 70,000 acres forming part of the Drakensberg Escarpment. Wildlife includes 12 species of antelope and 140 bird species, including bearded vulture. Fifty km of trails lead through the reserve.Hikers sleep in huts or caves. Two to four-day guided mountain rides. Brown trout fishing in Bushman's River and rainbow trout in Little Tugela River. Fishing licences obtainable from the Superintendent. Main Camp offers cottages, bungalows and upmarket Giant's Lodge.Injasuti has cabins. Camping.

HAROLD JOHNSON RESERVE
Box 148, Darnall 4480. (0324) 61574. Near Darnall in Zululand. Inhabited by blue, grey and red duiker, bushbuck, zebra and impala. Caravan camping.

HLUHLUWE GAME RESERVE
Natal Parks Board, P O Box 662, Pieter-maritzburg 3200. Tel. (03311) 47-1961. World-renowned game reserve about 280 km north of Durban and 30 km west of Lake St Lucia. Hluhluwe occupies 50,000 acres at the foothills of the first escarpment rising from the coastal plain, combining forest, woodland, savannah and grassland. Black and white rhinoceros, elephant, nyala, buffalo, zebra, blue wildebeest, kudu, impala, bushbuck, waterbuck, giraffe, warthog, bushpig, monkey, baboon, lion, leopard, wild dog, hyena and cheetah inhabit the reserve. Birds are numerous and varied. White-backed vulture, bateleur, crested guinea-fowl, green-spotted dove and trumpeter hornbill are frequently seen. Crocodiles and hippos in the rivers. Auto trail for self-drive visitors with their own transport, while boat trips on the Hluhluwe River

DLINZA FOREST RESERVE
Natal Parks Board, P O Box 662, Pieter-maritzburg 3200. Tel. (03311) 47-1961. At the town of Eshowe.Wildlife includes bushbuck, blue and red duiker, vervet monkeys and a rich bird life. No accommodation.

ENSELENI NATURE RESERVE
Natal Parks Board, P O Box 662, Pieter-maritzburg 3200. Tel. (03311) 47-1961. Thirteen km north-east of Empangeni. Supports nyala, impala, bushbuck, zebra, blue wildebeest and reedbuck. Crocodiles and hippos reside in the Enseleni River. No accommodation.

FALSE BAY PARK
Box 222, Hluhluwe 3960. Tel. (03562) Ask for 2911. On western shore of Lake St Lucia. Marshlands and coastal bushlands with abundant game. Provides sanctuary for the only pink-backed pelican breeding colony in Southern Africa. From December to April, hundreds congregate in the trees on the banks of the Hluhluwe River.

PARKS AND GAME & NATURE RESERVES - NATAL

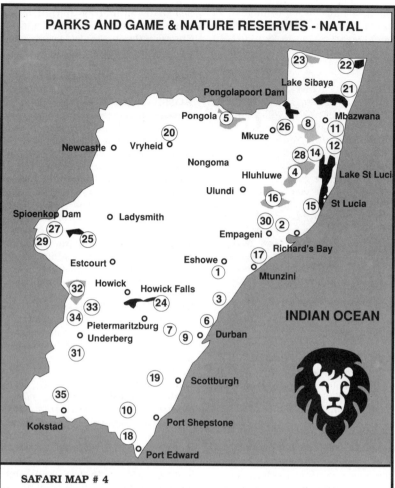

INDIAN OCEAN

SAFARI MAP # 4

1 Dlinza Forest Nature Reserve
2 Enseleni Nature Reserve
3 Harold Johnson Reserve
4 Hluhluwe Game Reserve
5 Itala Game Reserve
6 Umhlanga Lagoon Reserve
7 Krantzkloof Nature Reserve
8 Mkuzi Game Reserve
9 North Park Nature Reserve
10 Oribi Gorge Nature Reserve
11 Sodwana Bay National Park
12 St Lucia Game Reserve
13 Cape Vidal State Forest
14 False Bay Park
15 St Lucia Park
16 Umfolozi Game Reserve
17 Umlalazi Nature Reserve
18 Umtamvuna Nature Reserve
19 Vernon Crookes Reserve
20 Vryheid Nature Reserve
21 Baya Camp
22 Kosi Bay Nature Reserve
23 Ndumu Game Reserve
24 Umgeni Valley Reserve
25 Spioenkop Nature Reserve
26 Malachite Camp
27 Rugged Glen Nature Reserve
28 Ubizane Forest Camp
29 Royal Natal National Park
30 Nyala Game Ranch
31 Coleford Nature Reserve
32 Giant's Castle Game Reserve
33 Kamberg Nature Reserve
34 Loteni Nature Reserve
35 Mt Currie Nature Reserve

can be arranged. Self-contained cottages and chalets with access to communal showers, toilets and kitchens. Talks about wildlife and films and slide shows are held regularly.

ITALA GAME RESERVE

Box 42, Louwsburg 3150. Tel. (03882) 75239. In the Pongola Valley, north of the village of Louwsburg on the Transvaal border, this reserve measures 29,653 ha. Large variety of game including black and white rhinoceros, tsessebe, impala, waterbuck, warthog, reedbuck, giraffe, eland, kudu, baboon and cheetah on terrain varying from open bushveld to grassed hilltops, deep valleys, granite outcrops and rivers (safe for swimming). Over 300 bird species. Three-day hikes conducted from March to October. Hikers sleep in tents. Also 30 km self-guided *Ngubhu Loop Auto Trail.* Accommodation in bush camps. Camping.Picnic and *braai* (barbecue) sites on the Mbizo and Ngubhu Rivers.

KAMBERG NATURE RESERVE

Natal Parks Board, P O Box 662, Pietermaritzburg 3200. Tel. (03311) 47-1961. In the foothills of the Drakensberg. Wildlife includes reedbuck, blesbok, and other antelope.The four-km *Mooi River Self-guided Trail* is specially designed for the physically handicapped. Brown trout fishing in river and dams

Hippo mother and baby

stocked with rainbow trout. (Fishing season between 1 September and 30 April.) Licence and daily permit is obtainable from Camp Superintendent. Hutted camp. Rustic farmhouse provides accommodation for 10 guests.

KOSI BAY NATURE RESERVE

Kwazulu Bureau of Natural Resources, Private Bag X23, Ulundi 3838. Northeastern corner of Zululand, close to Mozambique border. Mangrove swampland with umdoni and fig canopy trees and palms around 4 interlinked lakes. Species include hippo, turtles and crocodiles. Fluff tail, palm-nut vulture, fish eagle, white-backed heron and crab plover are among 247 species of birds. Hiking trails, including overnight walk, conducted by rangers. Fishing. Three self-catering lodges. Camping sites. Four-wheel drive vehicles essential.

KRANTZKLOOF RESERVE

Box 288, Kloof 3640. Tel. (031) 74-3515. Some 26 km west of Durban. Bushbuck, bushpig and blue, red and grey duiker. Bird life includes raptors. Rambling trails. No accommodation.

LOTENI NATURE RESERVE

Natal Parks Board, P O Box 662, Pietermaritzburg 3200. Tel. (03311) 47-1961. In the foothills of Drakensberg. Reedbuck, rhebok, eland and other antelope and 150 bird species. Circular 12 km Eagle Trail offers magnificent views of the Drakensberg. Loteni River within the reserve stocked with brown trout. Fishing permits are obtainable from the Camp Superintendent. Bungalows and cottages. There is a Settlers Museum in the park.

MALACHITE CAMP

Rattray Reserves, Box 2575, Randburg 2125. Tel. (011) 289-2677. Named after malachite kingfisher. About 8 km south-east of Mkuze. Nearly 400 bird species. Fishing. Accommodation for a maximum of 10 in 4 thatched double rondavels. Meals provided. Unlicensed.

MKUZI GAME RESERVE

P O Box, Mkuze 3965. Tel. (0200) Ask for Mkuze 2. About 335 km from Durban on main North Coast road. Wildlife includes klipspringer, eland, mountain reedbuck, waterbuck, impala, giraffe, rhinoceros, nyala, kudu, reedbuck, suni, bushpig, hippopotamus and crocodile. Some 413 bird species. One-day walks and three-day Bushveld Trails twice a month from April to October.Self-guided 3 km Mkuzi Fig Forest Walk and Mkuzi Auto Trail. Accommodation, including meals, in huts, bungalows and cottages.Caravan camping. Four hides and bird observation platform overlook Nsumo Pan.

MOUNT CURRIE RESERVE

Box 378, Kokstad 4700. Tel. (0372) 3844. Close to town. Rhebok, reedbuck, oribi, grey duiker and other antelope. Birds include blue crane, rock kestrel and crowned eagle. No accommodation. Camping.

NDUMU GAME RESERVE

Kwazulu Bureau of Natural Resources, Private Bag X23, Ulundi 3838. About 470 km north of Durban.Riverine forest and bush. More than 400 bird species, including tropical East African types. Large crocodile population, as well as hippopotamus, nyala, bushbuck, duiker, rhino, bushpig and suni. Conducted walking trails and landrover tours. Self-catering hutted camp under *marula* trees.

NORTH PARK NATURE RESERVE

Box 288, Kloof 3640. (031) 74-3515. Near Durban. Bushbuck, blue and grey duiker and banded mongoose. Abundance of birds. No accommodation.

NYALA GAME RANCH

Private Bag, Empangeni Station 3910. Tel. (0351) 2-4547. Northwest of Empageni. Venue for environmental education. Large variety of mammals and birds. Mbondwe, Hlati and Umvumvu camps have huts.

Loggerhead turtle

ORIBI GORGE NATURE RESERVE

Natal Parks Board, P O Box 662, Pietermaritzburg 3200. Tel. (03311) 47-1961. Some 130 km south of Durban. 29 km circular drive leads through and around deep, forested Oribi Gorge. Wildlife includes leopard, bushbuck, reedbuck, baboon, samango and vervet monkeys, blue and grey duiker. Oribi, after which the gorge was named, is rarely seen. Close to 300 bird species. Accommodation in self-contained cottage and huts, as well as the nearby Oribi Gorge Hotel.

ROYAL NATAL NATIONAL PARK

Natal Parks Board, P O Box 662, Pietermaritzburg 3200. Tel. (03311) 47-1961. Royal Natal National Park Hotel P O Mount-aux-Sources 3353. Tel. (0364) 38-1051. About 100 km from Ladysmith. As part of the Drakensberg Escarpment, this park is dominated by the famous Amphitheater. Wildebeest, reedbuck, rhebok, blesbok and other antelope.Over 180 bird species, including black eagles bearded and Cape vultures and jackal buzzards.Thirtyone walking and horse-riding trails, ranging from 3 to 45 km.The *Tendele* Hutted Camp offers equipped cottages, bungalows and spacious lodge. Also modern, privately run Royal Natal National Park Hotel. Facilities include visitor center with wildlife film shows. curio shop, picnic sites and camping.

RUGGED GLEN RESERVE

Mount-aux-Sources 3353. Tel. (0364) 7011. About 98 km from Ladysmith. Habitat and wildlife are similar to those of the Royal Natal National Park. Camping.

SODWANA BAY NATIONAL PARK

Private Bag 310, Mbazwana 3974. Tel. (0356) 572. About 400 km from Durban Tidal pools and coral reefs and wildlife including suni, red and grey duiker, steenbok, reedbuck and bushpig. Abundant bird life with species such as Woodward's batis and Rudd's apalis. Coastal game fishing.Accommodation in 20 log cabins. Camping. Provisions.

African porcupine

SPIOENKOP NATURE RESERVE

Box 140, Winterton 3340. (0368) Ask for 78. Some 35 km south-west of Ladysmith.Tugela River runs through the reserve. Wildlife includes wildebeest, zebra, eland, hartebeest, blesbok, and white rhinoceros. One of trails leads to Spioenkop Battlefield. Fully equipped chalets. Caravan camping. Wildlife films during peak holiday periods.Picnic spots. Children's playground. Boating, water sports, tennis, badminton and horse-riding.

ST LUCIA GAME RESERVE

Natal Parks Board, P O Box 662, Pietermaritzburg 3200. Tel. (03311) 47-1961. The so-called Lake St Lucia complex comprises several sanctuaries, including the St Lucia Game Reserve. (See also St. Lucia Park, False Bay Park and

Cape Vidal State Forest. The Game Reserve stretches along the coastline and 3 km out to sea, from Sodwana Bay in the north to Cape Vidal in the south over an area of 72,000 acres. Hundreds of hippos and crocodiles. Sea contains the southernmost coral reefs in the world. Loggerhead and leatherback turtles breed on the beaches. Angling, ski boat and game fish spearing permitted. No accommodation.

ST LUCIA PARK

Private Bag, St Lucia Estuary 3936. Tel. (03592) Ask for 20. A 1 km wide strip of land surrounding Lake St. Lucia. Rich in hippo, crocodile, goliath heron and other fish-hunting birds, pelicans and flamingos. It is also the site for the interesting Crocodile Research Center. Accommodation varies from caravan and camping sites to furnished log cabins and camping sites. Rental boats, swimming pools, picnic sites.

UBIZANE GAME RANCH

Box 102, Hluhluwe 3960. Tel. (03562) 3602. Northern Zululand. Game includes rhino, giraffe, nyala and impala. Also abundant bird-life. The three-star Zululand Safari Lodge is on the ranch. Facilities include a restaurant, bar and swimming pool. Cruises are offered to the bird breeding areas. There are also 3 exclusive camps with reed and thatched huts for 20 guests. Meals available.Unlicensed.

UMFOLOZI GAME RESERVE

Natal Parks Board, P O Box 662, Pietermaritzburg 3200. Tel. (03311) 47-1961. Some 270 km north of Durban. Covers almost 100,000 acres of land between the White and Black Umfolozi Rivers. Wildlife includes rhino, duiker, steenbuck, elephant and nyala, Some 300 bird species. Wilderness Trails lead through Shaka's old hunting grounds. On the 'primitive trail' backpacks containing food, clothing and equipment are carried. The 67 km Umfolozi Mosaic Auto Trail takes 5 hours. Accommodation in self-contained cottages, a lodge, huts and bush camps. Hide at main rhino drinking pan.

UMGENI VALLEY RESERVE
Box 394, Howick 3290. Tel. (03321) 3931. Near Howick below Howick Falls. Supports giraffe, zebra, oribi and other antelope. More than 200 bird species. Network of trails. Five-bedded self-contained and four bush camps.

UMHLANGA NATURE RESERVE
Natal Parks Board, P O Box 662, Pietermaritzburg 3200. Tel. (03311) 47-1961. About 18 km from Durban. Large number of bird species. No accommodation.

UMLALAZI NATURE RESERVE
Box 234, Mtunzini 3867. Tel. (0353) 40-1836. About 128 km north of Durban Wildlife includes bushpig, blue, duiker, bushbuck and crocodile. Wide variety of bird species includes milkwoods, strangler figs, reeds and rushes. There are two self-guided hiking trails and fishing is allowed. Thirteen fully equipped log cabins are available, as well as camping and picnic sites. Water-skiing and boating are permitted on the lagoon.

UMTAMVUNA NATURE RESERVE
Box 25, Port Edward 4295. Tel. (03930) 383. Near Port Edward. Serval, baboon, reedbuck and small mammals. Diverse bird life. No accommodation.

VERNON CROOKES RESERVE
Scottburgh. Tel. (03231) 4-2222. Near town. Eland, zebra, blue wildebeest, bushbuck and abundance of birds. Three self-guided walks. Accommodation fully equipped camp.

VRYHEID NATURE RESERVE
Natal Parks Board, P O Box 662, Pietermaritzburg 3200. Tel. (03311) 47-1961. On Lancaster Hill overlooking Vryheid. Reedbuck, eland, zebra, oribi, bushbuck and blesbok. No accommodation.

CAPE REGION
SAFARI MAP #5 - PAGE 57

Game reserves in the Cape region vary dramatically from lush-green coastal forests to inland deserts. Wildlife ranges from elephant to moles, whales to minuscule water creatures.

This region contains Kalahari Gemsbok Park, the second largest game park after Kruger National Park in the Transvaal, and one of the world's foremost bird sanctuaries at Langebaan Lagoon. Its Addo Elephant Park, near Port Elizabeth, has developed into one of the prime destinations for conservationists.

Several of these parks are also prime destinations for botanists and floral societies as they represent a good cross section of the country's wealth of flora.

ACCOMMODATION

While the major parks offer accommodation and camping facilities, many of these reserves do not. Visitors will, however, usually find comfortable accommodation nearby.

Springbok

Following in alphabetical order is a selection of game parks and nature reserves in the Cape region. *(SAFARI MAP #5 ON THE OPPOSITE PAGE).*

ADDO ELEPHANT PARK

National Parks Board, P O Box 787, Pretoria 0001. Tel. (012) 343-1991. About 7 km north of Port Elizabeth. Large elephant population, as well as black rhino, buffalo and a number of antelope. Porcupine, ant-bear and bushpig among the nocturnal animals. More than 170 bird species .Self-contained rondavels and cottages. Camping. Restaurant, curio shop, *braai* (barbecue) facilities.

AKKERENDAM RESERVE

Box 28, Calvinia 8190. Tel. (02772) Ask for 11. Near town. Gemsbok, wildebeest, Hartmann's mountain zebra, steenbok, rhebok, jackal and bat-eared fox and 'black' springbok. Three dams attract birds. No accommodation.

ANDRIES VOSLOO KUDU RESERVE

Private Bag 1006, Grahamstown 6140. Tel. (0461) 2-7909. Some 32 km west of Grahamstown. Supports black rhino, kudu, springbok, warthog, blue and grey duiker and buffalo. Over 185 bird species. Two basic tent camps.

Chacma Baboon

AUGRABIES FALLS PARK

National Parks Board, P O Box 787, Pretoria 0001. Tel. (012) 343-1991. On Orange River, 120 km west of Upington. More than 160,000 acres with Augrabies Falls at center. Kokerboom and many other species of aloe as well as camel thorn, white karee, wild olive trees. Black rhino, eland, baboon and small antelope. It provides three hiking trails, complete with huts along the way. Rest camp with fully-equipped air-conditioned chalets. Caravan. Camping. Store. Restaurant.

BONTEBOK NATIONAL PARK

Box 149, Swellendam 6740. Tel. (0291) 4-2735. Some 7 km south of Swellendam. Set in botanical park covered with flowers in late winter and early spring. Large herds of once threatened bontebok, as well as rhebok, Cape grysbok, mountain zebra, steenbok, duiker and more than 192 bird species. Fishing in Breede River. Two hiking trails. Four six-berth caravans.

DE HOOP NATURE RESERVE

Private Bag X16, Bredasdorp 7280. Tel. (02922) 782. Some 60 km east of Bredasdorp. Diversity of bird species. This coastline is one of the most important mating and calving areas in the world for the southern right whale. Accommodation is in the form of two simple chalets and four camp sites.

DOORNKLOOF RESERVE

P O Box 94, Colesberg 5980. Tel. (05852) 1304. Some 45 km from Colesberg. Kudu, brown hyena, steenbok, bat-eared fox and aardvark (ant eater). Numerous bird species. Fishing. No accommodation.

GAMKA MOUNTAIN RESERVE

Private Bag X21, Oudtshoorn 6620. Tel. (04437) 367. About 35 km west of Oudtshoorn. Mountain zebra, klipspringer, duiker, steenbok, baboon and caracal, as well as 90 bird species. No accommodation.

GOOD HOPE NATURE RESERVE
Box 840, Cape Town 8000. Tel. (021) 22-1025. Tip of Cape Peninsula. Spectacular sea views and rich in flora. Eight antelope species, mountain zebra and chacma baboons. One of world's most prolific tortoise breeding grounds. Over 150 bird species. Restaurant, curio shop and information center. No accommodation.

GOUKAMMA NATURE RESERVE
Box 331, Knysna 6570. Tel. (0445) 22001. Between Knysna and Sedgefield,

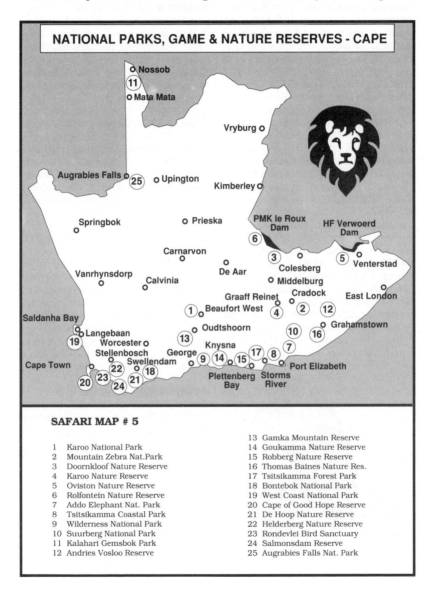

NATIONAL PARKS, GAME & NATURE RESERVES - CAPE

SAFARI MAP # 5

1 Karoo National Park	13 Gamka Mountain Reserve
2 Mountain Zebra Nat.Park	14 Goukamma Nature Reserve
3 Doornkloof Nature Reserve	15 Robberg Nature Reserve
4 Karoo Nature Reserve	16 Thomas Baines Nature Res.
5 Oviston Nature Reserve	17 Tsitsikamma Forest Park
6 Rolfontein Nature Reserve	18 Bontebok National Park
7 Addo Elephant Nat. Park	19 West Coast National Park
8 Tsitsikamma Coastal Park	20 Cape of Good Hope Reserve
9 Wilderness National Park	21 De Hoop Nature Reserve
10 Suurberg National Park	22 Helderberg Nature Reserve
11 Kalahari Gemsbok Park	23 Rondevlei Bird Sanctuary
12 Andries Vosloo Reserve	24 Salmonsdam Reserve
	25 Augrabies Falls Nat. Park

around freshwater lake, Groenvlei. Bontebok, duiker, eland, vervet monkey, bushpig and over 100 bird species. Two easy trails. No accommodation.

HELDERBERG NATURE RESERVE
Box 19, Somerset West 7130. Tel. (024)
51-4022. Disa orchids bloom from December to February. Inhabited by springbok, bontebok, steenbok, grysbok, duiker and a rich endemic bird life. No accommodation.

HESTER MALAN RESERVE
Private Bag X1, Springbok 8240. Tel.
(0251). Some 16 km south-east of Springbok. Gemsbok, Hartmann's mountain zebra, springbok, klipspringer, bat-eared fox, caracal, baboon and bird species. Succulent collection on display. No accommodation.

KALAHARI GEMSBOK PARK
National Parks Board, P O Box 787, Pretoria 0001. Tel. (012) 343-1991.
North-west corner of South Africa, wedged between Namibia and Botswana. Second biggest game park in South Africa after Kruger National Park. Covers 3702 sq miles. Most wildlife in the dry river beds. Large herds of blue wildebeest, springbok and eland, and smaller groups of gemsbok and red hartebeest. Carnivores include the distinctive Kalahari lion, cheetah, leopard, wild dog, spotted and brown hyena. More than 200 bird species. Rest camps at Twee Rivieren, Mata Mata and Nossob with fully equipped

Sea Otter

chalets. Twee Rivieren has swimming pool, restaurant and a 'lapa' (walled enclosure) where brunch and evening *braais* (barbecues) are served. Landing strips for light aircraft at Twee Rivieren and Nossob. Rental cars available.

KAROO NATIONAL PARK
Box 316, Beaufort West 6970. Tel. (0201)
52828. Just north of the town. Fifty species of mammals, including zebra, and gemsbok. Three-day Springbok Hiking Trail with overnight huts. Also luxury chalets, licensed restaurant, curio shop and supplies.

KAROO NATURE RESERVE
Box 349, Graaff-Reinet 6280. Tel. (0491)
23453. Bordering town. Game includes kudu, duiker, klipspringer, reedbuck, blesbok and Cape mountain zebra. Prolific bird life. Four trails, ranging from 2 to 20 km. No accommodation.

MOUNTAIN ZEBRA PARK
National Parks Board, P O Box 787, Pretoria 0001. Tel. (012) 343-1991.
Some 27 km west of Cradock. Mountain zebra and large herds of eland, springbok, blesbok and other antelope. Also African wild cat, black-backed jackal and Cape fox. More than 200 bird species, including black eagle. Three day hiking with overnight huts. Fully equipped chalets at restored farmstead. Caravan park. Restaurant.

OVISTON NATURE RESERVE
Box 302, Randfontein 1760. Tel. (011)
696-1442. Southern shore of Verwoerd Dam. Species include springbok, blesbok, Burchell's zebra and wildebeest. Over 140 bird species. Fishing. No accommodation.

ROBBERG NATURE RESERVE
Private Bag, Plettenberg Bay 6600. Tel.
(04457) 33741. Close to Plettenberg beach resort. Bird species include Cape gannet, crowned eagle, oyster-catchers, giant kingfishers and sunbirds. Fishing. No accommodation.

ROLFONTEIN NATURE RESERVE
*Box 23, Vanderkloof 8771.*On banks of P K le Roux Dam. Inhabited by eland, gemsbok, Burchell's zebra, rhino, kudu, cheetah and over 200 bird species. Self-guided 2 hour trail. Tented accommodation for groups.

RONDEVLEI BIRD SANCTUARY
Muizenberg. Tel. (021) 72-5711. Near Cape Town. More than 200 species of resident and migrant birds have been recorded. Hippo have been introduced. Museum features the birds, mammals, amphibians and reptiles of the region. No accommodation.

SALMONSDAM NATURE RESERVE
Box 5, Stanford 7210. Tel. (02833) 789. About 45 km west of Hermanus. Mountainous, with forests, deep kloofs, waterfall and many protea. Bontebok, klipspringer, small mammals and rich bird life. Huts. Caravan camping.

SUURBERG NATIONAL PARK
Private Bag X6052, Port Elizabeth 6000. Tel. (04252) Ask for 106. About 12 km north of the Addo Elephant National Park. Large numbers of grey rhebok, mountain reedbuck, bushbuck, grey and blue duiker, baboon, vervet monkey and caracal. Two short trails. No accommodation.

THOMAS BAINES RESERVE
Private Bag 1006, Grahamstown 6140. Tel. (0461) 2-8262. About 15 km south of Grahamstown. Cape buffalo, white rhino, eland, kudu and more than 170 bird species. No accommodation.

TSITSIKAMMA COASTAL PARK
National Parks Board, P O Box 787, Pretoria 0001. Tel. (012) 343-1991. Groot River mouth, near Humansdorp extending 5 km into sea. Yellow woods fringed by heaths and proteas, ferns, wild orchids and many species of lily. Hikers may encounter rock-rabbit, bushbuck, Cape grysbok, blue duiker, baboon and vervet monkey. More than 200 bird include 35 types of seabirds. Tidal pools are rich in marine life. Fishing limited.Self-contained beach cottages and luxury holiday apartments at Storms River mouth. Caravan camping. Store. Restaurant.

TSITSIKAMMA FOREST RESERVE
Private Bag X537, Humansdorp 6300. Tel. (04231) 5-1180. About 100 km east of Knysna. Ancient trees, dense forests, evergreen ravines, shrubs, creepers, ferns, moss and lichen. Bushbuck, bushpig and blue duiker and diversity of bird species.Several trails.Caravan camping.

WEST COAST NATIONAL PARK
National Parks Board, P O Box 787, Pretoria 0001. Tel. (012) 343-1991. About 100 km north of Cape Town. Includes 16 mile Beach and Langebaan Lagoon, stretching south of Saldanha.

This park is recognized by ornithologists as one of the great wetlands of the world and rated to be the world's fourth most important bird sanctuary.

Species present in the thousands include cormorants, sea gulls, common sandpipers, sanderlings, plovers, gannets and flamingos. In summer, the lagoon is populated by some 55 000 birds, including large numbers of migrants from arctic breeding grounds.

Bontebok

A section of the park has been zoned for water sports. The three star Langebaan Lodge provides accommodation nearby.

Educational boat trips are offered to the islands of Jutten, Schapen, Markus and Malgas. An environmental education center has been created to serve as a conservation school for the surrounding area.

WILDERNESS NATIONAL PARK
National Parks Board, Box 774, George 6530. Tel. (0441) 74-6924. Between Knysna and George. Comprises Touw River Estuary, known as Wilderness Lagoon, the Serpentine, Eilandvlei, Langvlei, Rondevlei, Swartvlei and Knysna National Lake. (Afrikaans word *'vlei'* means 'wetlands'.) Water ranges between fresh and sea-water. Swartvlei is largest natural saltwater lake in South Africa.

Mammals include golden moles, the Cape clawless otter, variety of bats and some antelope. Birds include marine, estuarine and evergreen forest species. Foremost waterfowl sanctuary. Water sports. Fishing. Fully equipped two bedroomed chalets. Camping. Rental caravans.

For more information about botanical gardens in the Cape and the other regions, see our chapter DOWN THE GARDEN PATH.

ORANGE FREE STATE
SAFARI MAP #6 - OPPOSITE PAGE.

Much of the large grassy plains once teeming with large herds of animals are now utilized as farmland in the Orange Free State.

Under the watchful eye of the provincial Directorate of Nature Conservation several new reserves and parks have been added to the famous Golden Gate Highlands National Park.

RECREATION

Most of these sanctuaries are situated around dams and often do double duty as recreational areas for humans as well. Several offer accommodation varying from self-contained chalets and huts to upmarket resorts.

Following in alphabetical order are the major points of interest for safari-goers who find themselves in this central part of South Africa :

FRANKLIN NATURE RESERVE
This reserve on Naval Hill in the center of Bloemfontein holds the distinction of being the only one of its kind in the middle of a city, anywhere in the world. Blesbok, springbok, bontebok, zebra and eland roam freely in the 400 acre sanctuary. No accommodation.

GOLDEN GATE HIGHLANDS PARK
National Parks Board, P O Box 787, Pretoria 0001. Tel. (012) 343-1991. On the scenic Highlands Route at the foothills of the Maluti Mountains. Its 24,000 acres cover a region with spectacular sandstone formations. The name Golden Gate comes from the sandstone golden gate-posts in the park. From spring to autumn a dazzling display of wild flowers covers the area, traversed by several hiking and auto trails.

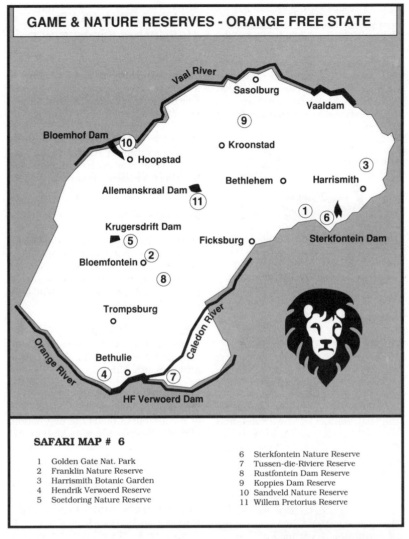

GAME & NATURE RESERVES - ORANGE FREE STATE

SAFARI MAP # 6

1 Golden Gate Nat. Park
2 Franklin Nature Reserve
3 Harrismith Botanic Garden
4 Hendrik Verwoerd Reserve
5 Soetdoring Nature Reserve
6 Sterkfontein Nature Reserve
7 Tussen-die-Riviere Reserve
8 Rustfontein Dam Reserve
9 Koppies Dam Reserve
10 Sandveld Nature Reserve
11 Willem Pretorius Reserve

Wildlife includes rhebok, oribi, wildebeest, blesbok, eland and zebra. About 140 bird species, including bearded vulture and the black eagle. Two-day Rhebok Hiking Trail leads through valleys and ravines, mountain streams and over hills to the summit of Generaalskop (2 757 m). Overnight hut accommodates 18. Main rest camp, Brandwag (Sentinel), offers fully equipped single and double accommodation and restaurant, bar, curio shop, laundromat, information center, tennis, bowling greens.. Glen Reenen has chalets. Caravan camping. Picnic and *braai* (barbecue).

HARRISMITH BOTANIC GARDEN

Box 43, Harrismith 9880. On outskirts of town. Several trails lead through botanic gardens with its variety of small mammals including rock dassies, common duiker and yellow mongoose.No accommodation.

HENDRIK VERWOERD RESERVE

Private Bag X10, Hendrik Verwoerd Dam 9922. Tel. (052172) Ask for 45. Extends between Hendrik Verwoerd Dam and Bethulie. Springbok, wildebeest, red hartebeest and the Cape mountain zebra. Fishing. Full equipped chalets and camping in adjacent resort offers luxury rondavels.

KOPPIES DAM RESERVE

Box 151, Koppies 9540. Tel. (016152) Ask for 2640. Northeast of Kroonstad.Surrounds Koppies Dam on the Rhenoster River. Game includes black wildebeest, blesbok, springbok, Burchell's zebra, impala and buffalo. Dam attracts large number of water birds, No accommodation. Camping. Boating. Fishing.

SANDVELD NATURE RESERVE

Box 414, Bloemhof 2660. Tel. (01802) 1103. About 20 km north-west of Hoopstad. Giraffe, eland, gemsbok, hartebeest and springbok. Bird-life includes spurwinged and Egyptian geese, yellowbilled duck, redbilled teal and South African shellduck. Boating permitted on Bloemhof Dam. Caravan camping.

Spotted hyena

SOETDORING NATURE RESERVE

Box 517, Bloemfontein 9300. Tel. (051) 33-1011. About 40 km from Bloemfontein at Krugersdrift Dam. Antelopes as well as predator park inhabited by lion and cheetah. No accommodation.

STERKFONTEIN DAM RESERVE

Box 24, Harrismith 9880. Tel. (01436) 2-3520. Some 25 km from Harrismith. Habitat for bearded and Cape vulture. Fishing. No accommodation.

TUSSEN-DIE-RIVIERE GAME FARM

Box 16, Bethulie 9992. Tel. (05862) 2803. Some 17 km east of Bethulie. More game than any other reserve in the Free State. Species include springbok, wildebeest, hartebeest, reedbuck, kudu, eland, blesbok and white rhino. Birds include several raptors. Two nature trails. Self-catering accommodation available between 1 November and 30 April.

WILLEM PRETORIUS RESERVE

P O Ventersburg 9450. Tel. (01734) 4168. At Allemanskraal Dam, between Winburg and Kroonstad. Springbok, eland, white rhino, giraffe, buffalo, impala and the largest herd of wildebeest in the world. Over 900 bird species. Chalets, cabins and apartments. Licensed restaurant. Caravan camping.

RUSTFONTEIN NATURE RESERVE

Director of Nature Conservation, Box 577, Bloemfontein 9300. Tel. (051) 405-5245. Area surrounding the Rustfontein Dam is popular breeding ground for water birds and habitat for a number of mammals. No accommodation. Camping and basic facilities.

In the chapter KEY ADDRESSES under WILDLIFE a list of conservation and wildlife societies will be found. Contact any of these for further information and advice about game viewing and conservation.

DOWN THE GARDEN PATH

South Africa can promise you a rose garden.

Roses are the most popular culti-vated flowers in this country. Bloem-fontein in the very center of the country has become known as the rose capital of the Southern Hemi-sphere.

But going down the garden path in South Africa, means more than roses. With 22,000 different wild flowering plants the tip of the Afri-can continent has more than one-tenth of the world's total.

Today tens of flowering plants from South Africa are to be found all over the world. With more than 22 000 different types of wild flowering plants, it is not surprising to trace the roots of many a famous plant or flower back to the tip of the African continent.

STRELITZIA

South Africa gave the city of Los Angeles its emblem - the Strelitzia - and proteas from the Cape adorn the gardens of New Zealand. Australia has adopted more flowering trees, shrubs and bulbs from South Africa than any other part of the world. Cape arums have been known to survive an ordeal by ice in the gardens of England while Scots have long been familiar with the flora of the South African veld, favoring pink and white watsonias and great clumps of agapanthus.

VYGIES

All over Europe window boxes are flushed scarlet with the brilliance of South African pelargoniums, the same radiant heads that give color to New York's brownstones. And across the Americas, over Spain, France, Italy and the Middle East South African *vygies* (Mesembrianthemum) show off

their iridescent beauty. Also the Cape daisy family, the gazanias, arctotis and ursinias that are part of the miracle of spring flowering in semi-desert Namaqualand, have found their way into the gardens of the world.

CAPE

In the vicinity of the Cape Peninsula the vegetation is generally known as *fynbos* - shrubs with delicately shaped or attenuated leaves. Prevalent are the Cape heaths or heather, members of the *Erica* family. *Fynbos* also includes 'pincushions' the 'silver leaf tree' on the slopes of Cape Town's Table Mountain. Fynbos is, however, famous for the protea. One of them, the *Protea cynaroides* is the national flower of South Africa.

The Western Cape also has an infinite variety of smaller plants - bulbs, annuals and perennials, including the radiant and rare 'red disa' *(Disa uniflora)*, acknowledged as one of the most beautiful orchids in the world.

NAMAQUALAND

Inland to the dry north known as Namaqualand, the Cape floral kingdom performs a miracle every year during spring. A sea of flowers appear overnight as succulents storing water in their leaves, stems or roots and ephemerals such as the *Ixia, Moraea* and *Sparaxis* and other members of the daisy family, don their magic dream coats during August to late September.

Other parts of the southern and eastern Cape are also noted for their flora. The Karoo Botanic Garden at Worcester, rich in succulents is not too far from the fynbos of the Outeniqua Mountains and the temperate evergreen forests of Knysna and the Tsitsikamma Forest where towering yellowwood, stinkwood and ironwood trees form dark, cool forests. In the shadows ferns, wild orchids and many species of lily thrive, while at the eastern end of the Langkloof Valley the Eastern Cape bush makes a brief first appearance, only to surface later in the Addo Elephant National Park in a unique tangle of creepers and trees.

NATAL

In Natal humid air rushing inland from the Indian Ocean forms a mist belt as it hits against the cold barrier. It turns the hot coastal air into a temperate moist climate, giving Natal two distinct zones. Sub-tropical vegetation, dune forest, palms, mangroves and the occasional swamp on the coast blend with iris, lilies and other exotic flowering shrubs, trees and climbers. Close to the wildlife reserves of Zululand grow immense sycamore fig trees, mahogany, forests of wild thorn, monkey rope and marula and raphia palm with leaves big enough to lay a table for a family dinner. Inland, every summer, the slopes of the Drakensberg mountains come alive with wild orchids, proteas, watsonias, species of gladiolus and a host of perennials.

TRANSVAAL

The Eastern Transvaal known both as the Bushveld and the Lowveld is another favorite haunt of naturalists. The umbrella-shaped *Acacia* prevail, often in clusters, interspersed with ilala palm, wild fig, fever trees, baobabs, aloes, cycads and impala lilies.

FREE STATE

In the Orange Free State the Drakensberg Botanic Garden near Harrismith and the foothills of the Maluti Mountains contain a variety of flora, while Bloemfontein houses the largest orchid collection in South Africa. Exotica thrive in the Free State and the Lombardy poplar lends special color to the highways in autumn.

William Burchell

English naturalist. Burchell was sent by the British government to St. Helena in 1805 and he arranged for his fiance to follow him to the island. On the voyage over she fell in love with the captain of the ship and married him instead.

For the next two years a tormented Burchell travelled far and wide in the South African interior, seeking solace in nature. This short, slight man of great courage and talent, collected more than 60,000 objects of scientific interest, made drawings and kept extensive records. Two of his finds, the white rhino and a new type of zebra were named after him.

On his return to Britain his plant collection was incorporated into the Kew Royal Botanic Gardens and the entomological finds in the Oxford University museum.

William Burchell's *Travels to the Interior of Southern Africa* was published in the 1820s. His original drawings form part of the Gubbins Trust Collection at Johannesburg's Witwatersrand University.

A drawing of the Protea Nerifolia in an exotic plant book produced by Carolus Cladius in 1605, made it the first of South Africa's 22,000 flowering plants to make it into print. The drawing was based on a dried out specimen brought back all the way from the Cape. Not surprisingly, the Nerifolia was assumed to be a thistle.

Naming these thousands of new and exotic plants was a task that involved among others Carolus Linnaeus, the famous Swedish botanist. Putting his unusual gift for classifying and christening plants and animals to work, Linnaeus came up with names for at least twenty five percent of the flowers found in the Cape Peninsula.

Although Linnaeus never went to the Cape, he encouraged others to go and worked from specimens and drawings brought back to him.

British naturalist and artist, William Burchell, who undertook valuable animal research in the eighteenth century, also distinguished himself as a botanist in South Africa.

With such variety of indigenous flowering plants it is not surprising to find South Africa high on the list of garden clubs and botanists - both for individual and group tours. Various tour operators offer coach tours incorporating visits to the main attractions. Some of these are seasonal and vary in length from one day to a week's duration. Alternatively special interest tour itineraries encompassing the entire country may be booked through a travel agent. For those visitors who prefer to make their own arrangements the following places may be of special interest (SEE FLORAL MAP ON THE OPPOSITE PAGE) :

KIRSTENBOSCH BOTANIC GARDENS. Curator, Private Bag X7, Claremont 7735. Tel: (021) 77-1166. This is the headquarters of the National Botanic Gardens of South Africa, devoting itself exclusively to the cultivation of wild flowers and other indigenous plants. Set against the slopes of Table Mountain, the garden's acreage includes flatlands, gorges, natural springs and streams. Kirstenbosch is one of the most famous gardens of the world. (See also CAPE OUTSKIRTS in the chapter CITY SIGHTS).

CAPE TOWN COMPANY GARDENS. Director of Parks and Forests, Cape Town Municipality, Box 1694, Cape Town 8000. Tel: (021) 210-2622. These gardens in the center of Cape Town occupy part of the site originally planted by founder father, Jan van Riebeeck. Originally intended to yield vegetables for passing ships, it has today a great variety of indigenous and exotic trees. (See also the chapter CITY SIGHTS).

CAPE OF GOOD HOPE RESERVE: The Chief Warden, Box 62, Simonstown 7995. Tel: (021) 86-7176. A typical example of Cape fynbos in an unspoilt area at the southern tip of the Peninsula. Frequently described as Cape

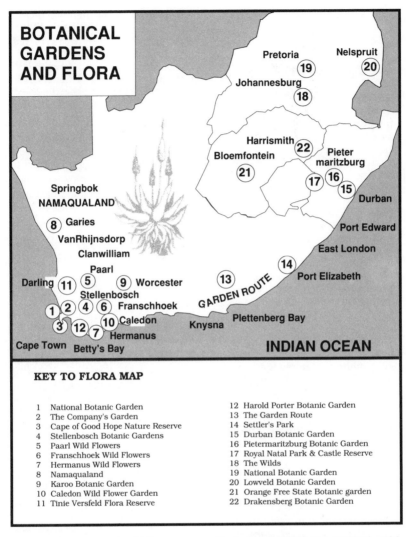

BOTANICAL GARDENS AND FLORA

KEY TO FLORA MAP

1 National Botanic Garden	12 Harold Porter Botanic Garden
2 The Company's Garden	13 The Garden Route
3 Cape of Good Hope Nature Reserve	14 Settler's Park
4 Stellenbosch Botanic Gardens	15 Durban Botanic Garden
5 Paarl Wild Flowers	16 Pietermaritzburg Botanic Garden
6 Franschhoek Wild Flowers	17 Royal Natal Park & Castle Reserve
7 Hermanus Wild Flowers	18 The Wilds
8 Namaqualand	19 National Botanic Garden
9 Karoo Botanic Garden	20 Loweld Botanic Garden
10 Caledon Wild Flower Garden	21 Orange Free State Botanic garden
11 Tinie Versfeld Flora Reserve	22 Drakensberg Botanic Garden

Town's biggest natural wild flower garden this nature reserve contains, apart from some game, a wealth of wild flowers, including proteas, heaths, red-hot pokers and members of the crassula family. *(See also the chapter ON SAFARI).*

PAARL, FRANSCHHOEK, STELLENBOSCH, HERMANUS: *Curator, Botanical Gardens of the University of Stellenbosch 7600. Tel: (02231) 4223.* This whole region offers the full range of Cape flora among scenic mountains and in and around the wine estates with their classic Cape Dutch homesteads. The *Hortus Botanicus* at Stellenbosch also features rare members of the Welwitschia family and rare species of cycad. *(See also the chapters on WINE COUNTRY, ON SAFARI and RURAL ROUTES).*

General Jan Smuts

Revered around the world as a great leader, thinker and philosopher, General Smuts, author of the Preamble to the UN Charter, found time to practise botany.

Well-read in botany, both in English and German, Smuts never ventured into the veld without his shears and magnifying glass.

To Smuts botany was a study of living things set in their natural surroundings. Man-made gardens did not interest him. The plant specimens he took home from the veld he would either put in his presses or study carefully before discarding them. But he went to great pains identifying and collecting specimens.

Even in his late seventies he remained a familiar figure on the slopes of Table Mountain as he climbed to the top, scouring the slopes for interesting stubbles and plants.

"Botany", Smuts wrote, " is one of the basic sciences of human welfare. Plants should be studied as societies, as communities, as groups in their togetherness. Plants, like human beings, should be studied in their social relationships."

NAMAQUALAND: *SA Tourism Board, Box 6187, Roggebaai 8012. Tel: (021) 21-6274.* A semi-desert area centered around Clanwilliam, VanRhynsdorp, Garies, Springbok and Langebaan, north and north-west of Cape Town. During August to September, the desert miraculously turns into a multi-colored carpet of wild flowers.

KAROO BOTANIC GARDEN: *The Curator, Box 152, Worcester 6850. Tel: (0231) 3785.* This popular botanic garden specializes in indigenous succulents such as aloes, euphorbias and stone plants. The garden is ablaze with color in August and September.

CALEDON WILD FLOWER GARDEN: *The Curator, Box 24, Caledon 7230. Tel: (0281) 2-1611.* One of the premier wild flower venues in South Africa. Heaths, bluebells, proteas, everlasting flowers and a host of annuals and perennials are to be found in this garden.

TINIE VERSVELD FLORA RESERVE: *The Curator, Private Bag X7, Claremont 7735. Tel: (021) 77-1166.* Situated about 100 km north of Cape Town this reserve has a large variety of Sandveld flowers such as the scabious, the nemesia, the hybrid ixias and other ephemerals.

HAROLD PORTER BOTANIC GARDEN: *The Curator, PO Box 35, Betty's Bay 7141. Tel: (02823) 9711.* Situated at Betty's Bay, between Cape Town and Hermanus, this area has a wide variety of Cape flora.

THE GARDEN ROUTE: *SA Tourism Board, Box 312, George 6530. Tel (0441) 73-5228.* Starting roughly at Mossel Bay and extending beyond the Tsitsikamma Forest and Tsitsikamma Coastal National Parks, near Knysna and Plettenberg Bay, towards Port Elizabeth, this is one of the world's most popular scenic highways. Its sights include fields of arum and watsonia, a bewildering array of other bulbous plants, shrubs, annuals, perennials and forests of indigenous trees to ferns and wild orchids. *(See also our chapters RESORTS AND SPORTS and RURAL ROUTES).*

SETTLER'S PARK PORT ELIZABETH: *Superintendent of Gardens, Private Bag 1006, Grahamstown 6140. Tel: (0461) 7216.* This park along the Baakens River Valley close to the city represents four floral regions: the *fynbos* of the Western province flora; the Karoo flora, in the form of succulents and the strelitzia family; the Coastal Belt flora of the north-east; and the Addo Bush flora, including the *spekboom*. *(See also the chapter CITY SIGHTS).*

DURBAN'S BOTANIC GARDEN: *The Director of Parks, Recreation and Beaches Department, Durban Municipality, PO Box 3740, Durban 4000. Tel: (031) 21-1303.* Renowned for its large collection of exotic orchids and plants from the region. *(See also the chapter CITY SIGHTS).*

PIETERMARITZBURG BOTANIC GARDEN: *The Curator, 2 Swartkop Road, Pietermaritzburg 3200. Tel: (0331) 2-3585.* Azaleas are in full bloom from August to October while exotica thrive at the Botanic Garden. Plants include rhododendrons, camellias and a wide variety of plane trees. One section of the garden is reserved for the flora of Natal and more particularly the specimens from its mist belt.

ROYAL NATAL AND GIANT'S CASTLE RESERVE: *Public Relations Officer, Natal Parks Game and Fish Preservation Board, PO Box 662, Pietermaritzburg 3200. Tel: (0331) 5-1221 or The Curator, Drakensberg Botanic Garden, PO Box 157, Harrismith 9880. Tel: (01436) 2-3212.* These areas are representative of the rich indigenous flora of this summer rainfall region. The slopes

and bridle paths of the mountains are verdant with trees, shrubs, bulbs, annuals and perennials. *(See also the chapter ON SAFARI).*

THE WILDS JOHANNESBURG: *General Manager, Parks and Recreation, Johannesburg Municipality, Box 2824, Johannesburg 2000. Tel: (011) 77-1111.* An extensive area set aside exclusively to the cultivation of South African wild flowers. Best seen in spring, September to October. The Johannesburg Botanic Garden is also worth including, especially in spring when it has thousands of roses in bloom. *(See chapter CITY SIGHTS).*

NATIONAL BOTANIC GARDEN, PRETORIA: *Director, Private Bag X101, Pretoria 0001. Tel: (012) 86-1164.* Named the Jacaranda City after the thousands of trees which paint the city blue-mauve in October and November. There are several other parks worth including on a visit to the city.

LOWVELD BOTANIC GARDEN, NELSPRUIT: *The Curator, Box 1024, Nelspruit 1200. Tel: (01311) 2-5531.* Features include the River Walk,

clothed in the natural vegetation of the Lowveld, with specimens of trees such as the kiaat, combretum, marula and wild fig. Barberton daisies add color.

ORANGE FREE STATE BOTANIC GARDEN, BLOEMFONTEIN: *The Curator, Box 1536, Bloemfontein 9300. Tel: (051) 3530.* Local flora grows between trees such as the karee and white stinkwood, many succulent plants and members of the daisy family. The Bloemfontein Orchid House, the most modern facility of its kind in the southern hemisphere, houses the largest orchid collection in South Africa. *(See also the chapter CITY SIGHTS).*

DRAKENSBERG BOTANIC GARDEN, HARRISMITH: *The Curator, Box 157, Harrismith 9880. Tel: (01436) 2-3212.* Situated around two lakes below the rugged slopes of the Platberg, 2,700 m above sea level. It has rare aloes, forests of oldwood and other flowering plants typical of the Drakensberg range.

EVENTS

Visitors who wish to combine their visit with important shows, have a wide choice.

In the **vicinity of Cape Town** wild flower exhibitions are during September to the end of October, including the Caledon Wild Flower Show (September) Ceres Wild Flower Show (October), Bredasdorp Wild Flower Show (September), Clanwilliam Flower Show (Late August); Darling Flower Show (September), Hermanus Flower Show (September), Tulbagh Agricultural Wild Flower Show (September) and the Villiersdorp Wild Flower Show (October).

Other major events are the February Dahlia Flower Show, the August Spring Flower Show and the September Orchid Show at **Kirstenbosch**. The Rose and Garden Show in The Civic Centre at Cape Town's Foreshore is another major item on the floral calendar. *Contact the Honorary Secretary of the South Western Cape Horticultural Society, 28 Barlinka Road, Meadowridge 7800. Tel: (021) 72-3709 or Captour, Box 1403, Cape Town 8000. Tel: (021) 25-4090.*

The **Johannesburg** January Wild Flower Show in the Sima Eliovson Floreum of the Botanic Garden is followed by the February Autumn Flower Show and the August Early Spring Flower Show and a Special Wild Flower Show is held at The Wilds in September. *For detail contact the Honorary Secretary, The Transvaal Horticultural Society, PO Box 7616, Johannesburg 2000. Tel: (011) 52-4222.*

In **Pretoria** October is not only the peak month for jacaranda trees and rose and flowers in the city parks. It also marks the massive Rose and Summer Flower Show, preceded by the September Flower Fantasia. *Contact the Secretary, Pretoria Horticultural Society, PO Box 1186, Pretoria 0001. Tel: (012) 6-5242. (The Society welcomes visitors to their monthly meetings on the fourth Wednesday of each month).*

In the **Durban/Pietermaritzburg** region sub-tropical favorable weather makes for year-round shows. *Contact the Secretary, The Durban and Coast Horticultural Society, PO Box 2266, Durban 4000. Tel: (031) 28-6224.*

Port Elizabeth starts its calendar with the popular January Dahlia Show in Feathermarket Hall followed by the February Summer Flower Show in Walmer Town Hall. In September it stages an Orchid Show at City Hall and in October the Spring Flower Show in Walmer Town Hall. Its November Rose exhibition is combined with a home craft show. *Further detail can be obtained from the Secretary, Walmer Horticultural and Industrial Society, 68 Fordyce Road, Walmer 6065. Tel: (041) 51-3416.*

HISTORIC TRAILS

A little bit of history helps.

There are a growing number of travellers who realize that some knowledge of a country's history can make a visit more enjoyable and rewarding.

It makes monuments and museums come alive. Yes, even the living themselves acquire new dimensions as their actions, characteristics and behavior are being weighed against those of past generations. A little knowledge of the past heightens the enjoyment of the present.

History comes in handy, not simply as a reference to identify monuments or to enjoy museums and historic sights. It helps also in the understanding of current events.

Attending the negotiations towards the creation of a new apartheid-free South Africa, are leaders from a dozen or so interested parties ranging from Afrikaner and English-speaking whites, to Colored, Indian and a few black tribes. Although the major parties attending this Convention for a Democratic South Africa (CODESA) all lay claim to broad bipartisan support they are all only parts of the mosaic that is South Africa.

Lord de Villiers

Gandhi 1900

Smuts 1908

Almost a century ago South Africa had an equally momentous national convention to try and bring together four provinces that evolved from the long struggle between Briton and Boer. Only then blacks were serving tea instead of helping to set the agenda.

The National Convention of 1910 was an all-white affair. Representing white Afrikaner interests were Boer generals Louis Botha, Jan Smuts and Barry Hertzog and looking after the interests of English-speaking whites were such notables as Lórd Milner, Dr Leander Jameson and Percy FitzPatrick.

WISDOM

The goal then was to join the two former British colonies of the Cape and Natal together with the two former Boer Republics of the Transvaal and Orange Free State. The wounds left by the Anglo-Boer War of 1899-1902 were still fresh and painful and it took great wisdom and tact on the part of Lord Henry de Villiers, the Chief Justice of the Cape who presided over the negotiations to keep the hurt of the past from wrecking the plans for the future.

Born an Afrikaner and educated in London, De Villiers had an intense admiration for things British, from common law to customs and culture. If anyone could strike a compromise between the two erstwhile enemies, this titled man from the backwoods of South Africa was the one to do so.

CAPITALS

But he also had to contend with regional claims. Natal wanted a guarantee against domination by the other bigger provinces. So local powers were vested in provincial councils. The other three provinces all wanted to be the seat of the new united South Africa. In an act that would have done Solomon proud, Cape Town in the Cape Province became the legislative capital, while Pretoria in the Transvaal was made the administrative capital. Bloemfontein in the Orange Free State became the seat for the highest court in the land, the Appellate Court and was named the judicial capital. South Africa adopted two official languages, Afrikaans and English.

The British flag was left untouched for a while and only later transformed into today's orange, white and blue with a composite of the Union Jack and the two old Boer Republican flags in the middle.

COLOR

The question of color was hardly mentioned in these 1909 deliberations. Smuts, who as Attorney-General of the Transvaal, had already had a few skirmishes with a young Indian lawyer named Mahatma Gandhi over the rights of the oppressed, suggested that the color problem be shelved until after independence. He feared that widely differing viewpoints and practices over this issue may wreck the talks. The founding fathers of the Union of South Africa all concurred.

Gandhi came to South Africa from India as a young lawyer at the turn of the century. He turned up in Natal at the invitation of a wealthy Moslem to handle a corporate case, but soon turned his undivided attention to the plight of the Indian "coolies". They were brought to the sugar cane fields as indentured laborers to make up for the lack in willingness on the part of the proud Zulu tribe to undertake this menial task.

SATYAGRAHA

British-trained barrister Gandhi in his Indian headdress resorted to passive resistance to protest against injustices against his own kind, first in Natal and Transvaal and after 31 May 1910 when South Africa became an independent nation, on a countrywide basis. His method of satyagraha as it was called, was later used with great effect against British colonial rule in India.

Independently from Gandhi, black South Africans were also beginning to become impatient about their situation in the newly independent nation. In 1913 their leadership joined forces in the African National Congress to protest new laws adopted by the new government under the leadership of General Louis Botha.

Hottentot Woman

Several restrictive laws were passed. One removed Blacks in the Cape from the common voters roll and allowed them to vote merely for three white representatives, while another enlarged the territories reserved for black rule.

APARTHEID

Apartheid had been a practice long before 1948 when the National Party came up with the word. Segregation according to race had been the law of the land ever since Jan van Riebeeck landed at the Cape in 1652, and when the British took over in the early eighteenth century they followed suit.

The British actually introduced the first of South Africa's so-called black homelands or Bantustans by declaring British Kaffraria exclusively for the Xhosa tribe and separating it from white-owned land. In 1894 the territory received limited self-rule from the British colonial government, becoming one of the pillars of an edifice that would later be known as grand apartheid.

Until recently it has been fashionable in South Africa to argue about who laid claim to which portion of the country. This debate has subsided somewhat as the realization set in that it is as unrealistic to try and unscramble an egg as

The original Dias Cross
A 5,000 piece puzzle

The oldest and most famous South African relic is kept at the University of Witwatersrand in Johannesburg. The Dias Cross was painstakingly reconstructed from 5,000 fragments sifted from the sand at Kwaaihoek, near Alexandria at the Eastern Cape where Portuguese explorer Bartholomeu Dias erected it more than five hundred years ago.

Until Professor Axelson of the University of Cape Town excavated the fragments in the 1930s, everyone assumed that Dias' cross had totally disappeared from the site where he and his weary men went ashore on 12 March 1488 to commemorate the first successful voyage around the Cape. In Portuguese fashion Dias and his men set up a stone pillar and cross, a *padrao*, to mark the turning point of their discovery voyage. Axelson also found the fragments of an old hand-blown bottle that must have held the sacramental wine used on the occasion.

Today a replica marks the exact spot on South Africa's east coast where the remains of Dias's original beacon was found.

it is to divide all the different factions into neat separate areas according to historic rights and claims.

ON FIRST

So who was on first anyway?

Bartholomeu Dias was the first European to set foot on South African soil. Setting out from his native Portugal with two caravels and a small supply ship in August 1487, he managed to round the Cape early the following year. On 3 February 1488 he spotted the east coast near today's Mossel Bay.

The Portuguese explorer called it Angros dos Vaquiros because they could discern cows watched over by herdsmen. The herdsman were Hottentot or Khoi people, who together with the Bushmen or San, were the original inhabitants of South Africa. A few days later Dias and his party disembarked at Cape St. Blaise and made contact with the natives. They tried to barter for sheep and cattle but an incident erupted which forced his party to return to their ships in a hurry. They resumed their northeastern journey stopping briefly at Algoa Bay (today's Port Elizabeth) before continuing on to Kwaaihoek, west of the Bushman's River mouth.

PADRAO

Here Dias planted a cross or padrao to indicate the furthest point of this historic journey. Back in Portugal sixteen months after his departure, Dias' sensational discovery hardly caused a ripple. The Portuguese were conducting a roaring trade with west Africa and had no immediate need to venture past the Cape to the Far East.

A few years later priorities had changed and in 1497 Dias was asked to accompany fellow Portuguese navigator Vasco Da Gama on the first leg of a journey around the Cape that would actually lead to India and back. The Dutch and British followed the Portuguese once Da Gama had opened up a lucrative sea trade route to India and the Far East. Soon the Cape at the tip of the Africa became a post office and a place for barter with the locals.

Mrs Ples

But were the Hottentot and the Bushmen really the first inhabitants of South Africa. In April 1947 the cranium of what was claimed to be not only South Africa's but the world's earliest man, was discovered at the Sterkfontein caves near Krugersdorp. Initially the scientist who made the discovery, Dr Robert Broom, was the target of much ridicule from experts abroad who dismissed the skull as that of an ape instead of man.

But subsequent discoveries seemed to have confirmed Dr Broom's belief that the Sterkfontein ape-man *(Plesiianthropus transvaaliensis)* may well have been the missing link between ape and man. Mrs. Ples, as this discovery had become known, has been joined since by the fossilized remains of many other early beings who are reputed to have been the first ever to walk upright in human fashion. South Africa, it seems, harbored the world's earliest upright citizens.

Van Riebeeck

Ask white South Africans and they will tell you that South Africa started on 6 April 1652 when Jan van Riebeeck arrived at the Cape with his wife Maria, his four month old son, and a small party. Their original purpose was of course only to establish a halfway supply station to feed the company ships sailing to and from the Far East.

Van Riebeeck was told to build a fort, erect a flagpole to signal the passing ships and to establish a garden to grow

VOC One Guilder

Jan van Riebeeck was not sent to the Cape by the Dutch Government. He went on company business for the *Vereenigde Oost-Indische Compagne* (Dutch East India Company).

Known simply by its acronym VOC, this trading house had received from the Dutch government exclusive trading rights east of the Cape and the authority to establish and run colonies. The VOC was a law onto itself. It meted out punishment in its own courts, including the death sentence. It had its own flag, issued its own money, made its own treaties and even declared war.

Van Riebeeck and his successors were responsible, not to the Dutch government, but to the VOC's ruling Council of Seventeen. So pervasive was the influence of the VOC in their daily lives, that the colonies would simply refer to it as Jan Compagnie (John Company).

Today visitors will find the VOC's initials on much of the finery, cutlery, silverware, crystal and other remnants of the early Cape era in South African museums.

Jan van Riebeeck

produce for the passing crews. He tried to accomplish all this as quickly as he could. To Van Riebeeck this assignment was punishment for suspicion of insider trading while serving the Dutch East India Company in Batavia. The *Vereenigde Oost-Indische Compagne* or *VOC*, as it was known, promised to reassign him to the more desirable Far East on condition that he first does community service, so to speak, at the tip of the Dark Continent.

PRAISE

But Van Riebeeck did not find his tenure at the Cape altogether miserable. His journals contain many happy stories, not least of which is an entry on 2 February 1659: "Praise be the Lord, wine pressed for the first time from Cape grapes." He had started not only a nation, but one of the world's most renowned wine industries.

After seven years, Van Riebeeck volunteered to stay an additional three years and when he finally left in 1662 to become the commander in Malacca, he had started a nation. This time, however, it was with company approval as the VOC had instructed him to send out company men as farmers into the interior. The company gardens were simply not producing the desired volume of food and it was felt that free farmers (vryburgers) would help to fill the need.

When Van Riebeeck landed in 1652, the Hottentots were there to welcome him. Relations were quite cordial as the Dutch bought cattle and sheep from these native herdsmen with bangles, brass, beads and brandy. But in 1657 this sweet relationship soon soured as white farmers began encroaching on traditional Hottentot grazing fields.

THEFT

The Khoi resorted to stock theft and killing and the settlers went after them with guns. But diseases from Europe proved to be a more deadly foe than white pioneers' primitive flint guns. A small pox epidemic in 1713 decimated these native people as those Khoi were infected fled inland, rapidly spreading the killer disease to the interior. Finally the remaining Khoi found themselves caught between the expanding white settlement and the warring black tribes moving southward from other parts of the African Continent. Some sought refuge on white farms where they lost their identity, while others intermingled with the black tribes on the eastern border.

EXTINCT

Many years ago the Khoi Khoin or Hottentot became an extinct race. Apart from drawings by the early explorers and relics in museums, the only traces of these original inhabitants are to be seen in the facial features of the Cape Coloreds and the Xhosa tribes of the Eastern Cape.

We know today that at least some of the *strandlopers* or beach combers first encountered by the Portuguese explorers and Dutch settlers were not Hottentot or Khoi but Bushmen. These aloof little people were called Bosjemans by the Dutch, a name that later changed to Boesman (Bushmen).

Hunters by nature, these Bushmen turned to stock theft instead as farmers denied them access to their traditional stomping grounds. Soon they became the hunted instead of the hunters as killing expeditions were organized to remove the Bushmen menace.

Despite heavy losses inflicted on the Bushmen they continued to raid white farms and kill herd boys - mostly "domesticated" Khoi. In barely ten years from 1786 until 1795 the Bushmen stole an estimated 19,000 cattle and 85,000 sheep and killed almost 300 people. But even these bush-wise people eventually had to give way to the march of modern man.

Those who managed to escape the systematic genocide (in 1795 more than 2,500 were shot and close to 700 taken prisoner in the Graaff Reinet district alone) moved further north. Some sought work on white farms, while others found refuge in the Kalahari.

HUGUENOTS

The arrival of the French Huguenots in the 1680s added measurably to a growing resistance among the farmers against the sometimes dishonest officials at the Cape. At the beginning of the 18th century a certain Adam Tas of Stellenbosch had accused Governor Willem Adriaan van der Stel of widespread corruption in a protest letter signed by himself and sixty fellow farmers and sent to company offices in Batavia. Van der Stel made the mistake of arresting Tas and four of his henchmen, deporting them to Holland and unwittingly giving them the opportunity to state their grievances in person in front of the ruling council of the VOC. Van der Stel was sacked and Tas and his men allowed to return vindicated.

This victory emboldened the settlers to the point where they showed little respect for authority. In

March 1707 French-Dutch Hendrik Bibault heckled an unpopular local official, Starrenburg. When commanded to shut up or leave. Bibault exclaimed in bravado: *"I will not go! I am an Afrikaner!"* This is said to have been the very first time when the word Afrikaner had been used by a settler to describe his nationality. A new nation was born.

MIXING

In 1795 the population at the Cape stood at about 20,000 Europeans, an equal number of slaves (imported mostly from the Far East) and about 15,000 Hottentots. Mixing had taken place despite strenuous efforts by the authorities to keep the races apart. These mulatto people became known as the Cape Coloreds.

At the start of the Napoleonic wars in 1795 the British occupied the Cape at the invitation of the Dutch who dreaded the idea of a French occupation. In 1802 when hostilities between France and Britain ended with the signing of the Peace Treaty of Amiens, the Cape and its mounting problems were given back to the Dutch. Serious border problems had surfaced as the black Xhosa tribes were beginning to spill across the Great Fish River, joining the Khoi or Hottentots in their attacks on Dutch frontier farms.

Bushmen hunt ers-by C D Bell 1835 (Africana Museum)

Shaka from a drawing by Lt. James King who met him in 1825. (S A Library).

Britain's peace with France was, however, short-lived. This time Britain did not wait for an invitation. In January 1806 a British fleet of sixty ships turned up to take possession of the Cape. Britain stayed for a hundred years, giving cause to much turbulence, but at the same time leaving in their wake culture vastly enriched and advanced.

BRITISH

At first the new masters of the Cape cared little about the interior. To Britain, Table Bay was *'the Gibraltar of the Indian Ocean.'* A strategically important harbor halfway between Europe and the Far East. The interior may as well not have existed. In 1814 when the Napoleonic Wars came to an end thou-, sands of demobilized soldiers were left jobless as the Industrial revolution had eliminated much of the manual labor opportunities that existed before the war.. Britain's rulers offered assisted passage and free land in the colonies .

On 9 April 1820 the first group of British settlers were welcomed at Algoa Bay (Port Elizabeth) by the acting Governor of the Cape, Sir Rufane Donkin. They were mostly tradesmen from the cities and knew little about farming and eventually most of them would end up in the towns.

"Soon after our arrival we exchanged our books for guns," wrote a settler to his relatives in far off England. Instead of the idyllic promised land they found themselves not only battling nature but marauding black tribes from the north.

GREAT TREK

Relations between the British newcomers and the Dutch frontiersmen were cordial. The Boers (Farmers) as these descendants of the original Dutch and French settlers called themselves, were, however, perturbed by meddling from Britain. In 1834 more than 360 men, women and children departed from the Eastern Cape under the leadership of Piet Retief. Uys and others followed Retief's example, pushing northwards into Natal. The Great Trek had started.

On reaching the British coastal settlement of Port Natal (Durban), these Voortrekkers (Pioneer Trekkers) were welcomed with open arms by the British who migrated by sea. They felt that the Boers would strengthen their defenses against the belligerent Zulu *impis* (armies) of Dingane.

BLACK TRIBES

Archeological findings confirm the existence of black peoples in West and East Africa as early as 500 BC. These Iron Age people migrated southwards and reached southern Africa between 400 and 700 AD. Their descendants are to be found among the Nguni, Sotho, Venda and Tsonga peoples of South Africa.

In their southward move Nguni stuck close to the eastern coastline, while the Sotho stayed inland. Eventually this powerful tribe split into the North Nguni (comprising the Zulu of Natal and the Swazi peoples) and the South or Cape Nguni (the Xhosa-speaking people of the Transkei and Ciskei). The Sotho fragmented into the North Sotho, West Sotho (or Tswana) and South Sotho (or Basotho) tribes.

The Venda arrived much later than the Sotho and Nguni and settled in the northern inland region of South Africa, while the Tsonga, who congregated in the northeast region of the country, were later so thoroughly subjugated and influenced by a rebel Nguni group that they became known as the Tsonga-Tshangana (after Soshangana).

SEGREGATION

It was only a matter of time before the southward moving Xhosa became embroiled in a struggle with the white settlements moving northwards in search of new grazing land. In 1778 Dutch Governor Joachim van Plettenberg laid the groundwork for apartheid by introducing territorial segregation to try and keep the peace. He reached agreement with a few minor black chiefs to respect officially drawn boundaries between themselves and the whites.

FRONTIER WARS

Soon, however, serious frontier wars erupted as the black tribes raided and plundered white farms. Eventually no fewer than nine wars were fought on the eastern frontier of the Cape during the late 1700s and early 1800s. The toll taken in these wars between black and white, however, pales in comparison with the cost in human life that accompanied the constant battle for supremacy among the various black tribes and clans.

In the early nineteenth century mere mention of the names Shaka, Dingane, Mzilikazi, and Soshangane would strike terror in the hearts of many. They would show no mercy in fighting each other and in subjugating lesser tribes.

SHAKA

But Shaka stands out as the most feared and fearless of them all. In a short time he built the Zulu tribe into a mighty war machine. They nicknamed him Nodumehlezi - the one who causes the earth to rumble when he sits. It is estimated that during his short life-span of forty years, from 1788 until 1828, Shaka caused the death of at least a million people as he conquered and subjugated all of Natal.

The Voortrekkers did not exchange books for guns. They took both on their arduous trek to the north. This Bible was a parting gift from British fellow frontiersmen.

His watchword for his warrior was *Victory or Death*. He named his capital *Kwa-Bulawayo* (The Place of Murder). When his mother died he had several thousand of his own followers killed so that their families could genuinely share his grief.

In 1818 Shaka had set in motion large-scale warfare that lasted until 1838 and left hundreds of thousands of blacks dead and destitute. Referred to in the Nguni language as the *Mfecane* and in Sotho as the *Difaqane*, this was a period of extermination, carnage, cruelty and cannibalism.

Young Zulu in gala dress by GF Angas (Africana Museum)

Realizing, however, that the white man with his more advanced weaponry posed a more formidable challenge than his rival black tribes, Shaka instructed subjects to live in peace with them. The Zulu king appreciated their gifts, admired and adopted their life-style, acquired their firearms and even enlisted their help against rival tribes.

On 22 September 1828 Shaka was assassinated by his bodyguard and two half-brothers, Dingane and Mhlangane. As he bled to death from stab wounds, Shaka said to Dingane: "Do you think you will rule the land? No, you will not - for the swallows have come." (The swallows he was referring to were the whites who had begun to settle Natal).

DINGANE

In part driven by Shaka's disturbing prophecy Dingane harbored a deep dis-trust of the white intruders. From his capital at the White Mfolozi River, Mgungundlovu (the Place of the Great Elephant),Dingane viewed the arrival of increasing numbers of whites with growing concern. This distrust turned to obsession when large numbers of Voortrekkers entered the region in their covered wagons in search of land.

First Dingane ambushed and killed Voortrekker leader Piet Retief and one hundred of his followers and then sent his impis out to destroy several Boer laagers. After several laagers were obliterated and hundreds lost their lives, the Boers braced themselves for the final onslaught at the Buffalo River.

COVENANT

Leading the besieged Boers in prayer, preacher Sarel Celliers promised God that 16 December 1838 would always be celebrated and a church built in the honor of the Lord, should victory be granted. With 470 men, primitive frontloaders and two small cannons, the Voortrekkers under leadership of Andries Pretorius dealt the Zulu army of 12,500 a crushing defeat. More than three thousand Zulu lost their lives before the rest took off in disorderly fashion.

The river was renamed Blood River (as it was reported to have turned red with Zulu blood). A special church was built at nearby Pietermaritzburg and the Day of the Covenant has been observed ever since.

Dingane and his remaining army fled northwards where he was dealt a crushing blow by his rival Mpande at the Battle of the Qongqo Hills, near Maugudu. Although Dingane escaped, he was later killed by the Nyawo tribe in the Ubombo Mountains.

MPANDE

Mpande who succeeded Dingane as ruler of the Zulu lived in relative peace with the British rulers of Natal. Only occasionally would he allow his battle-starved and bored impis to on raids against neighboring tribesmen. The same tolerant Mpande showed no compassion when it came to personal comforts. An aide assigned to provide shade for the ruler with his shield would be liable to execution should he allow but a trickle of sunlight to streak across his master's face.

Next to rule the Zulu was Cetshwayo who proceeded to press land claims against both the Voortrekkers in the newly established Transvaal Republic and the British in Natal. When Cetshwayo attacked a rival chieftain and abducted and executed his wives, the British in Natal demanded that the Zulu army be disbanded. Cetshwayo refused and the British attacked.

ISANDHLWANA

In January 1879 the British regiment was almost totally wiped out at Isandlwana. The Zulu impis promptly proceeded to nearby Rorke's Drift where the British had occupied a Swedish mission as a hospital. Thirty five sick men and about one hundred armed soldiers held out for twelve hours inflicting heavy casualties on the Zulu impis. Seventeen British died, while more than 350 Zulu perished. Eleven Victoria Crosses were awarded for gallantry, most of them posthumously - still a record for any single battle.

BROKEN

Reinforcements were sent and eventually Cetshwayo was defeated at his capital Ulundi. The might of the Zulu was finally broken and the territory split into thirteen regions.After several years in prison, Cetshwayo was allowed to spend his final years in the splintered remains of the Zulu empire. In February 1884, his son Dinuzulu tried unsuccessfully to reunite the old Zululand, calling at one stage the help of the Boers in the Transvaal to defeat rival chieftains. Eventually the British annexed Zululand and banished Dinuzulu to St. Helena - where Napoleon spent his last days.

Further south the Cape Nguni, pressured from the north by the ripple effect of Shaka's *Mfecane* or period of destruction spilled onto white farmland, plundering as they proceeded. Despite their inferior weaponry these black tribesmen often managed to ambush and defeat their well armed white adversaries.

XHOSA

The Eastern Cape where the British settlers tried to manage on their own after the departure of the Voortrekkers, was the scene of several Frontier Wars against Xhosa tribesmen. First as military officer and later as governor, Harry Smith, was short in tact and long on cruelty in his dealings with the Xhosa. Chief Hintsa was captured by Colonel Smith. When he tried to escape he was shot to death and, in a senseless act, his body was mutilated.

In 1846 the British were on another punitive expedition, chasing the Xhosa into the Amatola Mountains where the tribesmen used the dense vegetation to ambush their pursuers, capturing sixty-five supply wagons. Emboldened by this success the Xhosa invaded the white settlements, causing great damage and destruction. British Governor, Sir Harry Smith, retaliated by proclaiming the area settled by the Xhosa a colony and called it British Kaffraria.

Harry Smith in pursuit of Chief Hintsa

Cecil John Rhodes

Colossus. This is the word most often used to describe Cecil John Rhodes. It refers not to his physique, but the impact of his brief life on the lives of the many millions not only in South Africa but the world.

In 1870 he arrived in South Africa, a sickly youth of seventeen. Unlike Barney Barnato, his toughest business rival, Rhodes came to South Africa not to seek a fortune but better health. In the next thirty years, however, until his death in 1902 he built one of the world's largest financial empires on diamonds and gold. Rhodes used money as a means to accomplish political goals. He was most serious and effective empire builder of his time.

Rhodes established Rhodesia (named after him and since renamed Zimbabwe), and became Prime Minister of the Cape Colony but he never managed to fulfill his ultimate dream of a British South Africa stretching from Cape to Cairo. In 1896 he was implicated in an abortive coup attempt in the Transvaal and destroyed politically.

Today the outside world knows him as the man behind the Rhodes Scholarships, awarded annually to deserving students in English-speaking countries.

He would visit many an insult upon the Xhosa, placing his foot on one chieftain's neck and another to kiss his boot. Eventually the Xhosa, angered by Hintsa's killing and Smith's behavior, struck back. On Christmas eve they attacked Smith and his troops at Bhuma (Boomah) Pass in the Amatola Mountains. Thirteen soldiers were killed and many wounded.

BOOMAH PASS

The Battle of Boomah Pass was the start of the Eighth Frontier War. A humiliated Smith was trapped in Fort Cox for several days, waiting for reinforcements. Before the war ended, he was replaced as governor by Sir George Cathcart who gave the Xhosa chiefs authority over their own subjects in terms of their own laws. Cathcart's successor, Sir George Grey, tried even harder to win the friendship of the Xhosa.

Good deeds were, however, to no avail. Hurt by decades of colonial abuse and several military campaigns that cost them dearly in terms of land and lives, the Xhosa were susceptible to prophecies and promises of supernatural victory over the white intruders.

SUICIDE

In 1856, Nongqawuse, the young niece of a respected Xhosa chieftain reportedly met with the spirits of long deceased black tribesmen who promised deliverance from the British on condition that the tribesmen kill all their own livestock, destroy all their grain and stop cultivating the land. Those who did not heeding this command, would be swept into the sea with the British when the saviors of the Xhosa appear on the assigned day.

Both the British colonial authorities and the missionaries tried in vain to dissuade the Xhosa from this suicidal course. The day of deliverance came and passed,leaving thousands of Xhosa starving and destitute. The might of the Xhosa was finally broken by this act of desperation.The tribal leaders behind the tragic National Suicide of the 1850s were imprisoned on Robben Island, near Cape Town - a site that would gain worldwide prominence more than a century later when another prominent Xhosa, Nelson Mandela, the leader of the African National Congress, was incarcerated there for a quarter of a century.

BOER REPUBLICS

In 1838 Dingane's power was broken and the Boers had their independent republic in Natal. Barely five years later, however, the British rulers had caught up with the Afrikaners once again.

Irked by the Voortrekkers' decision to resettle thousands of displaced Zulu tribesmen on the Cape border, British governor Napier sent troops to Natal. The Voortrekkers responded by surrounding Port Natal. The siege was finally lifted when British settler Dick King managed to slip through the Boer lines and ride six hundred miles on horseback to Grahamstown to get reinforcements.Once again the Boers were on the move, inland where two independent republics of the Orange Free State and Transvaal evolved. Jan Brand, who became president of the Orange Free State, was a man of great tact and a great sense of justice, well respected overseas - even in Britain. Monies flowing from the discovery of diamonds were wisely spent to build a model republic. To the north, the Transvaal Republic had a much more turbulent history. After considerable infighting the Boers of the Transvaal suffered the ultimate indignity in 1877 when the politically insecure President Thomas Burgers invited the British to raise the Union Jack in the capital of Pretoria (named after Andries Pretorius).

For three years the Boers tried to talk the British into lowering their flag and leaving. Eventually Boer patience ran out. On 16 December 1880 they held a mass demonstration at Paardekraal to elect a provisional government under the leadership of a triumvirate consisting of Paul Kruger, General Piet Joubert and M W Pretorius. After several skirmishes with the British the Boers dealt the enemy, led by Sir George Pomeroy Colley, a crushing defeat at Amajuba.

FIRST BOER WAR

The First War of Independence, as the Boers called this encounter, ended with the signing of the Pretoria Convention on 3 August 1881. Barely five years later the discovery of large deposits of gold in the Witwatersrand would, once again set Boer and Briton on a collision course.

The gold was hidden deep below the surface in hard rock. To get to it men with money and machines were needed. Men with the likes of Barnato, Rhodes, and Beit - the Randlords as they would

President Kruger meeting a deputation

soon become known. And with the machines and supplies came foreigners - mostly British - who soon developed grievances and demanded rights.

As God-fearing men, President Paul Kruger and his Volksraad in Pretoria viewed the greedy cosmopolitan crowd in Johannesburg with distaste. But they were willing to be tolerant, even forgiving, as long as they received much-needed monies from the *uitlanders* (foreigners) who owned and worked the gold mines.

COUP

On 2 January 1896 a little medical doctor, Leander Starr Jameson, attempted a coup on behalf of his fellow *uitlanders*. He failed miserably. It became known that Cecil Rhodes was behind the attempt and it meant the end of his illustrious career. He had to resign his post as Prime Minister of the Cape and pay Kruger's government a fine of 100,000 pounds each to have Jameson and three other key men in the attempt, released from jail.

DEMANDS

Britain pressed on with demands. In the beginning of 1899 British High Commissioner in South Africa, Sir Alfred Milner, delivered an ultimatum to Kruger. Extend the vote to the *uitlanders* in Johannesburg or suffer the con-

Lord Roberts

Lord Kitchener

Gen. Piet Joubert

Gen. Louis Botha

sequences, it said. The British were convinced that the vote would enable foreigners to vote the Boers out of office and place a new government in power, receptive to annexation by Her Majesty Queen Victoria.

CONCESSIONS

President Marthinus Steyn, successor of Jan Brand in the Free State, pressed Kruger into making concessions. The Transvaal President even agreed to extend the vote to uitlanders after five years residence instead of fourteen.

But Britain was in no mood to compromise. It mobilized its troops on the Natal-Transvaal border, demanding Kruger's capitulation. Britain had once again caught up with the Boers. Kruger sent the British a 48-hour ultimatum that expired on Wednesday, 11 October 1899. The Anglo-Boer War had broken out.

WAR

What started as a "gentlemen's war" with men sometimes leaving their trenches to exchange tobacco and food before they resumed the fight, soon turned sordid as the outnumbered Boers persisted and pressures built in Britain for a quick end to the war. To hasten war's end Queen Victoria sent Lord Frederick Sleigh Roberts, the hero of Kabul and Kandahar and as his chief-of-staff, Lord Kitchener of Khartoum. The men disembarked at Cape

Town on 10 January 1900 promising to take Pretoria before the year was out. In the north Boer General Piet Joubert of Amajuba fame waited as supreme commander of the joint Free State and Transvaal forces.

In March 1900 Roberts took Bloemfontein, the Orange Free State capital, and on 5 June he rode triumphantly into Kruger's capital, Pretoria. The Transvaal President had left for Europe and his troops retreated to the north.Roberts departed for Britain and left Lord Kitchener behind to mop up remaining resistance. But the real war had only just begun.

SCORCHED EARTH

The Boer guerillas drove Kitchener to desperation. He built block houses and fortifications to protect railroads and supply depots. And when that failed he turned a page to one of the darkest chapters in British war history.

Kitchener's scorched earth policy was designed to force the Boer commandos to surrender. Farmsteads and crops were systematically burnt to the ground and livestock killed indiscriminately. Women and children were carted off to concentration camps where the mortality rate reached alarming proportions. When the Boers finally decided to lay down their arms to save their families from further annihilation the death toll stood at 28,000.

PEACE TREATY

In an ornate room at Melrose House in Pretoria, which served as Kitchener's headquarters, General Louis Botha, who took over as supreme commander of the Boers after Joubert's death, signed the Peace Treaty of Vereeniging on 31 May 1902 together with other notables such as Smuts and De Wet. British rule was extended across South Africa.

Winston Churchill in the Boer war

"So they were not cruel men, these enemy," wrote Churchill after he was captured by the Boers. *"That was a great surprise to me, for I had read much of the literature of this land of lies, and fully expected every hardship and indignity."*

Captured at Frere in Natal in November 1899 as he got involved in battle as a correspondent for the *Morning Post*, Churchill was briefly held by the Boers at the State Model School in Pretoria, before his daring escape on 12 December. This was the beginning of a lifelong friendship with the Afrikaners.

Today a plaque at Frere, a poster offering a reward for his recapture, and the Pretoria State Model School where he was held, are a few reminders of Churchill's Boer War years.

Lord Robert Baden-Powell

His experiences as a British soldier in conflicts with the Zulu and the Boers led to the formation of the Boy Scouts and the Girl Guides. Impressed with the dedication and performance of the boys during the long siege of Mafeking by the Boers, Lieutenant Robert Baden-Powell formed the Boy Scout movement in 1907, and a little later, the Girl Guides.

Baden-Powell incorporated much of what he learned and experienced in South Africa in the training, recreation and rules of the scouts. As a member of the British forces that captured chieftain Dinuzulu in Natal 1888, he heard a Zulu chant that was later adopted by the Boy Scouts. The Zulu chief's necklace served as the model for the Scout's Wood Badge.

During the 217 day siege of Mafeking Baden-Powell had ample experience of food-rationing and scouting around enemy lines. He also incurred the wrath of Queen Victoria when he had issued special Mafeking postage stamps with a portrait of himself instead of Her Majesty's face.

In 1926 on his eighth visit to South Africa after the Boer War, Lord Baden-Powell, pioneered the establishment of the Scout movement among the Zulu themselves.

In 1906 the Union (Conservative) government that had waged the imperialist war against the Boers, was defeated in the 1906 election by the Liberals under Sir Henry Campbell Bannerman. As a champion of the Boer cause during the war years, Sir Henry promptly decided to grant self-rule to the former republics. He enjoyed full support from Winston Churchill.

In the Transvaal the former supreme commander of the Boer forces, General Louis Botha, became prime minister with Smuts as his minister of justice and right hand man. In the Free State Afrikaner Abraham Fischer took over as prime minister and appointed General Barry Hertzog as his deputy.

INDEPENDENCE

Soon there was serious talk of complete independence for a unified South Africa consisting of the two former Boer republics and the two British colonies of the Cape and Natal. A united South Africa made good sense both economically and politically.

UNION

So it happened that former foes in the Boer War, Afrikaner and English-speaking South Africans, gathered at the National Convention in 1909 to iron out the details for the new Union of South Africa, comprising the British colonies of Natal and the Cape and the former Boer republics of the Transvaal and Orange Free State.

The years from 1910 until 1948 saw growth and crisis as South Africa groped its way through strikes, schisms and new alliances towards white nationhood. It joined the Allied forces in the First and Second World War over violent objection from neutralists. These were issues that pitted Afrikaner against Afrikaner. These descendants of the Boers dominated every facet of public life. Most exceptions English-speaking whites seemed content to leave politics to the Afrikaner and to concentrate on business.

RACE LAWS

Segregation that had become the official policy of South Africa after independence, was ensconced in many a law determining where a black or a Colored or an Indian can sleep, vote, eat, work and be buried. During General Barry Hertzog's tenure as Prime Minister the territories set aside for the Xhosa, Zulu and other black tribes were enlarged. In London during the twenties General Smuts, as Prime Minister, would earn standing applause with this policy of segregation.

Then the Second World War happened and a world stung by the excesses of Nazi Germany became aware of injustices elsewhere, including South Africa.

SLOGAN

When Smuts was defeated at the polls in 1948 and replaced by Daniel Malan and his National Party the target came into sharper focus. After all, Smuts had a considerable body of support among the English-speaking while Malan was almost totally relying on Afrikaners.

Nelson Mandela

FW de Klerk

Mangosuthu Buthelezi

Apartheid (apartness) was the slogan that won the 1948 election. The policy that it stood for was as old as South Africa. It was segregation with bells and whistles. After Malan came Dr Hendrik Verwoerd, who resented the word apartheid and preferred to call his grand plans for a commonwealth of independent black nations and a white South Africa, separate development.

ARCHITECT

Since 1913 the African National Congress had been actively speaking out on behalf of the disenfranchised blacks. But, as one black leader would complain, it was like speaking over a toy telephone. No one listened. Dr Verwoerd was not the originator of apartheid, but he pursued the dream of separate nations with a greater vengeance than any of his predecessors. So he became known as the *Architect of Apartheid*.

In March 1960 the police, confronted by mass black demonstrations at Sharpeville, fired into the crowd and killed 67. This incident further galvanized the black struggle and world opprobrium against apartheid and South Africa's white rulers.

Prominent at the time was a distinguished man of royal Zulu lineage, Albert Luthuli, who pleaded for peaceful solutions despite

the Verwoerd government's unwilling-
ness to negotiate. When Luthuli, who
received the Nobel Peace Prize in 1961
died in 1967, the ANC and its allies,
the Indian Congress and the South
African Communist Party, as well the
Pan African Congress were already ban-
ned and operating underground.

PRESSURES

In 1964, several prominent members
of the ANC, including Nelson Mandela,
a Xhosa lawyer, who had been involved
a plotting the violent overthrow of the
white government, were convicted of
treason. They were given sentences
ranging from ten years to life. Mandela
spent the next twenty five years at
Robben Island while world censure
and increased incursions into South
Africa from neighboring countries by
the ANC's military wing, *Imkonte We
Sizwe*, built pressures for change.

THE EIGHTIES

John Balthazar Vorster who took over
the reigns after Verwoerd's assassina-
tion in 1966, was receptive to limited
change only. Towards the end of his
tenure and during the PW Botha leadership from 1978 until 1989, a new tri-
cameral parliament consisting of a
white, Colored and Indian chamber,
was introduced.

Blacks were still expected to seek their
political future in the tribal homelands.
Botha also combined the position of
Prime Minister and President (the latter was hitherto a purely ceremonial
post) with a president's council representing all three chambers.

In February 1990 newly elected State
President FW de Klerk stunned the
world and South Africa with drastic
reforms. He released Nelson Mandela
and all his fellow prisoners from jail
and unbanned the ANC, the PAC and
the South African Communist Party.

He started talks with Nelson Mandela,
Mangosuthu Buthelezi and other
prominent black leaders about a future New South Africa, free from in-
equality and racism.

CODESA

A few days before Christmas of 1991
representatives of 18 different parties
and groups turned up at a hotel near
Johannesburg for the first meeting of
the Convention for a Democratic South
Africa (CODESA). They represent the
various peoples who had staked a claim
in South Africa over the past three and
a half centuries. White, Black, Indian
and Colored. The judge who chairs
these deliberations will need even
greater tact and wisdom than Lord
Henry de Villiers at the 1909 all-white
National Convention. CODESA aims at
finding unity between not only whites,
but many tribes, nations and races
who all lay claim to the country.

MAIN PLAYERS

The three main players are the current
State President, Afrikaner FW de Klerk
and Nelson Mandela, Xhosa-born
leader of the ANC, and Dr Mangosuthu
Buthelezi, head of the Zulu-dominated
Inkatha Freedom Party. Trying to influence events from the sidelines are
several other factions ranging from far
left to far right, with the strongest
single force the white Conservative Party
under leadership of Andries Treurnicht,
who believes that some form of apartheid is necessary.

It took De Klerk less than two years to
dismantle the segregation system constructed over eighty years by successive white governments. In June 1991
the last pillars of apartheid crumbled.
In return, the outside world, acknowl-
edging these strides towards equality,
dismantled economic, cultural and
sports sanctions imposed against South
Africa over the past forty years.

CITY SIGHTS

Cape Town 1848

Cape Town used to be the port of entry for foreign visitors.

That was in the days before air travel. Nowadays most visitors come by way of Johannesburg's international airport.

But Johannesburg and Cape Town are only two of several interesting cities in South Africa. All of these cities offer, apart from sophistication in accommodation, restaurants and travel arrangements, a whole range of worthwhile, often unique, sights and sounds.

In the old days of the big ocean-liners foreigners visiting South Africa were usually welcomed by a flat-topped Table Mountain rising majestically out of the mist as their vessel entered the harbor. Today, the first sight to greet them as their aircraft tips its wing towards Johannesburg, are the mine dumps of *Igoli* - City of Gold.

BY AIR

Instead of disembarking amidst the smell of salt and fish and the sound of ships horns, visitors nowadays begin their South African journey by stepping into the cool, polished marble interior of Johannesburg's Jan Smuts airport terminal.

There are of course also direct overseas flights to Cape Town and Durban, but most of the foreign traffic flows through Johannesburg.

Chances are therefore strong that foreign visitors will spend at least one or more days in Johannesburg.

BEACHES

Those who have a bit of time on their hands after their safari experience will often go to either Cape Town or Durban, or both. Cape Town's reputation as a stylish old world city in unique surroundings, is well deserved, while

Durban is quite popular with sun-worshippers.

The other beach resort, Port Elizabeth, is not yet often included for its own sake but as part of the popular Garden Route. But as word of its magnificent beaches and surf spread it is becoming increasingly popular with foreigners for its own sake.

INLAND

Pretoria has no beach, but lots of history, interesting buildings and beauty and it is only about an hour's drive from Johannesburg. It is where government spends most of its time and therefore gets its fair share of overseas attention from both official and casual visitors.

The other two major cities, Kimberley and Bloemfontein, that are often bypassed by foreigners (and locals) who have not as yet discovered their country charm and character.

SOPHISTICATION

When stopping over in any of these seven cities or any of a number of smaller towns and rural resorts the visitor encounters a sophistication in accommodations, restaurants and transportation that matches any in the world.

This is what sets South Africa apart from any other major safari destination in Africa. Sophisticated cities within easy reach of unspoilt nature and abundant wildlife.

The following pages offer a brief history of each major city together with a description of special attractions.

(Important details about hotels, restaurants, car rental and other services can be found in the relevant sections of the guide).

BLOEMFONTEIN

City of Roses

CITY MAP #1 PAGE 93
Judicial Capital of South Africa
Capital of the Orange Free State
Population - 260,000

CLIMATE

Summers are hot, but not uncomfortable as the city is situated on a high plateau. Thunderstorms in summer. Dry and comfortable days during winter, cold at night.

HISTORY

Bloemfontein shares with Pretoria and Cape Town, the status of national capital. It is the seat of the nation's court of appeal.

Ever since President Jan Brand first built the Orange Free State into a model republic in the late nineteenth century, Bloemfontein has often been the site of peace conferences. In May 1899 Brand's successor, President M T Steyn,arranged for President Paul Kruger and British High Commissioner Alfred Milner to meet in Bloemfontein for five days in a last-minute effort to avert the Anglo-Boer War.

NAME

No one is certain how the city of Bloemfontein got its name.The original farm had a fountain with an abundance of flowers around it. So it is generally assumed that the name is derived from *Bloem* (flower) *fontein* (fountain). But there was also a Korana chief by the name Bloem in this area at the time and the town could have been named after him.

Today the city certainly lives up to its name with an abundance of flowers bordering neat wide streets and growing profusely in public parks and private gardens.With South Africa's largest public rose garden it is nick-named the City of Roses. Every year its annual two week Rose Festival attracts large numbers of tourists.

President Brand

In 1846 the British convinced Johannes Brits to sell his farm to them for £37 sterling. After giving the transaction some more thought he did not consider the sale such a sterling idea any longer and went back to renege on the deal. Major Henry Warden who bought the land on behalf of the British, persisted and finally satisfied the farmer with another payment of £50.

At first the transaction did not sit too well with Brits' fellow Afrikaners, who resented this intrusion by the very British from whom they tried to escape when they left the Cape. Still Cape Governor, Sir Harry Smith, managed to convince the folks that they should accept the Britain as their protector.

SECOND THOUGHTS

Like Brits these farmers also had second thoughts. Shortly after Harry Smith left town they chased his appointed representative, Major Warden, out. A month later, in August 1848, the persistent Harry Smith was back with reinforcements, repossessing Bloemfontein. Six years later the British ceded the town to the newly formed Boer Free State Republic, but on 15 March 1900 the city once again fell into British hands when Lord Roberts' forces took it by force during the Anglo-Boer War.

Much of today's noteworthy sights relate to this epic struggle between Boer and Briton. Naval Hill with a giant white horse laid out in stone on its eastern slope, is one of the first to attract a visitor's attention. This is not a promotion for a well-known brand of scotch, but was placed here by members of the British Wiltshire Regiment during the occupation. President Brand Street is full of historic sites and other remnants of old model Boer Republic.

POINTS OF INTEREST
CITY MAP #1 - ON OPPOSITE PAGE

1.**VROUEMONUMENT:** The Women's Memorial, as it is called, is dedicated to the 28,000 Boer women and children who died in British concentration camps during the Anglo-Boer War. This 37 meter (100 feet) high sand-

Dome - Fourth Raadsaal

stone obelisk has at its base statues by the well-known Afrikaans sculptor, Anton van Wouw, depicting two women gazing over the Free State plains, one with a dying child in her arms. A British woman, Emily Hobhouse, who volunteered assistance and championed the cause of the interned Boers, is also buried at the base of the monument. Also has a museum with war relics and artifacts by Boer prisoners of war and a research library.

2. BOTANICAL GARDENS: A 50 acre area at the northern outskirts of the city, divided into formal gardens and natural woodlands and wetlands. Facilities include a nursery, herbarium, tea room, summer house, a display of Iron Age potsherds and a petrified tree between 150 and 300 million years old. A man-made lake is frequented by waterbirds. Best times are February-May and September-November. Open daily. Guided walks are arranged.

3. NAVAL HILL: Bloem-fontein is probably the only city with a wildlife nature reserve at its center. The **Franklin Nature Reserve** on top Naval Hill contains a variety of species in their natural habitat, including red hartebeest, eland, springbok, blesbok and zebra. Open daily. **Naval Hill** derives its name from the naval guns placed there during the Boer War by the conquering British forces. It was the site for the Lamont Hussey Observatory where more than 7,000 binary stars have been logged before its American sponsors shut it down. The building is used today as a cultural center and theater.

Hamilton Park at the foot of the hill has an orchid house with more than 3,000 flowers under transparent domed roof, thriving in a landscape of pools, bridges, weathered stone formations and waterfalls. A specially designed fragrance garden caters to the blind. Best viewed from May through September. Open daily.

4. FIRST RAADSAAL: This modest dung-floored building in St. George's street is the oldest in Bloemfontein. Built in 1849 by British Major Henry Warden shortly after he bought the land from farmer Johannes Brits.. In 1854, the first Volksraad (parliament) of the old Free State Republic gathered here and it became known as the First Raadzaal (Assembly) once a larger and more appropriate parliament was built. Today it is a national monument, open to the public together with the adjoining Wagon Museum.

5. NATIONAL MUSEUM: Extensive collection of fossils, including the Florisbad skull, reputed to be one of the earliest of men. Depicts the development of

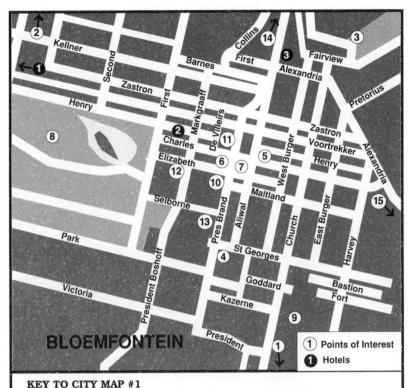

BLOEMFONTEIN

① Points of Interest
❶ Hotels

KEY TO CITY MAP #1

POINTS OF INTEREST

1. Vrouemonument & Boer War Museum
2. Botanical Gardens
3. Naval Hill
   Franklin Nature Reserve
   Hamilton Park
4. First Raadsaal & Museum
5. National Museum
6. Court of Appeal
7. Fourth Raadsaal
8. King's Park

9. Queen's Fort
10. Afrikaans Literary Museum
11. City Hall
12. Sand du Plessis Theater
13. Old Presidency
14. Oliewen House Art Gallery
15. To Maselspoort Resort

MAJOR HOTELS

1. Landdrost Sun ★★★★
2. Halevy House ★★★
3. Holiday Inn ★★★

man from the earliest single-cell creatures to man as well as black cultures and early Bloemfontein. Open daily.

6. COURT OF APPEAL: South Africa's highest court established in 1910 when the four British provinces joined in Union. Bloemfontein became the judicial capital in a compromise deal that gave Pretoria, administrative capital

status and made Cape Town the legislative capital.

7. FOURTH RAADSAAL: Formally opened in June 1893, by President Frederik Reitz this stately new parliamentary building was in use for only seven years before the British forces occupied Bloemfontein in March 1900 and turned it into a field hospital.

Much of the original furniture disappeared, but the building had since been restored to its original state. Today it is the seat of the Orange Free State provincial council (local legislature). A statue by Coert Steynberg of Free State Boer General Christiaan de Wet on horseback can be seen in the gardens at the front.

"The town is so quiet and seems to be so happy and contented, removed so far away from strife and want and disorder, that the beholder as he looks down upon it is tempted to think that the peace of such an abode is better than the excitement of Paris, London or New York."

Anthony Trollope
Famous British author
on visit to Bloemfontein in 1870.

---

8. KING'S PARK: This 700 acre park gave Bloemfontein its fragrant nickname, *City of Roses*. More than 4,000 rose bushes grow in the Rose Garden, opened by the Prince of Wales in 1925.

Since 1900 more than 125,000 trees have been planted. The park also sports a lake (Loch Logan) and a small but interesting zoo. Special features are an extensive collection of apes and monkeys from all over the world and the *liger* - a cross between a lion and tiger, first bred here some twenty years ago.

Die Volksblad, the local newspaper, arranges monthly art market in the park - one the largest in the country.

9. QUEEN'S FORT: In 1848 when Sir Harry Smith took Bloemfontein by force, he constructed this fort to protect Her Majesty's territory against the Boers. Today it is a military museum, with special emphasis on South Africa's role during the Second World War. There is a monument to Free State Boers who perished in the Basotho Wars at the entrance to the fort.

10. AFRIKAANS LITERARY MUSEUM: Housed in the Third Raadsaal (Parliament building) it contains an extensive collection of manuscripts, old photographs, autographed books and other memorabilia of Afrikaans authors, poets and playwrights - the men and women behind the thought process and culture of the Afrikaans nation. It also serves as a research center for students of the development of the world's youngest western language.

11. CITY HALL: Landmark building designed by Sir Gordon Leith and opened by the Duke of Kent in 1935. Situated opposite the Hertzog Square fountains and gardens.

12. SAND DU PLESSIS THEATER: Modern complex dedicated to the arts, featuring music, opera, dance and drama. Home to the Arts Council of the Orange Free State.

13. OLD PRESIDENCY: The site where Johan Brits' original farmstead stood, this stately building served as the official residence of the various presidents of the Orange Free State Republic. Today it is a museum open to the public on a daily basis.

14. OLIEWENHUIS ART GALLERY: This Cape Dutch manor house was originally erected as a guest house for visiting dignitaries and is today utilized as an art gallery by the National Museum.

15. MASELSPOORT RESORT: Opportunity for swimming, rowing, fishing and other recreation at this pleasant resort on the banks of the Modder River. Not far from the city. It offers restaurants and picnic areas.

CAPE TOWN
The Mother City

CITY MAP # 2 - PAGE 97
Legislative capital of South Africa
Capital of the Cape Province
Population - 1,043,000

CLIMATE

Mediterranean. Winter rains. Damp cold in winter and pleasant, dry summers. The odd heat wave is usually moderated by sea breezes and at times blown away (together with germs) by the strong Southeast winds or *Cape Doctor* as it is called by Capetonians.

HISTORY

Port Elizabeth and Mossel Bay further up the east coast lay claim to have been visited by Portuguese explorers long before Dutchman Jan van Riebeeck landed here in the shadows of Table Bay. But the Portuguese left only stone crosses while the Dutch started a new nation.
Cape Town is the Mother City. It oozes history from every pore and measures traditions and buildings in centuries. Its praises as a pleasant resort with magnificent beaches, classy hotels and restaurants and breathtaking beauty are sung far and wide.

HALFWAY HOUSE

The Dutch East India Company *(Vereenigde Oost-Indische Compagne or VOC)* that sent Van Riebeeck to the Cape in 1652 had no intention to build a new nation at the tip of Africa. He received specific instructions to establish a modest halfway house between the Far East and Holland to provide the company's passing ships with fresh supplies. Barely five years later, however, permission is given to officials at the Cape to go farming inland in the belief that this would stimulate pro-duction of vegetables and supplies for the passing ships. The halfway station became a permanent settlement and a new nation.

BRITISH

Visitors to Cape Town will see traces of VOC rule all over this city, blending with the influences of the British who took control of the Cape barely fifty years after it was first settled. It is a city of monuments and museums, old houses and pleasant gardens. It is dominated by one of the most spectacular mountains in the world.

Eventually when the Cape and Natal joined the former Boer Republics of the Transvaal and Orange Free State in the Union of South Africa in 1910, Cape Town became the legislative capital of the nation.

Castle Entrance

95

POINTS OF INTEREST
SEE CITY MAP #2 - PAGE 97

1. THE CASTLE: South Africa's oldest building and still in use. Jan van Riebeeck's first priority was to build a castle, but a few years after his departure his mud-walled effort was replaced by a more permanent one.

Started in 1666 by Commander Zacharias Wagenaer, the new castle was completed in 1679. Its stone walls are in the shape of a five-pointed star. Each point formed a bastion with gun placements, living quarters and storerooms and dungeons below sea level. Every one of the five bastions was named after the titles of the Prince of Orange, who ruled Holland at the time.

Inside a stylish residence was built for the governor and named De Kat (The Cat). From its ornate balcony all proclamations and criminal sentences were read. Today the residence houses a collection of paintings, Cape Dutch furniture and antiques, open to the public. A changing of the guard is performed by the Castle Guard at noon on Fridays.

Van Riebeeck Statue

2. VAN RIEBEECK STATUE: Since 1899 this statue of the founder of South Africa, Jan van Riebeeck, in his knickerbocker pants, knee breeches, low shoes, broad-skirted coat and shovel hat has been welcoming visitors to Cape Town. It is a gift from Cecil Rhodes to the city of Cape Town. He paid the Scottish sculptor John Tweed one thousand pounds on condition that the artist's name would not appear on the work. Seventy years later Van Riebeeck's statue was joined by one of his wife, Maria de la Quellerie - a gift from the Dutch government.

3. COMPANY GARDENS: The lower slopes of Table Mountain where Van Riebeeck planted pumpkins and potatoes for the passing ships three and a half centuries ago. Barely ten years after Van Riebeeck departed Governor Simon van der Stel had his slaves build an irrigation canal and turned the company gardens into an Eden of roses, oak trees, pines and exotic plants collected from around the world. Today visitors from all over the world stroll along shady Government Avenue to enjoy the gardening efforts of many generations of enthusiastic South African botanists and gardeners. The gardens are decorated with ponds where Japanese Koi, larger members of the carp family, abound. They are fed at 09h00 and 15h00.

4. BO-KAAP & MALAY MUSEUM: During the first half of the eighteenth century the Dutch East India Company (VOC) brought several thousand slaves from Java, Ceylon and other Far Eastern regions to the Cape. They were mostly Muslim craftsmen with interesting customs and an exotic cuisine that influenced Cape cooking. *Bobotie, blatjang* and *bredie* are a few examples of modern-day Cape dishes based on "Malay cooking". Joining these migrants from the Far East were several aristocratic Muslims - dissidents such as Sheik Yusuf and the Rajah of Tamora who were causing trouble for the VOC in the Far East. When slavery was abolished by the British in the 1830s they settled in the upper reaches of Cape Town (*Bo-Kaap* means Above Cape). Today a stroll around this area gives visitors a flavor of old Malay life-

Bloemfontein's President Brand Street, the only street in South Africa which in it's entirety has been declared a National Conservation area. Pictured here is the Fourth Raadsaal, one of the many historic buildings in this street.

South Africa

A WORLD IN ONE COUNTRY

ee a world like no other. Go on safari through wilderness country teeming with game. Enjoy friendly welcome of a diverse peo- —their crafts, dances and lifestyles. nple international award-winning es from historic vineyards. Shop ere the world buys its diamonds and gold. You can count on world class hotels and reliable services throughout. And save. With exchange rates decidedly in your favor, prices are amongst the lowest of any major vacation destination. See the world in our country. Call 1-800-822-5368. On the west coast, 1-800-782-9772.

satour

Catching the bre
off Humewood Be

Hooking the big o
at Maitland.

Fun in the sun
at Sardinia Bay

Here's where fun-seekers come to play.

From golden, uncrowded beaches to sparkling surf and sea, the sun smiles on holiday-makers seeking fun and adventure in the Friendly City. Our visitors flock in year after year for thrilling watersports, safe bathing, exciting outdoor activities, great entertainment and sheer relaxation.

Come and grab your share of the action. And while you're here, take a day-trip or two and explore those unique seaside havens along the spectacular Sunshine Coast. You can do it all at a price that won't ruffle your feathers.

When next you want to spread your wings, try Port Elizabeth — just for fun!

 **ELIZABETH**

The Friendly City.

For more information, post this coupon to PE Publicity Association, PO Box 357, Port Elizabeth 6000.

Name: Address: Code:

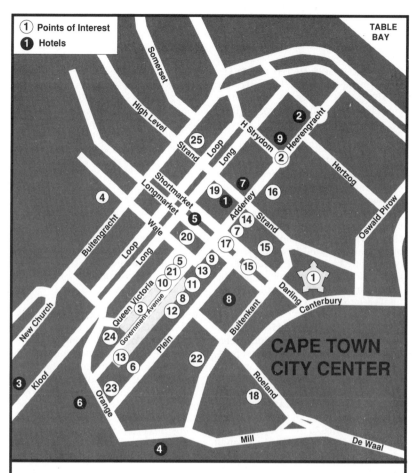

KEY TO CITY MAP #2

POINTS OF INTEREST

1. Castle
2. Van Riebeeck Statue
3. Company Gardens
4. Bo-Kaap & Malay Museum
5. St. Georges Cathedral
6. Great Synagogue & Jewish Museum
7. South African National Gallery
8. Houses of Parliament
9. SA Cultural History Museum
10. Cecil John Rhodes Statue
11. Queen Victoria Statue
12. Tuynhuys
13. Jan Smuts Statues
14. Golden Acre
15. Old City Hall & Grand Parade
16. Station
17. Groote Kerk
18. Cape Archives
19. Koopmans de Wet House
20. Old Townhouse
21. South African Library
22. Rust en Vreugd
23. Bertram House
24. South African Museum
25. Lutheran Church & Melck House

HOTELS

1. Cape Sun ★★★★★
2. Capetonian Protea Hotel ★★★★
3. Cape Swiss Hotel ★★★
4. De Waal Sun ★★★★
5. Inn on the Square ★★★★
6. Mount Nelson ★★★★★
7. St. Georges Hotel ★★★★
8. Town House ★★★
9. Tulbagh Protea Hotel ★★★

style and customs. An elegant house with a parapet has been turned into a museum.

5. ST. GEORGE'S CATHEDRAL: Designed by the famous Sir Herbert Baker in 1897, this serves as the mother church of South Africa's large Anglican community headed by Bishop Desmond Tutu.

6. GREAT SYNAGOGUE: Classic Baroque building on Government Avenue, consecrated in 1905 and shortly afterwards almost repossessed by its mortgage holders who wished to turn it into a cinema. Threat was averted and the Great Synagogue remained as a landmark place of worship for the Jewish community.In nearby Bouquet Street is the Old Synagogue, constructed in 1863, turned into a museum with exhibits relating to Jewry in South Africa.

7. SOUTH AFRICAN NATIONAL GALLERY: Exhibitions of local and foreign artists change regularly. Prints, postcards, and ethnic basket work, may be purchased.

8. HOUSES OF PARLIAMENT: After an elaborate foundation stone laying ceremony in 1875 the Cape government decided to abandon the original plans for parliament as they were "too expensive". The building based on second more modest plans was completed in 1885, at a much higher cost than the original figure. When Union was formed in 1910 Cape Town was named the legislative capital of the nation and these buildings became the seat for the national parliament. There were several expansions over the years - the latest, completed in 1988. Parliament is usually in session from January to June and visitors are allowed access to the public gallery. Tickets are available at parliament and visitors are required to show proof of identity. Passports will suffice.

Apart from their parliamentary functions, these buildings also house a museum with works of art and other memorabilia dating back to the first Cape Parliament of 1854. The **Library of Parliament** includes the **Mendelssohn Collection of Africana**, open to researchers.

9. SOUTH AFRICAN CULTURAL HISTORY MUSEUM: Opened in 1680 as the Dutch East India Company's official slave quarters, it also doubled as a brothel. Since the freeing of the slaves in the 1830s the building has been used as government offices, a supreme court and, until 1885 when the Houses of Parliament were opened, as a gathering place for the Cape Legislative Council. Today it provides a roof for an interesting collection of silver, glass, paintings, furniture, clothing, stamps and weapons relating to South African history.

Houses of Parliament

10. CECIL RHODES STATUE: Cecil Rhodes is honored not only at the Rhodes Memorial on the slopes of Table Mountain, but also with a statue in the Company Gardens.

11. QUEEN VICTORIA STATUE: One of five statues in South Africa of the ruler of the British Empire. Others are in Kimberley, Durban, Pietermaritzburg and Port Elizabeth. They are all made from marble, showing Her Majesty in flowing robes, with a scepter in the right hand and in the left an orb with a cross.

12. TUYNHUYS: *Tuynhuys* means Garden House. This landmark started as a lodge for official visitors in the 1680s. Nowadays it serves as the offices for the State President.

13. JAN SMUTS STATUE: A heated controversy erupted over this statue of the distinguished South African soldier and statesman when it was unveiled in front of the National Gallery in the company gardens in 1964. British sculptor Sydney Harpley was accused of ridiculing the revered statesman, and a committee was formed to commission a new, realistic statue of Smuts. The result is a more conservative work by Ivor Mitford-Barberton which stands outside the Cultural History Museum.

14. GOLDEN ACRE: Built in the 1970s, it looks like any of many modern shopping centers around South Africa. Underneath the modern facade there is, however, quite a bit of history. A bronze strip in the floor indicates the original shoreline where Van Riebeeck and his followers disembarked in 1652. The Foreshore area on which this and many other modern skyscrapers stand skyscrapers has been reclaimed since the 1940s. A diarama at the basement level of Golden Acre explains it all - replete with models of the old settlement, a wooden jetty and mud fort. In the process of excavation the builders of the shopping center also came across the remains of an old reservoir, which was preserved in place under a glass cover for posterity. Another interesting find on display is an engraved 'post office stone' used to exchange mail

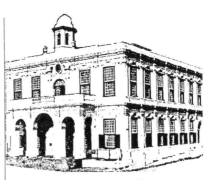

Old Town House

between in and outward bound Dutch ships in 1635 for collection.

15. CITY HALL AND GRAND PARADE: The Grand Parade was used for garrison parades long before the Castle was completed. Although it is only half its original size as new buildings encroached over the years, the oak-lined parade is still the city's largest open area. Wednesdays and Saturdays it is transformed into a colorful open-air market. Facing the Grand Parade is City Hall - a sandstone building completed in 1905 where symphony concerts are held on Thursdays and Sundays. Today it houses the Central Library and CAPTOUR, the local tourist organization. The city administration has moved to a new Civic Centre on the Foreshore.

16. STATION: South Africa's first locomotive is displayed on the concourse of the new railroad station. In 1859 this puffing billy was shipped in pieces from Scotland and re-assembled. It ran between Cape Town and Wellington in the 1860s. The driver William Dobbs came out with the engine and drove it until his death. One of the comforts afforded Dobbs was a roof to protect him against the fierce African sun.

17. GROOTE KERK: Literally Big Church, this is the "mother church" of the Dutch Reformed faith to whom the

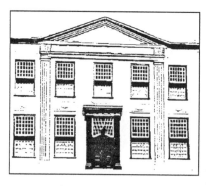

Koopmans de Wet House

majority of Afrikaners belong. First opened its doors in January 1704, earning a handsome income by selling and renting out of burial vaults inside the church. Governors Simon van der Stel and Ryk Tulbagh are among the rich and famous who found a last resting place here. The old building was closed in 1836, rebuilt and reopened in its present more elaborate form in January 1841. Old gravestones have been incorporated in the walls and as paving stones. Displays a rare collection of Cape silver and old family crests.

18. CAPE ARCHIVES: In a building behind the Old Rocland Street Jail archival records are kept dating back to the arrival of Van Riebeeck and his men in 1652. Most of these historic documents are available to the public.

19. KOOPMANS DE WET HOUSE: Situated in Strand Street (or Sea Street as it was originally called), this historic residence dates back to 1701 when merchant Reynier Smedinga built a one story thatched house. At the end of the eighteenth century a second floor was added and the well-known architect Louis-Michel Thibault commissioned to design its present Louis XVI facade. Named after socialite Marie Koopmans de Wet who owned the house in the nineteenth century, its serves as

a museum with an extensive collection of Cape Dutch furniture and other antiques. Open Mon-Sat.

20. OLD TOWN HOUSE: Originally constructed in 1716 as the first Burgher Wachthuis (Citizen's Watch House) and extended in 1755 it served as the city's administrative center or Town House for more than a century before it became the site for the Michaelis Collection of Dutch and Flemish oil paintings. It faces on cobble-stoned Green market Square, established as a market for farm produce three and a half centuries ago. Today it serves as a flea market.

21. SOUTH AFRICAN LIBRARY: This library housed in a classic building in Victoria Street is the South African counterpart of the famous US Library of Congress. A copy of every publication in South Africa has to be deposited in this library. It is a treasure house of rare Africana books and historic papers of notables. Open Mon-Sat.

22. RUST-EN-VREUGD: Built by a bureaucrat, Willem Boers, who apparently spent ample official time working towards his own enrichment. *Rust-en-Vreugd* (Rest and Peace) houses most of the William Fehr collection of Africana and watercolor paintings. The rest is in the Castle. Open Mon-Fri.

23. BERTRAM HOUSE: Built by attorney John Barker in the 1820s, this residence has been restored to its original state by the Cultural History Museum. A good example of the late Georgian style transplanted to the Cape in the early days of British rule.

24. SOUTH AFRICAN MUSEUM: Displays life-sized very realistic models of the San (Bushmen) as well as rock art exhibits. Also includes a planetarium, whale gallery and exhibits of indigenous birds, fish, insects and mammals.

25. LUTHERAN CHURCH & MELCK HOUSE: Across from the Koopmans de Wet House in historic Strand Street is a cluster of 18th century buildings, including the old Lutheran Church and Martin Melck House. The Lutheran church was disguised as a warehouse in 1774 by Martin Melck as the local authorities allowed "free worship" only as long as it took place in the Dutch Reformed Church. Five years later this restriction was lifted. The church interior includes an Anreith octagonal pulpit. The parsonage was built after Melck's death in 1781.

CAPE OUTSKIRTS
CITY MAP # 3 - PAGE103

The outskirts of Cape Town presents the visitor with a wealth of pleasant beaches, interesting drives and pleasant walks, while no visit seems complete without Cape Peninsula tour that reaches down to Cape Point. *(RURAL ROUTES - Page 143)*.

Within easy reach of the center city are the beach resort areas of Sea Point, Clifton, and Camps Bay *(See RESORTS & SPORTS - Page 191)*, and on the east-side of the mountain, the suburbs of Rondebosch, Newlands, Wynberg and Constantia. The obvious first consideration is, however, Table Mountain itself that so dominates the city.

POINTS OF INTEREST
CITY MAP #3 - PAGE103

1. TABLE MOUNTAIN: Until the world got wings, so to speak, and everyone was content to spend days and weeks by sea instead of hours in the air reaching their destination, Table Mountain was there to welcome most visitors to South Africa. (Some, of course, who shipped in from the Far East disembarked at Durban or Port Elizabeth). Never before or since has there been a mountain more often sketched, drawn, painted in the whole world. It is not simply size, but shape and situation that make this mountain so impressive and famous. It has a majestic presence much large than its life-size 3,500 odd feet.

The first man to climb its slopes was a Portuguese admiral, Antonio de Saldanha, who named it *Taboa do Cabo*, the Table Cape or Head in 1503. So this flat-topped colossus at the tip of the African continent became known as Table Mountain.

FOLKLORE

But it is not only an object. Through the years it has assumed a life and soul of its own in folklore. There are stories of how a certain Jan van Hunk challenged the devil to a pipe-smoking con-

Table Mountain and its companion mounts as seen by John Seller, "Hydrographer to the King" in 1675. At the time Seller, who obviously owed his allegiance to the British crown, dubbed Devil's Peak, "Charles Mount or Crown Hill", Lion's Head he called "Sugar Loaf", and Signal Hill, "James Mount or Lion's Rump".

test. In the end both of them disappeared in a puff of smoke. Whenever clouds form along the top of Table Mountain, Van Hunk and the Devil are supposedly at it again. In reality this white table cloth (the French calls it *"la perruque"* or the wig), that rolls down from the top on certain days, is caused by a south-east wind that precipitates moisture on the sandstone-covered mountain top. This same wind has been called the Cape Doctor as it is believed to blow away every virus and germ.

> *The fairest Cape we saw in the whole circumference of the earth."*
>
> **Sir Francis Drake**
> *After sailing around the globe in 1580*

Table Mountain greatly influences the weather and it dictates where people build and live. Cape Town and its suburbs are scattered around the foot of Table Mountain like crumbs along the bottom edge of a huge table cloth.

CONSERVATIONISTS

Some enterprising builders have been vying to go further up along the slopes, but famous and thoughtful conservationists have fought hard to protect the fauna and flora against undue intrusion. Among them were General Jan Smuts, the famous South African and world statesman, who was at his happiest scouring the slopes for new species of fauna.

There are more than 3,000 species of indigenous flowering plants to be found along the slopes of the mountain. Apart from proteas, including the silver tree, its is also known for the *Disa uniflora* (Pride of Table Mountain) - a type of orchid. Wildlife range from baboons to grysbok, duiker, rhebok, civet cats, porcupine and rock-rabbit or dassies.

Table Mountain is not only an impressive background for Cape Town, but provides the visitor with a birds-eye view of the city and its suburbs as well as the ocean and the inland regions. On the Atlantic ocean side, stretching from Camps Bay to Llandudno runs a line of steep sandstone elevations. These were named the **Twelve Apostles** in the early 19th Century by British Governor, Sir Rufane Donkin.

Towards the False Bay side of Table Mountain is **Devil's Peak**, so named after the Malay legend of Van Hunk and the Devil having their smoking contest whenever the clouds roll from the mountain top. **Signal Hill** and **Lion's Head** are, however, the first to attract attention as they are situated closer to the city center.

FACILITIES

The same Portuguese navigator, Antonio de Saldanha, who first used the word "table" to describe Table Mountain in 1503, named the natural harbor Agoada de Saldanha. In the 17th century a Dutch fleet commander, Joris van Spilbergen, renamed it **Table Bay**, It straddles strategically between two oceans - the Indian and the Atlantic. **Facilities** at the top of Table Mountain include a restaurant and souvenir store (where letters and postcards are postmarked with a special Table Mountain stamp).

There are two ways of getting to the top of Table Mountain - climbing or by cable car.

CLIMBING

For the energetic with time on their hands, there are more than 350 routes to the top, ranging from relatively easy walks to climbs that should only be attempted by experienced mountaineers. The *Mountain Club of South Africa (Tel: 021-45-3412)* is on 24-hour call.

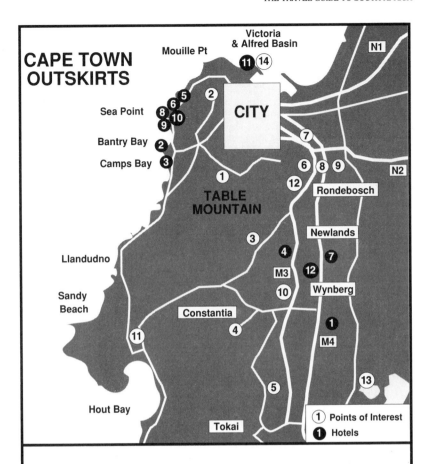

CAPE TOWN OUTSKIRTS

Mouille Pt

Victoria & Alfred Basin

N1

Sea Point

CITY

Bantry Bay

Camps Bay

TABLE MOUNTAIN

Rondebosch

Newlands

Llandudno

Sandy Beach

Constantia

Wynberg

M3

M4

N2

Hout Bay

Tokai

Rondevlei

1 Points of Interest

1 Hotels

KEY TO CITY MAP #3

POINTS OF INTEREST

1. Table Mountain & Cable Car
2. Signal Hill & Lions Head
3. Kirstenbosch Botanical Gardens
4. Groot Constantia
5. Tokai Forest & Arboretum
6. Rhodes Memorial
7. Groote Schuur Hospital
8. Mostert's Mill
9. Irma Stern Museum
10. Wynberg Park
11. The World of Birds
12. Groote Schuur Estate
13. Rondevlei Bird Sanctuary
14. The Waterfront

HOTELS

1. Alphen Hotel ★★★
2. Ambassador by the Sea ★★★
3. The Bay (P)
4. The Cellars Country House (P)
5. Don Protea Hotel ★★★
6. Karos Arthur Seat ★★★
7. Newlands Sun ★★★★
8. Peninsula Hotel (P)
9. President Hotel ★★★★★
10. Ritz Protea Hotel ★★★★
11. Victoria & Albert Hotel (P)
12. Vineyard Hotel (P)

The description (P) indicates new hotels that were still awaiting grading by the authorities at the time of publication.

Rudyard Kipling

British writer Rudyard Kipling was a young man of twenty six when he first visited South Africa. The *"color, light and half-oriental manners"* of this country, Kipling confessed, *"bound chains round his heart for years to come"*.

"South Africa is a most fascinating place," Kipling told a reporter after his first visit.

Every December for the next ten years Kipling and his family *"were all off to South Africa to play about in the sunshine until April."*

They stayed in a cottage specially built for them on the famous Groote Schuur estate by Cecil John Rhodes. In The Woolsack, as it was called, Kipling did much of his writing.

Together with Rhodes, Kipling would tour the wine estates and fruit farms of the Cape and on the drawing room mantelpiece of one farmstead he carved a poem:

This is the blossom of the fruit
I cleared the land, I set the trees
I led the water down the sluit.
Earth gave me fiftyfold increase
This is the blossom of the fruit.

Several of these walks wind through the **Table Mountain Nature Reserve**, including the Pipe Track from Kloof Nek above Camps Bay and the circular path around Lion's Head which starts from the Signal Hill Road. Although maps and guidebooks detailing the various routes are available, prudent visitors usually go with local experts. Weather can change rapidly and make basic climbing quite treacherous. Those who are adventurous enough to go by themselves should never stray from the defined paths and leave word beforehand with their hotel or a responsible person of their intended route.

CABLE CAR

Most visitors prefer to go by cable car. The bottom station is situated at the top of Kloofnek - easily accessible by car or a bus that departs regularly from Adderley Street. Established in 1929 and regularly upgraded since, the cableway has provided safe rides for millions during its accident-free existence. It is open every day, depending on the weather - and during summer evenings it runs until 10.30 pm. A flashing green light from the top station is an indication of night-time operation. The trip up or down takes five minutes and visitors who wish to complete either leg by foot, are allowed to purchase one-way tickets. *For reservations or guides call 21-4715 and for information 21-4205.* (Visitors who find the cableway closed due to windy conditions, may wish to continue past the lower cable station on Table Mountain Road to get a good view of Cape Town and Table Bay).

2. SIGNAL HILL & LION'S HEAD: Easily accessible by car, Signal Hill provides its own interesting vista of the city. At its thousand feet high summit is Lion's Battery and a signalling gun which makes its presence known every day as it is fired electronically exactly at noon-time. Also connected to Table

Mountain at Kloofnek is the 1,500 feet high Lion's Head. Some insist that its name derives from its shape resembling a lion's head, while others claim that the name signifies the place where the last lion was shot in the Cape. It is possible to climb to its top.

3. KIRSTENBOSCH BOTANIC GARDENS: This 1,000 acre property once belonged to Cecil Rhodes before it was turned into National Botanical Gardens in 1913. The upper portion is a forest with indigenous yellowwood, stinkwood and ironwood trees amidst an undergrowth of proteas,Cape anemone, erica, rare disa and nerine. In the lower portion more than 4,000 species of indigenous flora from around the country are cultivated in a setting of attractive rock gardens, springs and other special landscaping.

Flowering plants are at their best in springtime, but there is color even in winter, when aloes, ericas and proteas flower. A *braille trail* is provided for the blind, winding through a fragrance garden of indigenous aromatic herbs. A raised garden with paved paths makes it easier for the physically handicapped to enjoy their visit. The Compton Herbarium exhibits 200,000 plant specimens and indigenous plants and seeds are on sale throughout the year. There is an information center and restaurant, while the South African Botanical Society, which has its headquarters in the gardens, operates a bookstall stocked with souvenirs. Open daily. A modest entrance fee is charged. *(See also DOWN THE GARDEN PATH - Page 63).*

4. GROOT CONSTANTIA: Cape Governor Simon van der Stel spent his years here in retirement from 1699 until his death in 1712. He named the property after Constantia, the daughter of the senior company official, Baron van Reede, who had granted the land to him. The homestead represents the finest in Cape Dutch architecture. Although Van der Stel had the pleasure of tasting fine wines produced from his own vineyards, it was a subsequent owner, Hendrik Cloete, who acquired the estate in 1778 and made Constantia wines famous in Europe. Constantia red and to a lesser extent the white wines became popular in palaces and prominent households in France. Napoleon, when he went into exile at St. Helena, chose French champagne and Constantia wines to be served to him in captivity. Today the estate belongs to the government and still makes quality wines.

The house furnished in 18th century style, and the wine museum and cellar are open to visitors. Guided tours are conducted through the cellars every hour from 10h00 until 16h00 and wines can be purchased on the property. There are two restaurants: the **Jonkershuis** (Bachelor's House) with traditional Cape dishes and teas and the **Tavern** which serves buffet meals. Visitors are also encouraged to bring along a picnic basket and relax on the lawns under the oak trees behind the cellars. *Tel: 021-794-5178/9.*

5. TOKAI FOREST AND ARBORETUM: A great variety of tree species along the slopes of Constantia. It has

Bronze statue at Rhodes Memorial

105

pleasant walking trails and a shady picnic area close to the old homestead. Open winter, when forest fires are less of a hazard. Entry permits required.

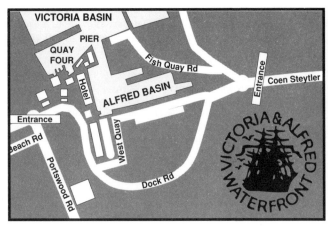

6. RHODES MEMORIAL: A tribute to Cecil John Rhodes who bequeathed this site as part of the Groote Schuur Estate to the nation when he died 1902. The centerpiece, an equestrian bronze created by the British sculptor G F Watts, is entitled *Energy*. The monument was designed by Rhodes' friend Herbert Baker. Another Rhodes admirer and confidant, Rudyard Kipling, wrote the words inscribed under the bust: *The immense and moving spirit still shall quicken and control.Living he was the land and dead his soul shall be her soul.*

7. GROOTE SCHUUR HOSPITAL: On their way to the Rhodes memorial, Groot Constantia and Tokai, visitors pass Groote Schuur Hospital where Dr Chris Barnard performed the world's first heart transplant in 1968 - and several subsequent innovations that helped to improve the quality of life of patients around the world with incurable heart ailments. Dr Barnard was also the first to perform so-called piggyback heart transplants, leaving the patient's own heart in place while implanting a second one onto it.

8. MOSTERT'S MILL: Built in 1796 and named after Sybrand Mostert, who used to ground wheat here. Restored in 1936 and declared a national monument. Open daily.

9 IRMA STERN MUSEUM: The Firs in Cecil Road, Rosebank, where internationally acclaimed South African art-ist, Irma Stern, lived for almost 40 years until her death in 1966. Today it is a museum, displaying not only Stern's art, but her personal collection.

10. WYNBERG PARK: This is where Van Riebeeck planted a vineyard and a hedge of bitter almonds *(Brabeium tellafolium)* indicate the original border of the settlement. Today it is a tranquil park.

11. THE WORLD OF BIRDS: The largest of its kind in South Africa, attracting more than 100,000 visitors every year. Specially designed aviaries create simulate natural habitat for more than 450 species.

12. GROOTE SCHUUR ESTATE: This huge estate on the slope of Devil's Peak once belonged to the empire builder Cecil Rhodes and comprised also the land on which Groote Schuur hospital, the Rhodes Memorial, Cape Town university and medical school, the small zoo and nature reserve and Mostert's Mill stand. Today this estate is, however, largely associated with the mansion which serves as the official residence of the Head of State. Designed and built in by Sir Herbert Baker the Cape Dutch mansion took its name from the old farmstead *Groote Schuur* or Great Barn. Also on the property is Woolsack which Rhodes built as a guest house for his author friend, Rudyard Kipling, who spent many working summers here.

13. RONDEVLEI BIRD SANCTUARY: This nature reserve has a small herd of hippo, and more than 200 bird species. There are a museum, information center and lookout towers. Open daily.

14. THE WATERFRONT: In the old days of stylish departures and arrivals by ship the Victoria and Alfred basins were the life of the city. Since then the area has fallen into disrepair. Recently private enterprise started restoring the waterfront. In this multi-billion rand venture they drew their inspiration from Boston's Quincy Market, San Francisco's Granville Island Fish Market, New York's South Seaport and similar developments in Sydney and Vancouver harbors. The old warehouses and historical buildings were converted into hotels, museums, restaurants, markets, stores and entertainment centers.

DURBAN
Subtropical Paradise

CITY MAP # 4 - PAGE 108
Capital of Natal
Population - 795,000

CLIMATE

Subtropical weather ideal for holidaymaking around the year, although the humidity can be quite high during the mid-summer months from January to March. Rainfall is mostly in summer.

HISTORY

Durban or Durbs as it is was nicknamed, is the prime beach resort for Transvalers. It is built around the natural harbor of Port Natal.

When explorer Vasco da Gama first landed here on Christmas Day 1497 he named the harbor Rio de Natal (Christmas River) in the mistaken belief that it was a lagoon at the mouth of a river. The name was changed to Port Natal by others who discovered Da Gama's mistake.

Although the harbor had seen its fair share of pirates, shipwrecked souls and slave traders in the intervening years, no one stayed until November 1823 when a group of British merchants from the Cape went ashore and liked it so much that they decided to return the next year.

PORT NATAL

Benjamin D'Urban

Under the leadership of Francis Flynn a contingent of British pioneers arrived by ship and started a settlement at Port Natal. In June 1835 Port Natal was renamed Durban in honor of Cape Governor Sir Benjamin D'Urban.

Although the settlers maintained cordial relations with the powerful founder of the Zulu nation, to their north, matters changed for the worse when Dingane took over. While Shaka instructed his citizens to live in peace with the white settlers, Dingane showed open animosity and aggression.

VOORTREKKERS

The British settlers at this outpost were therefore quite happy to welcome the Voortrekkers in their midst in 1838.

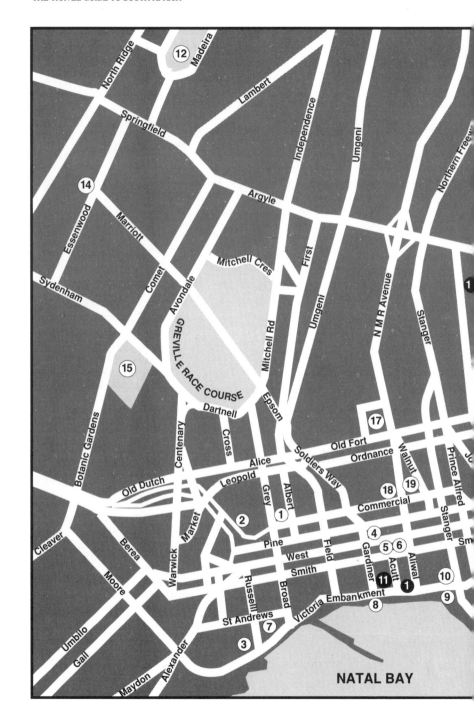

DURBAN CITY MAP

KEY TO CITY MAP # 4

POINTS OF INTEREST

1. Oriental Arcades
2. Juma Mosque
3. Victoria Street Market
4. Old City Hall
5. Natural History Museum
5. Art Museum
6. Local History Museum
7. Old House Museum
8. Dick King Statue
9. Vasco da Gama Fountain & Clock
10. John Ross Statue
11. Sea World
12. Mitchell Park
13. Umgeni Bird Park
14. Campbell Library
15. Botanic Gardens
16. Snake Park
17. Old Fort Warrior's Gate
18. The Workshop
19. Exhibition Center

HOTELS

1. Albany ★★★
2. Beach Hotel ★★★
3. Blue Waters ★★★
4. Edward ★★★★
5. Elangeni ★★★★
6. Four Seasons ★★★
7. Maharani ★★★★★
8. Malibu ★★★
9. Marine Parade Holiday Inn ★★★
10. Ocean City Holiday Inn ★★★
11. Royal Hotel ★★★★★
12. Tropicana ★★★★

① Points of Interest
❶ Hotels

These Boers who trekked from the Cape to escape British rule, found the people at Port Natal quite friendly and made plans to establish their own little republic nearby. But Dingane has his own agenda. First he ambushed and killed Piet Retief . Then he sent out his armies to destroy the white intruders.They were beaten back by the Voortrekkers at Blood River and crushed with the help of the British.

In 1842, the Voortrekker republic at Pietermaritzburg, named after leader Pieter Maritz, was included by the British when they annexed Natal. The Boers promptly retaliated by laying siege to the Old Fort in Durban.

HEROIC RIDE

Dick King came to the rescue. He escaped on horseback and rode to the Cape in ten days, informed the British authorities about the siege and got reinforcements by sea. Five weeks later the Old Fort was freed. The Voortrekkers retired to Pietermaritzburg and Natal officially became British.

RESORT

Today Durban is South Africa's busiest port and beach resort. Most of the province of Natal is populated by the North Nguni or Zulu and Durban has a strong infusion of tribal citizens. It also has the largest Indian population - descendants of indentured laborers who came in the 1860s to work on the sugar cane fields.

This is the city where Mahatma Gandhi started a political career that eventually led him to great prominence in the struggle for independence in India. Gandhi did not come as an indentured worker but as a lawyer at the invitation of a wealthy Moslem client in Durban.

Although Durban is viewed by most as a resort city with deluxe hotels, good beaches and interesting restaurants and night life, it does offer a rich cultural heritage and history.

POINTS OF INTEREST
SEE CITY MAP #4

1. ORIENTAL ARCADES: A trading area between Grey and Cathedral Streets crowded with small vendors offering Indian jewelry, cottons, silks, gold-threaded saris, incense and spices and other Indian specialities.

2. JUMA MOSQUE: Golden domed landmark built by large numbers of Moslems who emigrated to Durban in the 19th century, as traders and professionals. Tours can be arranged through the Islamic Propagation Center, Tel. (031) 306-0026.

Juma Mosque

3. VICTORIA STREET MARKET: This replaced the old Indian market that was demolished by a fire in 1973. This new building with its eleven domes was opened on Victoria and Russel streets in 1990. A hundred vendors sell herbs and spices, curries and other items on the ground floor, while fifty stores and several restaurants do business on the first floor. Popular with both regular shoppers and browsers, who come for the smells, sounds and color.

4. OLD CITY HALL: Used today as the General Post Office, the foundation stone of the Old City Hall was laid in February 1883 by Natal Governor Sir Henry Bulwer amidst dancing, fireworks displays and marching processions. The design submitted by a local architect, A P Dudgeon, was considered the best of 14 submitted from all over the country. A plaque on the eastern steps indicates the exact spot where Winston Churchill addressed a gathering in 1899 shortly after his escape from Boer imprisonment in Pretoria.

5. NATURAL HISTORY MUSEUM: Housed on the first floor of the "new" City Hall that replaced the old one in 1903, the Natural History Museum has earned international renown for the quality of its ornithological research. (As in the case with the Old City Hall, it was decided to hold a competition for the design of this newer **City Hall**. Although the winning entry came from a Johannesburg firm, the city fathers decided to have the building constructed in different sections and at different times, combining the designs of the winner and the runner-up). Exhibits include a mummy (one of only three in southern Africa); a life-size reconstruction of a dinosaur, and the egg of the giant (extinct) Aepyornis (Elephant Bird). Also on display is a skeleton of the extinct Dodo bird. Guided tours and film shows are arranged. (031) 30-40111.

5. ART MUSEUM: The Art Museum on the second floor of the "new" City Hall displays a collection of paintings by well-known English, French and Dutch artists.

6. LOCAL HISTORY MUSEUM: Situated in the old Natal Supreme Court building, it depicts the Natal colony's past. Among the exhibits are a replica of pioneer Henry Francis Fynn's wattle-

and-daub cottage, an 1860s sugar mill a drapery store and an apothecary. The building itself, when complete in the 1860s, was considered to be one of South Africa's finest. The first Chief Justice, Walter Harding, however, complained that the acoustics were so bad that he could not hear anything in the courtroom and it became a museum instead. Curio shop. Open daily.

7. OLD HOUSE MUSEUM: Next to the Local History Museum is a colonial-style home that seems out of place among the skyscrapers of the center city. Built in 1849 by John Goodricke, former mayor of Durban, it also displays items that belonged to a one-time owner and John Robinson, publisher of the Natal Mercury and the first governor of the Colony. Open daily.

8. DICK KING STATUE: A statue in honor of Dick King and his horse Somerset who travelled 600 miles in ten days in 1842 to get reinforcements in the Cape after the Voortrekkers besieged Durban. (See *DURBAN - HISTORY*).

9. VASCO DA GAMA FOUNTAIN AND CLOCK: The fountain was erected in 1897 to commemorate Portuguese discoverer Vasco da Gama's landing at this spot on Christmas Day four centuries ago. The clock that forms part of the structure was donated by the Portuguese government.

10. JOHN ROSS STATUE: Less well-known but equally important was the feat by sailor John Ross who walked 600 miles in 1826 to Delagoa Bay (today's Port Elizabeth) to get medical supplies for his compatriots in distress in Port Natal (later renamed Durban).

11. SEAWORLD: Sharks and a wide range of other sea creatures are on view in glass-walled tanks. They represent the wealth of sea-life in the sub-tropical waters, captured and kept in

Dick King

In 1842 when the Voortrekkers laid siege to Durban, it was Dick King and his horse that escaped by night and covered 600 miles in ten days, crossing, it is claimed, 122 rivers, to get reinforcements in the Cape. Five weeks later British troops arrived by sea to relieve Durban.

Ironically, the same Dick King, who came to South Africa with the 1820 British settlers, warned the Voortrekkers of an impending attack by the Zulu's only four years earlier.

His horse, Somerset, also had strong ties with both the British and the Voortrekkers. Somerset, named after Lord Charles Somerset, the British governor at the Cape, originally belonged to a British officer who sold him to a Voortrekker, Jan Hofmeyr.

At the battle of Blood River against the Zulu the Voortrekker leader, Andries Pretorius, borrowed Somerset from Hofmeyr. Afterwards Pretorius commented on the horse's good training and calm demeanor in the thick of battle. Shortly afterwards Somerset was stolen by an African and sold to the British. This is how he ended up taking Dick King on his epic ride in 1842.

near-natural conditions. Open daily and feeding time is at 11 am and 3 pm. Shows, starring dolphins, jackass penguins and Cape fur seals, are held in the **dolphinarium**, joined to Seaworld by underground tunnel. The entrance fee charged at both establishments goes back into conservation.

12. MITCHELL PARK: Famous for its colorful and artistic display of flowers, shrubs and trees. A mini-zoo is provided for children, as well as several well stocked aviaries. Teas, light meals and full lunches are offered in a **restaurant** in the park.

13. UMGENI BIRD PARK: Situated on the banks of the Umgeni River in Durban North. Offers walkways and hides for close-up views of colorful plumaged birds from around the world. Refreshments and light meals available. Open daily from 09h00-17h00. Tel. (031) 83-1733.

14. CAMPBELL LIBRARY: Established by the legendary Killy Campbell in Muckleneuk, the original home of her father - sugar magnate Sir Marshall Campbell. As a horticulturist, nurse, sportswoman and amateur historian Margaret Roach (Killie) Campbell had diverse interests. The Africana library contains a wealth of rare books, pic-

Dick King Statue

tures, maps and manuscripts, while another section displays the Campbell furniture collection. A third section consists of a collection of Zulu arts and crafts and paintings and the grounds are filled with exotic bougainvillea. Open daily except Sundays. Guided tours by appointment.

15. BOTANIC GARDENS: Established as an agricultural station by the early settlers in 1849, the Durban Botanic Gardens offers visitors a wealth of indigenous flowering trees and tropical plants and bird life. Facilities include an orchid house, cycad collection, herbarium and a garden for the blind. Refreshments offered in a tea garden. Open daily and guided tours on the last Sunday of every month. Tel. (031) 21-1303.

16. SNAKE PARK: Houses more than sixty South African species and a few from overseas, as well as crocodiles, terrapin and iguana. Apart from lectures about snakes, the park also demonstrates to visitors how anti-snake-bite serum is made. Open daily.

17. OLD FORT: This is where the British garrison survived a five week siege by the Voortrekkers in 1842 while Dick King rode on horseback six 600 miles south to get reinforcements. The Fort is well preserved and the grounds have been transformed into a garden. The original ammunitions magazine has been transformed into a chapel. Adjoining Warrior's Gate is shaped like an old Norman gateway and the place of safekeeping for trophies from battlefields in Natal and other parts of the world.

18. THE WORKSHOP: Completed in 1894 as one of the grandest railway stations in the country, This national monument has recently been converted into an upmarket office block. Adjoining old railway locomotive shed serves as a shopping mall.

19. EXHIBITION CENTER: Venue for many national and international exhibits and shows, as well as sports and other indoor and outdoor events. The South Plaza area offers Sunday flea market. Facilities include restaurants, bars and lots of parking.

JOHANNESBURG
City of Gold - Igoli

CITY MAP #5 - PAGE 115
South Africa's largest city
Population - 1,800,000

CLIMATE

Johannesburg lays claim to one of the best climates in the world. Summers are warm, seldom hot, without humidity. Occasional rainfall in summer is, however, at times accompanied by thunder and lightning. Although winter nights and early mornings may be chilly to cold, the days are mostly pleasant and conducive to outdoor activity.

HISTORY

In February 1886 prospector George Walker, out on a Sunday stroll, stumbled over a piece of gold-bearing rock on barren farmland. Others claim that it was his friend George Harrison who made the discovery.

Both Georges, Harrison and Walker, announced their finds almost at the same time. But neither George made much out of it. Walker did not have the funds to mine, so he sold his rights for a mere £350 and went to work for someone else, while Harrison peddled his claim for £10 and disappeared.

TENTS

Tents and shelters and shacks sprung up like toadstools on a compost heap.

They came by the thousands from overseas and the diamond diggings at nearby Kimberley. The biggest gold rush in history transformed the barren veld into a seething mass of disorganized humanity, mixed with machines and wagons and horses.

George Walker

JOHANNES

From Pretoria, the capital of the Boer Republic of Transvaal, came two commissioners to choose a site for a new city. Their names were Johannes Rissik and Johannes Joubert. They picked a vacant piece of government-owned land, Randjieslaagte, and started auctioning off stands for buildings and houses. Oom Paul Kruger decided to call this new mining town Johannesburg (after the two Johanneses who laid out its plans). By sheer coincidence the first mayor of Johannesburg was Johannes de Villiers.

SHACK & SHOVEL

So started the town built on the discoveries of the two Georges, planned by and named after the two Johanneses, and run in the beginning by another Johannes. Three years after the first tent was pitched, Johannesburg became South Africa's largest town.

During the first few years every one with a shack, shovel and servant could lay claim to a piece of land and start digging for gold. Soon there were more than two hundred "mining companies" registered in Johannesburg. In those days many a gold mine was, in the words of some cynics, nothing more than a hole in the ground with a fool at the bottom, a liar on top and a crook in a nearby office.

RANDLORDS

But the randlords changed all that. Monied men such as Cecil Rhodes, Barney Barnato, Julius Wernher and Alfred Beit, turned up with mighty machines to dig deep and fast in the bowels of the earth - leaving the amateurs no choice but to sell out. The big mining houses took over to make the Witwatersrand (White Waters Reef) as this rich strip was called, the prime producer in the world.

Gold to lay by and gold to lend,
Gold to give and gold to spend.
The Star newspaper's
description of
Johannesburg in 1887

While President Paul Kruger and his advisors detested this rowdy and rambunctious crowd of *Uitlanders* (foreigners) with their ungodly behavior and lust for gold, they did not resent the much-needed income from the mines.

WARLORDS

But soon the Randlords would invite the Warlords into this new eldorado. The pretext was better treatment by Oom Paul Kruger of the *Uitlanders* (foreigners), but it soon became clear that Britain wanted more than the vote for its subjects in Johannesburg. It wanted to make the Transvaal and all its gold part of the Empire. In 1899 the Anglo-Boer War broke out.

Overnight Johannesburg became a ghost town as the Uitlanders, anxious not to get caught in the cross-fire, scrambled out of the Transvaal. For three years a stillness descended on the shacks and the shanties, the bars and the brothels. When Britain won the war in 1902, they returned in full force and resumed digging down below and building on top - transforming Johannesburg into the City of Gold *(Igoli)*.

Today downtown Johannesburg is the hub for a metropolis stretching for fifty miles from east to west and growing rapidly northwards towards Pretoria. Sandton, Randburg and other new satellite cities have sprung up, making Greater Johannesburg the single largest and by far the most developed metropolis in Africa.

THE DUMPS

Visitors from abroad usually arrive by jet at Johannesburg. Clearly visible from the air are the yellowish flat-topped hills between skyscrapers and the houses and the swimming pools and the golf courses.

These mine dumps are square-shaped ant-heaps, yellow sand left after tons of rock brought from deep down below were crushed and washed to squeeze out every minuscule drop of gold. Some have been turned into drive-in theaters and when those went out of fashion, simply parking lots. Others have been carefully planted with tufts of grass to keep the dust down - like trying to make hair grow on bald palates.

Then suddenly a new process enabled the mining houses to squeeze some more gold out of the dust, so they began bulldozing the yellow waste back into the processing plants.

SHIFT

But the major activity for mining has shifted further west and east and down south as far as the Orange Free State. Johannesburg itself is left with a

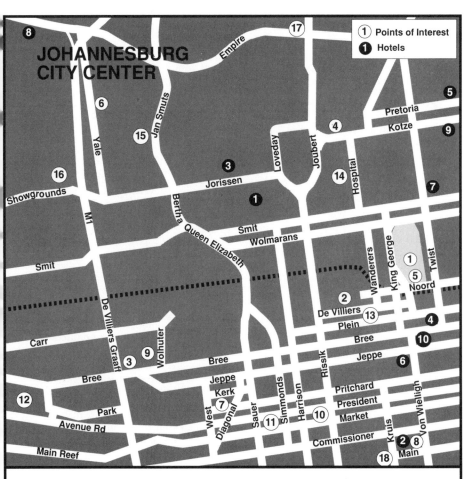

JOHANNESBURG
CITY CENTER

| 1 | Points of Interest |
| 1 | Hotels |

KEY TO CITY MAP # 5

POINTS OF INTEREST

1. Joubert Park
2. South African Railways Museum
3. Africana Museum in Progress
4. The Fort
5. Johannesburg Art Gallery
6. Planetarium
7. Stock Exchange
8. Carlton Center
9. Market Theater
10. City Hall & Post Office
11. Africana Museum
12. Oriental Plaza
13. St. Mary's Cathedral
14. Adler Museum of the History of Medicine

15. Smuts Library
    Gubbins Library
16. Bernard Price Museum
17. Bensusan Museum of Photography
18. Jewish Museum

HOTELS

1. Braamfontein Protea (4 star)
2. Carlton Hotel & Towers (5 star)
3. Devonshire (4 star)
4. Down Town Holiday Inn (3 star)
5. Hillbrow Protea (3 star)
6. Johannesburg Sun & Towers (5 star)
7. Karos Johannesburger (3 star)
8. Mill Park Holiday Inn (3 star)
9. Protea Gardens (4 star)
10. Rand International (3 star)

Disney-style reconstruction of the good old times at Gold Reef City. Today, Johannesburg is not only the City of Gold. It spent lavishly on the arts, on parks, zoos and nature reserves, top class hotels and restaurants.

SOWETO

To the southwest of Johannesburg lies SOWETO, a blend of First and Third Worlds, shanties, row houses and stylish mansions, donkey carts, minibuses and limousines, street vendors and supermarkets, music and misery, happy faces and stares of hopelessness.

It is a black city, developed under apartheid to replace the festering slums that resulted from mass migration of tribal folk to *Igoli* (the city of gold) in search of a better future.

SOWETO is an acronym for Southwestern Townships. It became known not only for its intriguing mosaic of tribal people and cultures or its artists and musicians, but for political reasons. In 1976 an uprising by the SOWETO youth against the white establishment, resulted in tragic clashes and the death of several hundred. Every year on 25 June SOWETO Day is commemorated by black South Africans. Most houses in SOWETO have electricity, television and access to more than 3,000 black-owned stores.

Community beer halls and shebeens (speak easy joints), recreation centers and football stadiums are popular places of entertainment. Many a musical hit from SOWETO has made the world charts. This township with its peculiar mix of African rhythm and Western influences has spawned a number of internationally acclaimed popular artists.

To cater for foreigners half-day tours to SOWETO depart regularly from the Carlton Hotel in Johannesburg. *(Tel. (011) 331-5072 & 331-4911)*

POINTS OF INTEREST
SEE CITY MAP #5

1. **JOUBERT PARK:** The original park that was laid out in 1887 and today is the site for the Johannesburg Art Gallery. Recently renovated fountains, a tropical plant hothouse. A floral clock, restaurant and theater are additional attractions.

2. **SOUTH AFRICAN RAILWAYS MUSEUM:** Situated at Park Station and displays the first locomotive used in the Transvaal, as well as other historic equipment and memorabilia relating to rail, roads, harbors, airways and other services. Also has a collection of Pierneef paintings and model railways. Store sells items relating to the South African railways, including model trains. Open Mon-Fri. Tel. (011) 773-9114.

3. **AFRICANA MUSEUM IN PROGRESS:** Portrays the African and Bushman cultures of South Africa. with a large ethnological exhibition featuring life-size tribal huts, as well as a collection of beadwork, hunting tools and dolls and toys. The museum is open to the public on weekdays. Tel. (011) 836-8482.

City Deep Gold Mine - Pierneef (Africana Museum)

4. THE FORT: Built as a prison in 1890 to accommodate unruly diggers and later utilized by the Boer artillery, this building with its heavy, studded wooden door under the coat of arms of the old Transvaal Republic, is one of Johannesburg's oldest.

5. JOHANNESBURG ART GALLERY: Situated in Joubert Park this museum contains one of the most extensive collections of South African art as well as a valuable array of famous overseas works, ranging from English, Dutch and French to Flemish. Overseas artists include Picasso, Rodin, El Greco, Van Gogh, and Henry Moore. Japanese woodcuts, textiles and furniture are recent additions. Special tours, lectures, film shows and concerts are offered to the public. The gallery is open Tue-Sun from I0h00-17h00. Tel. (011) 725-3180.

Rissik Street Post Office 1897

6. PLANETARIUM:Situated on the west side of the University of the Witwatersrand, this well-known planetarium changes its programs often but most presentations deal with the southern skies. Books, charts and equipment are on sale. Reservations necessary. Tel. 011-716-3199.

7. STOCK EXCHANGE: There were several other exchanges in South Africa before Johannesburg first started trading in gold stocks in 1887 "between the chains". The first JSE building was too small to accommodate the excited crowds and the area between Commissioner and Markets Streets had to be closed with chains to the traffic to allow traders to spill into the street.

The expression *"between the chains"* soon became world currency for stock trading as Johannesburg grew in importance. Today the JSE is housed in a modern building on Diagonal Street, handling not only gold, but all of South Africa's industrial and other shares. The JSE offers guided tours Mon-Fri at 11h00 and 14h30. Also open to visitors in the building is the South African Hall of Achievement. Tel. (011) 883-6580.

8. CARLTON CENTER: The highest building of a three tiered complex, is a 50 floor office complex with the Carlton Panorama observation deck on the top floor offering visitors panoramic views of the city and its suburbs stretching far beyond the mine dumps. Also has a gold exhibition. Open daily. Admission fee.

9. MARKET THEATER COMPLEX: Housed in an old classic restored building complex are three theaters, a photographic gallery, two art galleries, a live music bar, two restaurants, a shopping mall, book stores, an intimate bar and a music/drama facility called 'The Warehouse'. These old buildings originally served as the Indian Fruit and Citrus Market. Held on Saturdays on the adjoining square is a flea market with 300 stalls, a street theater, music and pavement shows.

10. CITY HALL AND POST OFFICE: The old Rissik Street Post Office was built in 1897 and is still in use. Right opposite is the Johannesburg City Hall, completed in stages between 1910 and 1915.

US President Hoover

In 1928 the mayor of Johannesburg got a letter from a man in Minnesota who wished to know whether a presidential candidate by the name of Herbert Hoover had voted in the city's elections while he was living there in 1912. All the records have long since been destroyed, the answer came.

Herbert Hoover became America's 31st President, but if it turned out that he had voted in the Johannesburg elections he would have been disqualified as a candidate altogether.

Coming to Johannesburg as a mining engineer, Herbert Hoover did not stay long. In the words of one observer at the time: Hoover came, saw and was hardly noticed himself. And he left , realizing that the swinging city of those days was not a good place for a Quaker.

Hoover may not have cast a ballot in the city elections, but he had another (quite profitable) connection with a certain Ballot.

John Ballot, who developed a new process for extracting copper, employed the American mining engineer and together they started the Messina Copper Mines in Northern Transvaal, which soon grew into a highly successful operation. This venture was one of many which helped Hoover to become a self-made multi-millionaire.

11. AFRICANA MUSEUM: Situated above the Johannesburg Public Library in Market Street, this museum features exhibits and documentation relating to Southern African history as well as priceless collections of Cape silver, antique toys and artifacts. Adjoining is the Geological Museum with an extensive collection of minerals and the Harger Archeological Museum with its emphasis on prehistoric southern Africa. Open daily, except Sunday mornings. Tel. (011) 836-3787.

12. ORIENTAL PLAZA: A shopping center with an eastern flavor featuring 270 stores and stalls and three restaurants. Features a minaret clock tower and peacock fountain. Open Mon-Sat.

13. ST MARY'S CATHEDRAL: One of the many memorable creations by Sir Herbert Baker, Rhodes' friend who also designed the Union Buildings and Groote Schuur.

14. ADLER MUSEUM OF THE HISTORY OF MEDICINE: Medical, dental and pharmaceutical items as they were developed over the years, collected by a husband-wife team, Drs. Cyril and Ester Adler. It takes the visitor from primitive witchcraft to Dr Chris Barnard who performed the world's first heart transplant in Cape Town. Has an African herb shop, divining bones and mutis (medicines) of all kinds for sale. Open weekdays 10h00-16h00.

15. SMUTS & GUBBINS LIBRARIES: The Smuts Library is situated in Witwatersrand University. Smuts' old farmhouse (a barracks transported to the farm) is still in place on Doornkloof near Pretoria, but this is where his book collection is displayed. The room imitates the original Smuts study in detail. Also on the campus is the **Gubbins Library**, famous for its extensive collection of Africana books. In 1930, John Gaspard Gubbins, a farmer in the Transvaal decided to donate his extensive collection of Africana books to the University as he felt that his thatch-roofed house posed a fire hazard to this priceless possession. In December 1931, when half of the books were transferred to the campus a fire broke out in the old building where it was temporarily stored. They were all destroyed. Undeterred Gubbins not only rebuilt the collection but expanded it in the ensuing years. Also displayed on the campus is the original Dias cross.

16. BERNARD PRICE MUSEUM: The Bernard Price Institute of Paleontology is respected world-wide as the premier museum for the study of extinct plants and animals - and early man. Contains a large collection of fossils, including bones and remnants found at various South African sites.

Featured among these are the bones and tools of the *Australopithecus africanus* (Southern Ape of Africa), discovered by Prof. Raymond Dart. This creature who is reputed to have lived three and a half million years ago turned out to be more man than ape.

Although small (three feet tall), it walked erect. Other famous contributors to these discoveries in the search for the Missing Link were Dr. Robert Room and Tobias. Visitors who have a special interest in the prehistoric past may wish to take a trip to Sterkfontein Caves, near Krugersdorp,or further afield to Makapansgat, near Potgietersrus.

17. BENSUSAN MUSEUM OF PHOTOGRAPHY: An extensive collection of photographic books, valuable prints and antique equipment started by a former mayor of Johannesburg - an ardent photographer. Recognized as one of the world's most extensive of its kind, the museum is situated on the corner of Showground and Raikes Roads. Open daily. Tel. (011) 403-1067.

Mark Twain

"In seven or eight years, they have built up in a desert, a city of a hundred thousand inhabitants, counting white and black together; and not the ordinary mining city of wooden shanties, but a city made out of lasting materials," wrote Mark Twain after his visit to the rapidly expanding City of Gold in 1896.

The famous American author had come to South Africa on a lecture tour, trying to recover financially after he lost nearly everything he owned through a bad publishing investment at home. Understandably a bit worn and unhappy, the South African experience seemed to have restored Twain's sense of humor.

Accompanied by his wife and daughter, he dropped in at the Colonial Parliament in Cape Town where debates were conducted in both English and Dutch. Said Twain: *"They quarreled in two languages, while I was there, and agreed in none."*

On the voyage back to America via Britain, Twain got his wish to meet a South African millionaire up close. Barney Barnato and his wife and daughter were on the same ship. Twain's visit to South Africa is recounted in *Following the Equator*, published in 1897.

18. JEWISH MUSEUM: In Sheffield House on the corner of Main and Kruis streets it is dedicated to Jewry in South Africa. Also displayed are art objects. Open Mon-Thu. Tel. (011) 331-0331.

JOHANNESBURG OUTSKIRTS
CITY MAP #6 - OPPOSITE PAGE

1. GOLD REEF CITY: Theme park few miles south of city, constructed around the gold mine museum, depicting Johannesburg in the gold rush days. Offers rides on a steam train and horse drawn omnibus, an underground visit, a gold pouring, a Victorian fun fair and mine dancing. Also has a variety of stores, restaurants, bars and live entertainment. Entrance fee includes free parking and access to all events except the underground mine trip. Group tours offered. *Tel. (011) 496-1400. Fax. (011) 496-1249.*

The Chamber of Mines arranges **underground mine visits** to a working gold mine on Tuesdays, Wednesdays and Thursdays. It is also possible for visitors to attend traditional African and 'gumboot' dancing on the first, second and fourth Sunday of every month. The venues change. Call the *Chamber* beforehand. Reservations are essential. *Tel. (011) 838-8211.*

2. JOHANNESBURG ZOO & ZOOLOGICAL GARDENS: One of the most impressive zoos in Africa and comparable to the best overseas. Five thousand different types of animals are housed on the well manicured grounds. Also on the grounds is the Museum of South African Rock Art with a collection of prehistoric rock engravings. Facilities include an open-air restaurant and souvenir kiosks. Open daily.

3. FLORENCE BLOOM BIRD SANCTUARY: A 20 acre sanctuary around two small dams. Hides are provided for birdwatchers. The sanctuary forms part of Delta Park, that also serves as the headquarters of the Wildlife Society of Southern Africa.

The Nature Conservation Center on the grounds has an auditorium, aquarium, exhibition halls with environmental displays, gift shop, information center, and a meditation room. The center is closed on Sundays but the bird sanctuary is open every day. Tel. (011) 782-1531.

4. ZOO LAKE: Offers row boats for rental, a swimming pool, tennis courts, a bowling club, an outdoor tea garden and indoor restaurant. There are breeding bird colonies on the islands in the center of the lake.

KEY TO CITY MAP # 6

POINTS OF INTEREST

1. Gold Reef City
2. Johannesburg Zoo and Zoological Gardens
3. Florence Bloom Bird Sanctuary
4. Zoo Lake
5. Emmarentia Dam and Botanical Gardens
6. Melrose Bird Sanctuary
7. Organic Village Market
8. Santarama Miniland
9. James Hall Museum of Transport
10. Lion Park
11. Gillooly's Farm
12. Sandton City
13. South African National Museum of Military History
14. The Wilds

HOTELS

1. Protea Balalaika Hotel ★★★
2. Gold Reef City Hotel ★★★★★
3. Karos Indaba Hotel ★★★
4. Rosebank Hotel ★★★★
5. Sandton Holiday Inn ★★★
6. Sandton Sun ★★★★★
7. Sunnyside Park Hotel ★★★

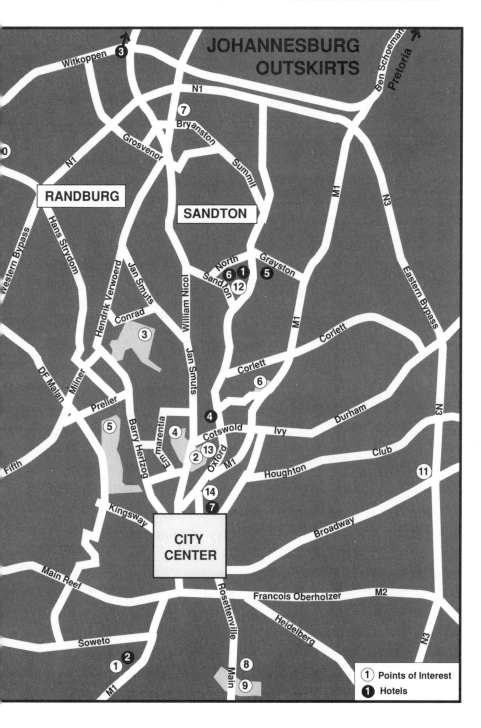

JOHANNESBURG OUTSKIRTS

RANDBURG

SANDTON

CITY CENTER

① Points of Interest
① Hotels

Randlord Mansion

5. EMMARENTIA DAM AND BOTANICAL GARDENS: Situated in the 250 acre Johannesburg Botanical Gardens and contains a herb garden amidst fountains and exotic trees.Also a boating center and serves as headquarters for the Model Boat Club.

6. MELROSE BIRD SANCTUARY: Provides a safe haven for about 120 species of birds among its thick reed beds on the dam. Has a hide for birdwatchers.

7. ORGANIC VILLAGE MARKET: Offers arts and crafts for sale on the grounds of the Waldorf School in Bryanston. Features organically grown vegetables and pony rides are provided for children. Refreshments are served. Open Thu-Sat from 08h00-13h00.

8. SANTARAMA MINILAND: Scaled down version of South Africa features models (to a scale of 1: 25) of historical and contemporary scenes. Styled after Madurodam in Holland. Cruises on a paddle-steamer, as well as train rides. Restaurant and souvenir shop. Open daily from 10h00 to 17h00.

9. JAMES MUSEUM OF TRANSPORT: In Pioneers' Park at La Rochelle, it features the development of transport in South Africa over the years.Open daily. tel. (011) 435-9718.

10. LION PARK: About 15 miles from the city center. Contains lions, zebra, antelope and other species along a 10 mile car trail. Opportunity to hold and be photographed with lion cubs. There is also a Ndebele village. Refreshments, picnic and braai (barbecue) facilities available. Open daily.

11. GILLOOLY'S FARM: Often used for dog and other shows and fetes or simply for picnicking under the trees. Facilities include a koppie (or hill), children's playground, and miniature railway that operates in summer. Tel. (011) 407-6111.

12. SANDTON CITY: One of the most extensive shopping malls in South Africa. It provides visitors with a full range of local and foreign wares.

13. SOUTH AFRICAN NATIONAL MUSEUM OF MILITARY HISTORY: Exhibited are weapons and memorabilia from the early wars in South Africa and the two world wars, where South Africa was heavily committed as a full ally. Open daily and offers audio-visual presentations on Sundays. Tel. (011) 646-5513.

14. THE WILDS: A pet project of General Smuts, the statesman-botanist, this 36 acre park close to the city center in Killarney, contains indigenous plants (including succulents and aloes), amidst waterfalls and walking paths. It has four plant houses.

KIMBERLEY
City of Diamonds

CITY MAP # 7 - PAGE124
Diamond Capital of the World
Population - 150,000

CLIMATE

Situated in a summer rainfall area. Rains usually in the form of thunder storms. Although summers can be quite hot, it is a dry heat. Evenings are cool.

Winter days usually start out with frost but warm up to become pleasant with lots of sunshine. Winter nights are cold.

HISTORY

Diamonds were first discovered near Hopetown, south of where Kimberley stands today. One Sunday in March 1867 Schalk van Niekerk saw the Jacobs children on a neighboring farm play with a big shiny pebble. He liked the look of it and wanted to pay Mrs Jacobs to have it.

You have got to be joking," the indignant Mrs Jacobs responded. *"I will never take your hard-earned money for a worthless pebble. Take it. The children, I am sure, will pick up many more."*

The Jewish shopkeepers in town were not particularly impressed with the stone so Van Niekerk took up an Irish travelling salesman on his offer to carry the stone to Colesberg to have it assessed by an expert.

EUREKA

The "expert", town chemist Kirsch, declared the stone a topaz, but agreed to send it to Grahamstown where Dr William Atherstone tested the stone. It turned out to be a 10 carat diamond and was bought by the Cape Governor Philip Wodehouse for £500. He had it exhibited at the Paris Exhibition in the hope that it would draw overseas interest to the economically depressed Cape Colony, but was hardly noticed among the array of new machinery displayed at the exhibition to herald the dawn of mechanization.

Eventually this first diamond, the Eureka, had a place of honor in the Library of Parliament in Cape Town before it finally came to rest in the Mine Museum in Kimberley.

Although Kimberley has earned the name as the Diamond Capital of the World, the largest diamond was found at Premier Mine, near Pretoria, on 25 June 1905. Measuring 4.5 inches (11 cm) by 2.25 inches (6 cm) by 2 inches (5 cm) it was named the Cullinan after the Chairman of the Premier Diamond Mining Company, Sir Thomas Cullinan.

The Cullinan was sold to the Transvaal Colonial Government for a nominal £125,000. (The surface manager, Frederick Wells, who actually found it, was rewarded with £2,000). The Transvaal Premier, Gen. Louis Botha, gave the diamond to King Edward VII.

The famous Asscher Brothers in Amsterdam cut it into nine large stones. The largest pear-shaped Cullinan I (530.2 carats) was renamed Great Star of Africa, and the second largest, an oblong Cullinan II (317.4 carats) became the Lesser Star of Africa. They both found their way into the scepter and Imperial Crown and are kept in the Tower of London.

Among those attending the Paris exhibition, at least one prestigious London diamond firm, Harry Emmaneul and Company, did notice the diamond. They decided to send the eminent Professor James Gregory to the Cape to make a personal report.

GREGORY

"The whole story of the Cape diamonds is false," Gregory concluded. *"It is simply one of many schemes for trying to promote the employment and expenditure of capital in searching for this precious substance in the Colony."*

Instead of luring thousands, only a few hundred impoverished fortune-seekers turned up from overseas.

STAR

In March 1869, two years almost to the day after he discovered South Africa's very first diamond on the Jacobs farm, Van Niekerk bought a second stone from a Griqua shepherd for 500 sheep, 10 oxen and a horse. His risk paid off when Lilienfeld Brothers in Hopetown offered him £11,200 for the diamond. It was a blue-white diamond weighing 83 carats.

The Lilienfelds called it the Star of South Africa and sold it to the Earl of Dudley for £30,000. Since then it changed hands several times and turned up in Switzerland in 1974 where it was sold for twenty times its original price.

The old Lilienfeld store in Hopetown has changed its name to A Rosen, but visitors can still see the two deep scratches that Van Niekerk made in the front display window to "prove" his diamond when he sold it.

A Gregory has ever since been used in South Africa as an expression to indicate bad judgment.

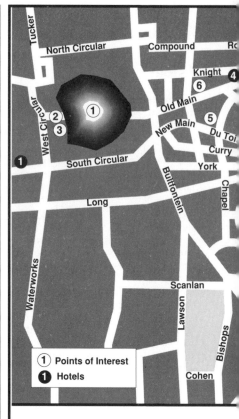

KEY TO CITY MAP # 7

POINTS OF INTEREST

1. Big Hole
2. Kimberley Mine Museum
3. Bultfontein
4. Cecil Rhodes Statue
5. Electric Tram
7. Steam locomotives
8. William Humphrey Art Gallery
9. Diggers' Memorial
10. Duggan-Cronin Gallery

The second find at Hopetown brought diggers by the thousands and short on their heels, buyers, traders, equipment and camp followers.

At first they raked the river banks and later as impressive discoveries were

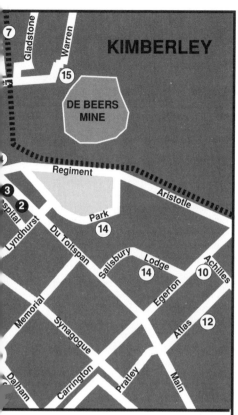

KIMBERLEY

DE BEERS MINE

11. Cape Corps Monument
12. McGregor Museum
13. Honored Dead Memorial
14. Dunluce
15. De Beers Mine
    Lookout Point
16. Pioneers of Aviation Museum

HOTELS

1. Diamond Protea Lodge ★★
2. Kimberlite ★★
3. Kimberley Sun ★★★★
4. Savoy ★★★

swift riches on farms with names which they could never hope to pronounce.

They renamed *Vooruitzicht* Kimberley after the Colonial Secretary of the day - and *Du Toitspan*, Beaconsfield after Lord Beaconsfield, the former British Prime Minister Disraeli.

The Boer farmers had been robbed of their pastoral peace, but they got compensation in other ways. Van Niekerk and other farmers sold their land at inflated prices to escape the rowdy fortune seekers and bought land elsewhere. Also the Cape Colony was blessed. At last the men and machines and new capital that Wodehouse was seeking when he displayed that first diamond in Paris, had come to the Cape and South Africa. The Machine Age had dawned on South Africa.

BIG HOLE

There were several diamond rushes, starting with the first in Hopetown and eventually leading up to the greatest called the De Beers New Rush, after the owner of the farm Vooruitzicht where the 50,000 settled within a matter of weeks, living in tents and shacks while they burrowed deep into the kimberlite or blue ground in search of gem stones. The activity centered on and around Colesberg koppie (named after the hometown of Fleetwood Rawstone who made the discovery) and soon the hill disappeared in what became known as the Big Hole of Kimberley.

BIG BOYS

At times 30,000 men were at work digging crushing and sifting at the same time. There seemed to be no end to the diamonds in this vertical shaft. Much merriment accompanied every new find. Women bathed in champagne and men would light cigars with bank-notes. Kimberley in the 1870s was a rambunctious, disorderly town -

made further north, their focus turned to barren farms with names like Koffiefontein, Jagersfontein, Bultfontein, Du Toit'span, Dorstfontein and Vooruitzicht. They came in shiploads from every corner of the globe with supplies and skills. Men in search of

Barney Barnato

as chaotic in many ways as the activity in the deepening big hole.So the big boys decided to step in and make both the mining area safe and to protect limb and life and the market from collapse.

Enter sickly, nineteen year old Cecil Rhodes, who eventually founded the De Beers Mining Company. And at the same time vaudeville entertainer and boxer, the Cockney Jew from London, Barney Barnato.

They both aspired to be king of this man-made earthhole with its millions of glittering carats. In the end Rhodes would buy Barnato and his Kimberley Central Diamond Mining Company out and make him a director of the powerful De Beers, which took control of diamonds first in Kimberley and later all over the world.

DE BEERS

Order was restored to the diggings and peace restored until the outbreak of the Anglo-Boer War when the Boer troops had it under siege and gun-fire for several months.

De Beers ruled from its Head Office in Stockdale Street, built in 1898 and used until 1974 when it moved to a modern skyscraper named after Harry Oppenheimer. Here in De Beers' board room visitors can still see the original check of £5,338,650 paid by Rhodes to Barney Barnato.

Harry Oppenheimer was not the first of his family to dabble in diamonds and to make a name in gold while he served as chairman of both De Beers and Anglo-American. His father, Sir Ernest Oppenheimer, the son of a cigar merchant in Germany, came to Kimberley at the age of 17 to work in the diamond trade at £1 per week. He ended up building a fortune first in diamonds and then in gold. He also served as mayor of Kimberley.

Several diamond pipes in the Kimberley area are still producing, but the original diggings have long been depleted. There are, however, dealers who would sell diamonds directly to visitors. Diamonds are also sold at the curio shop at the Mine Museum.

Kimberley also claims to have the only two drive-in pubs in the world. These establishments at Halfway House Hotel and the Kimberlite Hotel date back to the days when people wanted a drink in passing while still sitting on horseback.

POINTS OF INTEREST
SEE CITY MAP #7 - PAGE 124

1. BIG HOLE: This is where 30,000 men toiled away around the clock from the 1870s, seeking for diamonds. Every inch of this enormous hole in the ground was dug by manual labor. What started out as a hill named Colesberg Koppie soon disappeared as miners bore down like ants into the kimberlite blue ground pipe, taking the diggings to the surface in carts and trollies along hundreds of cables and ropes that reached like spider webs deep to the ever shifting bottom.

Between 1871 and 1892 about 22.5 million metric tons of earth were hauled out of in this fashion and before the Kimberley mine finally closed in 1914, about 14.5 million carats (3 tons) of diamonds were recovered. With a depth of 365 m (1200 ft), a surface area of 31 acres and a diameter of 1.5 km (1 mile), this is the world's largest man-made hole and capable of swallowing any skyscraper in the world. The water level has risen to a level of about 265 m (870 feet) from the top.

2. KIMBERLEY MINE MUSEUM: Actual buildings from the beginnings of Kimberley, demolished elsewhere and erected in this museum village. Includes the Lutheran church built of corrugated iron two years before the first house went up in 1877 and Barney Barnato's boxing academy, diamond dealer's offices, bars and beer halls and the private railway coach used by the directors of De Beers Mining Company. In the Mining Hall visitors are shown how diamonds were recovered in the old days, using locally designed pulsating grease tables. An extensive collection of photographs are supplemented with models and, in the adjacent De Beers Hall, diamonds ranging from pebbles to glittering 'fancies'. The world's largest uncut diamond, simply called the 616, is on display, as well as 'Eureka', the stone that started it all.

At Engelsmans Prospect visitors can pick up a license allowing them to fill a bucket with gravel and send it through the ancient machinery to the sorting table. A find of any of the artificial diamonds hidden in the gravel entitles them to prizes ranging from a tram ticket to a real diamond. There is a tearoom and gift shop, where real diamonds are sold. Open daily. Tel. (0531) 3-1557/8.

3. BULTFONTEIN MINE: Historic mine offers surface tours of the treatment and recovery plants from Tuesday to Friday at 09h00 and 11h00. Advance bookings are necessary for underground tours. Children under ten not allowed. Tel. (0531) 3-1557/8. (Johannesburg: (011) 638-5126)

4. CECIL RHODES STATUE: This is where the nineteen year old sickly youth from England made his first million and started out on his journey towards great wealth and power. He called Kimberley his 'foster-mother'.

5. ALEXANDER MCGREGOR MUSEUM: Also known as the Old Museum, it was built in honor of a former mayor of Kimberley. Rock and mineral specimens from all over the world are on display, as well as items relating to early life and fashions in the Northern Cape.

6. ELECTRIC TRAM: Operating from outside the old City Hall to the Mine Museum, these tramcars date back to the early 1900s.

7. STEAM LOCOMOTIVES: Between Kimberley and Bloemfontein there are still a few steam engines in use. These may be seen in operation in the marshalling yards at Austin Road in the Beaconsfield area. Permit to the yards must be obtained at the Paul Sauer Building at the Kimberley Railway Station. Tel. (0531) 288-2061. There is also a steam train service to De Aar for enthusiasts who wish to take a ride. Tel. (0531) 288-1111.

8. WILLIAM HUMPHREYS ART GALLERY: Situated in the Civic Center, it displays a wide range of South African and European paintings, furniture, sculpture and other art objects.

Long Cecil

Johannes de Beer

In July 1871 the world's richest gold diamond field was discovered on the farm Vooruitzicht that belonged to the De Beers brothers, Johannes and Diederik. Johannes actually held the portion where Colesberg koppie (hill) stood that soon disappeared and sunk into what became known as the Big Hole as thousands of diggers toiled away in search of gems.

The De Beer brothers wanted no part of all this activity that became known as the New De Beer Rush and resulted in the famous Kimberley Mine.

They sold their land to an agent, John Reitz, for a total of £6,000, moved on and bought farms further along the Vaal River, foregoing untold millions in royalties.

Cecil John Rhodes eventually consolidated the diamond mining activity in Kimberley under De Beers Consolidated Mines Limited, which today controls a multi-billion dollar industry world-wide. Johannes and Diederik de Beer whose names were used, never had a single share in the company or earned a single penny in dividends and profits. Both brothers remained farmers until their death. Johannes' original modest wattle-and-daub house has been reconstructed in Kimberley.

9. DIGGERS ' MEMORIAL: A memorial in the Oppenheimer gardens dedicated to the thousands of diggers who descended on Kimberley to find their fortunes.

10. DUGGAN-CRONIN GALLERY: Every country has its resident photographer of fame dating back to the early beginnings of photography. In South Africa, Alfred Duggan-Cronin rose from obscurity as a humble turn-of-the-century De Beers' night watchman with the help of a simple box-camera. His collection of more than 40,000 pictures vividly portray the life-style and character of the indigenous people of southern Africa. Open daily.

11. CAPE CORPS MONUMENT: Center piece of this memorial is a German field gun captured by the South African Cape Corps in the battle with the Turkish army during the First World War at Square Hill, near Jerusalem.

12. MCGREGOR MUSEUM: Started in as the Sanatorium Hotel for the wealthy in search of Kimberley's pure dry climate. Cecil Rhodes himself stayed in several of these rooms during the Anglo-Boer War. After a short spell as a convent school the building has been turned into a museum with period furniture and displays relating to religion and ecology. Open daily.

13. HONORED DEAD MEMORIAL: Designed by the famous Sir Herbert Baker and the inscription provided by author Rudyard Kipling. But the name that gets star billing is George Labram, an obscure De Beers engineer who designed the field gun placed in front of the memorial. With no previous experience Labram built the gun to be used against the Boers during the siege of Kimberley. *Long Cecil*, as it was named after Cecil Rhodes, was completed in 24 days and outgunned the Boers had - until they brought in one of their Creusot 'Long Tom' guns.

Ironically, George Labram was one of the first killed by the Boer shelling while he was relaxing in his hotel room. *Long Cecil* was also used as the gun carriage on which Rhodes' coffin was carried to the Cape Town station for its long journey to a burial place in Rhodesia (now Zimbabwe). The lathe used to machine the barrel is still in use, at the Kimberley Engineering Works.

14. DUNLUCE: One of two meticulously restored old mansions open to the public.The original owner Gustav Bonus of Dunluce instructed architect Greatbach to design a house fit for a member of the Diamond Syndicate. Originally called 'Lilianfield', this ornate mansion with its long verandahs certainly met the requirements. A shell from the Boers' Long Tom gun went through the roof during the siege of Kimberley in 1899 and caused extensive damage. In the early 1900s Bonus sold the house to another financier, John Orr, who renamed it 'Dunluce'. The other mansion, The Bungalow, belonged to Rhodes' confidant and compatriot, Cecil Rudd. Visits to these houses are by appointment. Tel. (0531) 3-2645/6.

15. DE BEERS MINE LOOKOUT POST: Underground operations can be viewed at the De Beers Mine Observation Post. De Beers also stage shows by its world-famous Alsatian dogs on the first and third Sunday of each month to entertain visitors and scare off potential thieves.

16. PIONEERS OF AVIATION MUSEUM: The site for South Africa's first flying school was started in 1913. The South African Flying Corps that had its beginnings here was the forerunner of the South African Air Force. Aviation history was made here in 1911 when a non-stop flight record of 8.5 minutes was set. On the site of the old hanger is a museum depicting South African aeronautical history.

PORT ELIZABETH
The Bay

SEE CITY MAP #8 - PAGE130
Second largest City in the Cape
Population - 620,000

CLIMATE

Geographically and weather-wise Port Elizabeth is almost midway between Cape Town and Durban. It offers a pleasant compromise between the winter-wet Mediterranean climate of Cape Town and the summer-humid Durban. Summers are pleasant along the coast although it becomes hotter and drier inland. Winter days cold in the morning, heating up during daytime. Sometimes windy.

HISTORY

Referred to by many as The Bay or PE, this resort city on the Eastern Cape is situated close to where explorer Dias went ashore in 1488 and left his famous cross. The actual cross at Kwaaihoek was restored from five thousand pieces found on the site and is kept at Witwatersrand University in Johannesburg, while a replica welcomes visitors to Dias' landing spot. Also on the Market Square, somewhat intimidated by the majestic old City Hall behind it, stands another replica of this famous. It was presented to Port Elizabeth by the Portuguese in 1954.

Sir Rufane Donkin

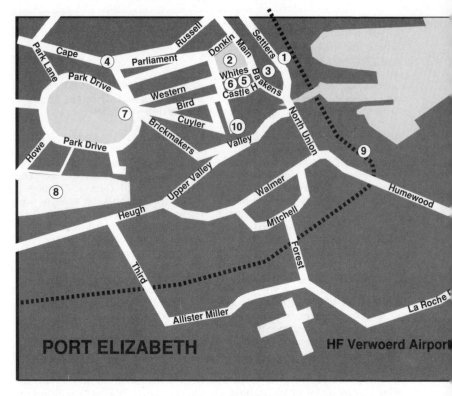

PORT ELIZABETH

HF Verwoerd Airport

FORT FREDERICK

In 1799 a military station, Fort Frederick, was established at what was then known as Algoa Bay. Some four hundred British soldiers were garrisoned out here to protect the harbor against attacks from the interior.

Today the fort can still be seen in its originally well preserved state. It is believed to be the oldest British construction in Africa south of the equator and is a national monument.

The actual founding of Port Elizabeth dates back to the arrival by sea of the first four thousand British settlers.

There to greet them was Sir Rufane Donkin, the popular Acting Governor of the Cape, who tried his utmost to make the new arrivals comfortable in their adopted new homeland.

Donkin named the new town after his wife, Elizabeth, who had died tragically in India at the age of twenty-eight only two years before.

TRIBUTE

In tribute to her, he erected a stone pyramid near the lighthouse, with the inscription: *One of the most perfect of human beings who has given her name to the town below.*

Thousands of visitors to this popular resort and important harbor city, talk in the glowing terms about the city itself. Its temperate climate makes for outdoor activity. Apart from some of the best surfing beaches in South Af-

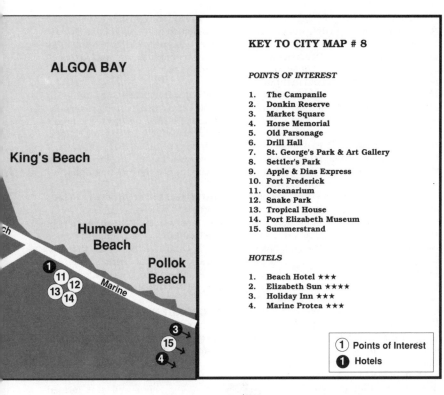

ALGOA BAY

King's Beach

Humewood
Beach

Pollok
Beach

Marine

KEY TO CITY MAP # 8

POINTS OF INTEREST

1. The Campanile
2. Donkin Reserve
3. Market Square
4. Horse Memorial
5. Old Parsonage
6. Drill Hall
7. St. George's Park & Art Gallery
8. Settler's Park
9. Apple & Dias Express
10. Fort Frederick
11. Oceanarium
12. Snake Park
13. Tropical House
14. Port Elizabeth Museum
15. Summerstrand

HOTELS

1. Beach Hotel ★★★
2. Elizabeth Sun ★★★★
3. Holiday Inn ★★★
4. Marine Protea ★★★

① Points of Interest

❶ Hotels

rica and the world, it has five golf courses and an array of recreational facilities for toddlers and adults.

Wool

Much of Port Elizabeth's initial development as a harbor came from the export of wool and mohair from the drier interior where the settlers crossbred flat-tailed Cape sheep with imported German merinos for a superior quality of wool.

The wool market is still centered in this city, but in recent years the establishment of automobile and other industries took prominence.

There is much of the past preserved in buildings and monuments and memorials in this resort city.

POINTS OF INTEREST
SEE CITY MAP #8 - ABOVE

1. **THE CAMPANILE:** The landing of the 1820 British settlers is celebrated by the 51.8 m (170 ft) Campanile, erected one hundred years after the historic event. It contains a carillon of 23 bells which ring different tunes three times a day at 8.32 am, 1.32 pm and 6.02 pm. For visitors who are willing to brave the 204 steps to the top, the Campanile offers a worthwhile vista.

2. DONKIN RESERVE: An 8 acre reserve in the heart of the city, proclaimed by Sir Rufane Donkin as a shrine to his wife. Contains a pyramid with an inscription to *"one of the most perfect human beings, who has given her name to the city below"* from *"the* *husband whose heart is still wrung by undiminished grief."* This was erected two years after Elizabeth Donkin's early death in India in 1818. Reserve has an open area from where visitors can get a good view of the bay. An old lighthouse has been converted into a military museum displaying medals, badges and other military items. Open daily.

3. MARKET SQUARE: In bygone days incoming ships dumped their cargo on the beach from where it was taken to nearby Market Square. On Saturdays visitors will still find heavy trading and interesting flea market activities on this historic square. It is bordered by the old City Hall, dating back to 1858, and according to his writings, a favorite of British author Anthony Trollope. In front of City Hall stands a replica of the cross planted by Bartholomew Dias when he landed at nearby Kwaaihoek in 1488, as well as a monument of Prester John, the mythical Christian king who supposedly ruled an empire somewhere in southern Africa. The massive stone Feather Market building erected in 1883, stands as a reminder of good old times for the ostrich feather trade. Also in the area is the old Opera House which survived since 1892 and the original railway station with ornate 1875 iron grills supporting its roof.

4. HORSE MEMORIAL: Port Elizabeth was a major port of entry for many of the remounts that arrived from overseas to replace the horses that were killed in the Anglo Boer War. It is therefore fitting that there should be a monument in this city to commemorate the senseless killing of 347,000 horses in battle - one third of the total number in service.

The inscription reads: *"The greatness of a nation consists not as much in the number of its people or the extent of its territory as in the extent and justice of its compassion."*

5. THE OLD PARSONAGE: Situated at 7 Castle Hill this English colonial house was built in 1827 by the settlement's first colonial chaplain, the Rev Francis McLeland. The oldest house in town, it serves as a museum, displaying period furniture and a collection of dolls.

6. DRILL HALL: Constructed in 1881, the Drill Hall houses a regimental museum. It served as the headquarters of Port Elizabeth's own regiment, Prince Alfred's Guard, which was the first volunteer unit in the British Empire to make a bayonet charge in battle against the Basotho tribe in 1880.

7. ST GEORGE'S PARK: South Africa's oldest sports grounds. In 1843 the country's first cricket club was formed here and in 1880 it was the site for the first athletics club. A year later the first cycling club was formed here and in 1882 the nation's first lawn bowling club. In 1889 the first international cricket match was played here against Britain and in 1891 the first international rugby test match. The Pearson Conservatory in the park features waterlilies, orchids and flowering plants. At the entrance is the King George VI Art Gallery with 19th and 20th century British and South African art. Open daily.

A snake handler has his hands full at the park

8. SETTLERS' PARK: A 100 acre sanctuary

on the banks of the Baakens River, close to the city center, containing four types of floral regions - Karoo, grassland, Cape *fynbos* and subtropical coastal flora. The Settlers' Park Nature Reserve also has an abundance of birds among its pools and streams, as well as small deer and other mammals. (Victoria Park, near the airport, is headquarters for the South African Dahlia Society). (See also the chapter DOWN THE GARDEN PATH - Page 63).

9. THE APPLE & DIAS EXPRESS: Operating on its narrow gauge since 1906, this is not simply a tourist attraction but a fully operative train. On Saturdays at certain times of the year, however, visitors can board the **Apple Express** for a special excursion into *Langkloof* (Long Valley). The journey winds hills and crosses the steel bridge over the 75 m (250 ft) deep Van Staden's River gorge. Reservations can be made at any railway station. Enquiries. Tel. (041) 520-2260. The **Dias Express** offers a shorter ride from the Campanile to King's Beach, making a stop at the Humerail railway museum. Tel. (041) 520-2400.

10. FORT FREDERICK: The ruins of the original old fort can be seen on the banks of the Baakens River. Built here in 1799, about thirty years before the British settlers arrived, to protect the bay against attacks from the interior. The original walls and an old cannon were preserved and is surrounded by manicured lawns.Open weekdays.

11. THE OCEANARIUM: Features a variety of South Africa sea creatures ranging from tropical fish to sting rays, turtles and sharks, but the dolphins who were caught in Algoa Bay area, steal the show. Two special performances per day together with Cape fur seals and jackass penguins.

12. SNAKE PARK: Lays claim to be number one of its kind in the world. It

is also here that its original director, F W FitzSimons, developed a serum that has since been widely used as an antidote to all snake bites. Instead of keeping snakes in cages enclosed by glass, hundreds of reptiles are allowed space and freedom in an open area with pergolas and trees, enclosed only by a moat and an inward curving wall. Also houses alligators, crocodiles and lizards. Snake handlers give demonstrations four times a day and draw venom to be used in the making of antidotes.

13. TROPICAL HOUSE: Adjoining the snake park is the Tropical House comprising an artificial landscape with jungle vegetation, waterfalls and pools and a stream, frequented by exotic birds. The Night House reverses day and night to allow visitors to observe the activities of nocturnal birds and animals. In the Reptile Rotunda exhibitions and video shows are held.

14. PORT ELIZABETH MUSEUM: Maritime hall shows shipwrecks, while in another section marine life in Algoa Bay is portrayed. Also on show are fossils and early humanoids (Boskop Man), as well as fashions from the Edwardian period until the Second World War.

A large elaborately decorated cast bronze cannon salvaged in 1977 from the wreck of the Sacramento, where it

Horse Memorial

had remained on the sea bed near Port Elizabeth for more than three centuries.

15. SUMMERSTRAND: This beach that has joined King's, Humewood and Pollok as popular playgrounds for holidaymakers with their thundering waves and crystal-white sand, once was part of a farm owned by a famous Voortrekker leader, Piet Retief. Most visitors, however, seem to be oblivious to the monument dedicated to its former owner as they set out on their surfboards.

PRETORIA

Jacaranda City

Administrative Capital
Capital of the Transvaal
Population - 800,000

Melrose House - Pretoria

CLIMATE

Warm to hot summers with occasional thunderstorms. Winter mornings and nights are cold and can be accompanied by frost, but days are usually sunny and pleasant. Pretoria tends to be warmer in winter and a few degrees hotter in summer than the elevated Johannesburg.

HISTORY

It was in the 1840s that a small number of Voortrekkers first discovered this pleasant valley among the hills. When the scattered little republics got together and debated over a seat for the new united Boer Republic, places like Lydenburg and Potchefstroom were in strong contention. Pretoria was still farmland, but there were strong petitions at the Volksraad (parliament) for a new capital on the banks of the Apies River. In 1855 Marthinus Pretorius had purchased three farms - Elandspoort, Daspoort and Nooitgedacht - prevailed upon his fellow Boers and established it as the seat of government.

The new town was called Pretoria in honor of Marthinus and his father, Andries, the hero of Blood River. In the beginning, it seems, some Boers had difficulty in accepting or remembering the name as it appears in forms such as Pretoriusstad (Pretorius City), Pretoriusdorp (Pretorius Town) and even Philadelphia on early documents.

PRETORIUS

In 1857 Marthinus Pretorius was elected first president of the new Boer South African or Transvaal Republic. In 1860 he also became president of the neighboring Orange Free State Republic to the south. The first and only leader to run two countries at the same time. After his resignation in 1871, Rev. Thomas Burgers became president and tried to procure outside assistance for the economically ailing republic and to the chagrin of his followers, got Britain in the bargain. Instead of giving aid and comfort, Cape Governor Shepstone arrived with a Union Jack in hand.

In 1881, the Boers defeated the British at Majuba and once again secured control of the Transvaal or South African Republic and its capital, Pretoria.

KRUGER

President Paul Kruger took over the reigns and for almost two decades the republic prospered (helped considerably by the discovery of gold) until Britain once again rose its flag in Pretoria as victors in the Anglo-Boer War. Finally in 1910, when the Union of South Africa was established, Pretoria became the Administrative capital of the newly independent nation, with Cape Town assigned the legislature and Bloemfontein, the highest court.

Over the years Kruger's former capital has become the symbol of South African nationhood and eclipsed all contenders as the internationally recognized seat of what is referred to as the Pretoria Government.

JACARANDA

Pretoria is not only a city of great historic importance, but an oasis of gardens and flowers and parks. Once called the City of Roses (a title now held by Bloemfontein), Pretoria is known as Jacaranda City.

The first two jacaranda trees were imported in 1888 at £10 a piece by a certain J D Celliers. Today there are more than 50,000 of these trees lining Pretoria's streets and parks - creating a profusion of purple and sapphire-blue as it flowers in October and November.

POINTS OF INTEREST
SEE CITY MAP #9 - PAGE 136.

1. CHURCH SQUARE: This is where it all started when a modest little thatched roof Dutch Reformed Church was dedicated on 22 February 1857. Through the years this square has been the site of many important events. In 1870 Church Square witnessed Cape governor Theophilus Shepstone's unwelcome intrusion when he raised the Union Jack.

It celebrated the return of the Vierkleur in 1881 when the British were defeated at Majuba. It saw Lord Roberts, commander of the British forces, raise the Union Jack once again in 1900.And it celebrated the raising of a South African flag after unity and independence in 1910. The northern side of Church Square is intended to resemble Paris's Place de la Concorde, while the south side imitates Trafalgar Square in London.

Church Square is surrounded by several classical buildings such as the Raadsaal, the Palace of Justice, the old Post Office, and the old Standard and Reserve Banks Towering on the south side is the more recently completed Provincial Administration Building. For guided tours of the square call (012) 814911 or 201-3223.

Paul Kruger Statue

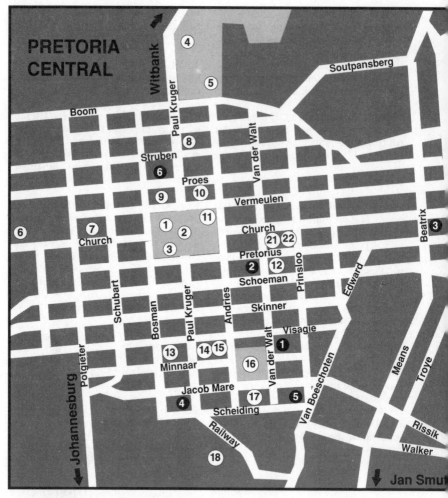

2. KRUGER STATUE: Sculptured by Anton van Wouw and commissioned by Jewish financier Sammy Marks, a close friend of President Kruger. Cast in Rome in 1898 by Francisco Bruno from where it was shipped to Lourenco Marques (to-day's Maputo). In the meantime the British had taken control of the Boer capital and the statue was kept in storage in Mozambique until 1913, when it was first set up in Prince's Park. Only in 1954 it found its way to Church Square after a short spell in front of the railroad station. The Boer figures who are seated on the four corners of the statue had an equally arduous journey. They had apparently reached Pretoria safely and then disappeared.

Eventually two were traced to Lord Kitchener's estate in England (who commanded the British forces after Lord Robert's left) and the other found at the British Military College in Clapham. They were returned to Pretoria in 1925.

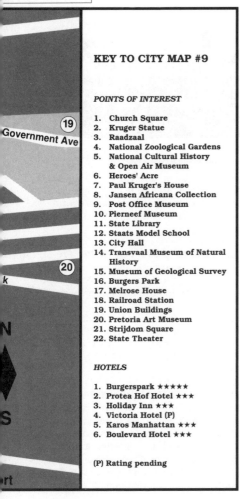

KEY TO CITY MAP #9

POINTS OF INTEREST

1. Church Square
2. Kruger Statue
3. Raadzaal
4. National Zoological Gardens
5. National Cultural History & Open Air Museum
6. Heroes' Acre
7. Paul Kruger's House
8. Jansen Africana Collection
9. Post Office Museum
10. Pierneef Museum
11. State Library
12. Staats Model School
13. City Hall
14. Transvaal Museum of Natural History
15. Museum of Geological Survey
16. Burgers Park
17. Melrose House
18. Railroad Station
19. Union Buildings
20. Pretoria Art Museum
21. Strijdom Square
22. State Theater

HOTELS

1. Burgerspark ★★★★★
2. Protea Hof Hotel ★★★
3. Holiday Inn ★★★
4. Victoria Hotel (P)
5. Karos Manhattan ★★★
6. Boulevard Hotel ★★★

(P) Rating pending

the Witwatersrand made for lavish expenditure. It also displays relics from the old republic. Open weekdays. The nearby **Palace of Justice** was not yet completed when the British took over and was commandeered as a military hospital before it returned to its originally intended role..

4. NATIONAL ZOOLOGICAL GARDENS: One of the biggest and best designed zoos in the world. Home for more than 3,500 different animals. Also includes an aquarium and reptile house. Seals are fed at 11h00 and 15h00 and carnivores at 15h30. Offers courses on ecology and bird-identification. Facilities also include refreshments, picnic spots, pony rides and a cable-car. Group tours on Saturday mornings. Special tours can also be arranged for the blind. Tel. (012) 28-3265 or 28-6020.

5. NATIONAL CULTURAL HISTORY MUSEUM: Has an open air section and features prehistoric rock engravings, a silverware collection and ethnological display. Archaeological room includes a 2,000 year old Egyptian mummy. Open weekdays. Tel. (012) 323-3128.

6. HEROES' ACRE: Several notable Afrikaans leaders are buried in this historic cemetery in Church Street West. Graves include those of Voortrekker hero, Andries Pretorius, Transvaal President Paul Kruger, and the late Prime Minister of South Africa, Dr. Hendrik Verwoerd, described by some as the architect of apartheid. Absent are the remains of Jan Smuts who stipulated in his will that his remains should be cremated and strewn over the hills at his farm Doornkloof, near Pretoria.

7. KRUGER HOUSE: At this modest house President Paul Kruger used to sit on the wide verandah, puffing his pipe and waving to passers-by. He lived here between 1883 and 1900. The two

At the time when the statue was first commissioned, Kruger's wife, Tant Sina, expressed the wish that the top of his hat be made hollow to hold water for the birds. Although her wish was not granted, pigeons still congregate on the president's broad shoulders and hat.

3. RAADSAAL: Dominating Church Square, the **Raadsaal** served as the parliament of Kruger's Republic. Funds from the newly discovered goldfields of

Union Buildings

imposing marble lion sculptures were a gift from his friend Barney Barnato, the British born Jew who made his millions on the diamond and goldfields. Kruger was a man without any pretense and the house reflects this character.

Introduced on one occasion to a British peer by someone who went on at length describing the lineage of this honored guest, Kruger looked unimpressed. At long last he put his pipe aside and said to his interpreter: *"Tell the gentleman that I myself was a cowherd and that my father was a farmer."*

Displayed in the house are Kruger's personal belongings and in the back the private railway carriage and the State coach. Open daily.

8. JANSEN AFRICANA COLLECTION: Display of early South African furniture and silver in Struben Street building. Open daily.

9. POST OFFICE MUSEUM: Opposite the headquarters of the General Post Office in Proes Street, there are displays dealing with various aspects of communication in South Africa and a collection of 750,000 stamps. Open Mon-Fri. Tel. (012) 293-1066.

10. PIERNEEF MUSEUM: Collection of paintings and sketches by a famous South African in 19th century house in Vermeulen Street. Has a tearoom. Open weekdays.

11. STATE LIBRARY: Collection of publications of all types relating to South Africa, including maps, government documents, newspapers and books. Open weekdays. Tel. (012) 21-8931.

12. STAATS MODEL SCHOOL: Preserved in its original form as an example of a typical Transvaal Republic school, but famous for another reason. For a while Winston Churchill was imprisoned here after his capture by the Boers during the Anglo-Boer War. Today it is used as a library by the Transvaal Department of Education. Open weekdays.

13. THE CITY HALL: Historic building features a huge clock tower with a carillon of 32 bells and statues in honor of Pretoria's founder, Marthinus Wessel Pretorius, and his father, Andries Pretorius, the hero of Blood River, fountains and murals, and a sculpture by South African sculptor Coert Steynberg.

14. TRANSVAAL MUSEUM OF NATURAL HISTORY: A huge whale skeleton welcomes visitors at the entrance of this extensive collection of mammals, birds, reptiles, amphibians and insects. The museum is also known for the Austin Roberts Bird Hall, featuring a collection of South African birds, and a large fossil display, including specimens of prehistoric man. This is where the renowned archeologist Robert Broom did much of his work on so-called man-apes. Open daily. Tel. (012) 322-7632.

15. MUSEUM OF GEOLOGICAL SURVEY: Next to the Museum of Natural History, it displays precious and semi-precious stones as well as fossils and rock formations. Has a skeleton in good condition of a Jonkeria reptile, reputed to have lived 250 million years ago. Open Mon-Fri.

16. BURGERS PARK: Named after Thomas Burgers, the second president of the South African or Transvaal Republic, is the oldest in Pretoria. Has statue of President Burgers and a memorial commemorating South Africans of Scottish origin who died in the First World War. Burger's wife, Mary Bryson, was Scottish.

17. MELROSE HOUSE: Lavishly furnished Victorian mansion in Jacob Mare Street where the Treaty of Vereeniging was signed on 31 May 1902, ending the hostilities between the two sides in the Anglo-Boer War. After the capture of Pretoria first Lord Roberts and after him Kitchener, used this as a temporary home and headquarters. Today it also serves as a museum where period furniture, porcelain, stained glass and works of art are exhibited. Open Tue-Sat from 10h00 to 17h00 and on Sundays from 13h00 to 19h00. Sometimes evening music recitals are held.

18. RAILROAD STATION: Ornate railroad station designed by Sir Herbert Baker and built in 1910. It has an old steam locomotive on display.

19. UNION BUILDINGS: Best known building in South Africa. Serving as the headquarters of the South African government since its completion in 1913 at a total cost of £1,180,000 this magnificent sandstone complex dominates Pretoria from Meintjieskop. Designed by Sir Herbert Baker who admits to having drawn some inspiration from the Acropolis in Athens. The two 'wings' of the building symbolizing the two

Baker is known as the man who designed Groote Schuur and the Union Buildings. Between these two

Sir Herbert Baker

magnificent creations in Cape Town and Pretoria, respectively, there are hundreds of other well-known Baker creations. Homes, cathedrals, schools and public buildings, carrying the imprimatur of Baker.

Soon after his arrival from England in 1892, the great Cecil Rhodes took a liking to Herbert Baker - 'because he doesn't talk too much.' First Baker concentrated on building and remodelling Cape Dutch houses - with Groote Schuur perhaps his most memorable legacy.

In 1900 Rhodes sent him on a study tour to Italy, Greece and Egypt - an experience that showed up in much of his work. In his perspective drawing of the Union Buildings in Pretoria with its large amphitheater, designed in 1909, Baker could not resist sketching in the background a likeness of the famous Parthenon.

In 1934 Baker wrote his own biography of Rhodes - *Cecil Rhodes, by his Architect.* Baker died at the age of 82 and was buried in London's Westminster Abbey.

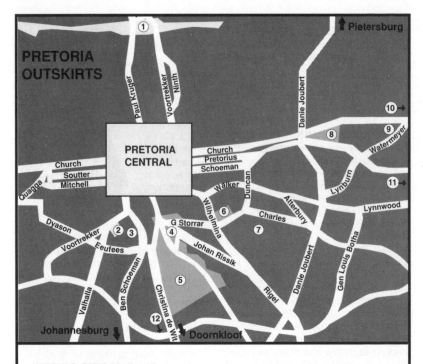

KEY TO CITY MAP #10

1. Wonderboom Nature Reserve
2. Voortrekker Monument
3. Fort Klapperkop
4. Fort Skanskop
5. Fountains Valley Nature Rserve
6. Austin Roberts Bird Sanctuary
7. Anton van Wouw House
8. Pretoria National Botanical Gardens
9. Pioneer Open-Air Museum
10. Sammy Marks Museum
11. Willem Prinsloo Agricultural Museum
12. Smuts House at Doornkloof

official languages, English and Afrikaans are surrounded by terraced gardens.

Wooded grounds also have statues of three former Boer generals who became Prime Ministers - Botha, Smuts and Hertzog - and in the Garden of Remembrance the Delville Wood Memorial and Pretoria War Memorial. Tearoom is open on weekdays and Saturday mornings.

20. PRETORIA ART MUSEUM: Works by major South African artists including Pierneef, Maggie Laubscher, Oerder,

Anton van Wouw, and Irma Stern are on display. The museum offers a library service, lectures, film shows and a variety of special presentations, also for children. Reprints are sold and light refreshments served in its tearoom. Open Tue-Sun. Tel. (012) 344-1087.

21. STRIJDOM SQUARE: Centerpiece of this square on the corner of Van der Walt and Church Streets, dwarfed by a whole complex of modern skyscrapers, is a giant bronze bust of J G Strijdom, South Africa's fifth prime minister. The sculptor is Coert Steynberg.

22. STATE THEATER: Adjoining Strijdom Square is an arts complex comprising five auditoriums for opera, ballet, drama and choral and symphony performances, respectively. Visitors are given tours of the facilities and art collection on Wednesdays and Fridays. Tel. (012) 322-1665.

PRETORIA OUTSKIRTS
CITY MAP #10 - OPPOSITE PAGE

1. WONDERBOOM NATURE RESERVE: Few miles north of Pretoria and named Wonderboom (Wonder or Magic Tree) after a one thousand year old fig tree growing on the 500 acre sanctuary. Reserve is also populated by monkeys, birds and dassies, and the remains of an old fort can be seen. Open daily.

2. VOORTREKKER MONUMENT: The Afrikaners' most important monument, inaugurated on 16 December 1949. Situated a few miles south of Pretoria, its 40 m (130 ft) cube-shaped granite structure commemorates the Voortrekkers who braved the interior in their trek north to escape British rule in 1834.

It was designed by the well-known South African architect Gerard Moerdijk and is surrounded by friezes of the 56 wagons which drew a *laager* against the attacking Zulu at the Battle of Blood River in Natal on 16 December 1838. Large granite sculptures of Voortrekker heroes Piet Retief, Andries Pretorius, Hendrik Potgieter and the Unknown Voortrekker are placed at the four corners of the monument. In the basement area is a cenotaph of polished granite with the inscription - *Ons vir Jou Suid-Afrika* (We for thee South Africa) - so positioned that at exactly 12 noon on 16 December every year, a ray of sunlight from the roof centers on it. (This Altar of Sacrifice is designed to commemorate the victory against Dingane's impis at Blood River on 16 December 1838, also known as the Day of the Covenant).

On the main floor, from where visitors can look down at the cenotaph, the walls are surrounded by frieze scenes depicting the Great Trek. The monument also houses a museum where Voortrekker relics are displayed. Its observation terrace reached by a circular stairway of 260 steps, offers panoramic views of Pretoria and its suburbs.

Every year on 16 December the monument becomes an important venue for Day of the Covenant meetings and celebrations. Facilities include a restaurant. Open daily.

3 & 4. FORT KLAPPERKOP AND SKANSKOP: Two forts built by Kruger's Republic after the outbreak of the Anglo-Boer War in 1899 to protect the capital against possible British attack.

They were, however, never put to use as the Boer forces had left when the British concluded their March to Pretoria. Today these forts have displays relating to South Africa's military history. Open daily.

Voortrekker Monument

Voortrekker ox-wagon

5. FOUNTAINS VALLEY NATURE RESERVE: Sanctuary and picnic spot south of the city, featuring indigenous and exotic plants and populated by a variety of birds. Has an open air theater, swimming pool, restaurant, and a miniature railway, as well as camp site and picnic area. Open daily until midnight.

6. AUSTIN ROBERTS BIRD SANCTUARY: Named after the internationally recognized authority on South African birds who wrote *'Roberts' Birds of Southern Africa'*.

More than a 100 species are represented, including blue crane, sacred ibis, heron and rare black swans. Observation hide and small museum. Open weekends and public holidays. Tel. (012) 344-3840.

7. ANTON VAN WOUW HOUSE: Sculptor Anton van Wouw, noted for his historical works in bronze (among them the Paul Kruger Statue on Church Square) lived at this home at 299 Clark Street. Today it displays some of his smaller pieces. Open Mon-Fri.

8. PRETORIA NATIONAL BOTANICAL GARDENS: A 150 acre area featuring indigenous plants from around the country can be seen.

Species are classified and grouped according to regions and labelled for the benefit of visitors. Group tours are arranged and include a slide show. Open weekdays. Tel. (012) 86-1180.

9. PIONEER OPEN-AIR MUSEUM: An authentic Voortrekker cottage was meticulously restored and the farmyard reconstructed with farming implements and animals completing the scene at Pioneer Park in Pretorius Street.. Picnic and braai (barbecue) facilities. Open daily.

10. SAMMY MARKS MUSEUM: Victorian home of President Paul Kruger's friend and confidant, the Jewish financier Sammy Marks, is now a museum. Situated east of Pretoria, *Swartkoppies Hall*, as its is called, contains period furniture and other household items that belonged to the Marks family. Open daily.

11. WILLEM PRINSLOO AGRICULTURAL MUSEUM: Comprises a homestead with Victorian furniture, blacksmith's shop, a working outside oven, dairy, water mill and peach brandy still. Also on the site is a modern exhibition center, cafeteria and lecture hall.Bread-baking in the oven, butter-making, sheep-shearing, and the distilling of potent peach brandy is demonstrated. Horse-rides and drives in a horse-drawn carriage are offered. Open daily.

Voortrekkers

RURAL ROUTES

The rustic remnants of a rich past awaits visitors who venture beyond the city limits on one of several interesting rural routes.

You will find cultural gaps as wide as the famous Blyderiver Canyon between the urbanized black South Africans and some of the different tribes who still maintain the cultures and customs of the past.

There are quaint frontier towns set in majestic landscapes and forest lands and oasis settlements in semi-desert arid territories.

Visitors who travel by road to Kruger National Park or any of the wide choice of game reserves described in our chapter *ON SAFARI*, will pass through rural regions known for attractions other than wildlife. The same goes for the wine tasting tours detailed in our chapter *WINE COUNTRY*, where gracious homesteads and scenery more than compensates for teetotallers who accompany the journey simply for the sake of sightseeing.

History buffs in search of battlefields where Boer fought Briton, and Dutch and English frontiersmen clashed with Zulu, Xhosa and other tribesmen, will find ample opportunities.There is even something worthwhile for archeologists in the shape of prehistoric rock paintings and the sites where man's missing link with the distant past has been unearthed.

WESTERN CAPE

For those who wish to go all the way instead of simply staying in the shadows of Table Mountain *(see CAPE OUT-SKIRTS under CITY SIGHTS)* there awaits a whole world of travel delights.

The **Cape Peninsula Tour** winds past Cape Town's beaches and Hout Bay, and Kommetjie to Cape Point at the tip of this famous peninsula. *(Peninsula Map - Page 193)*. This rocky point so impressed ancient mariners that they

mistakenly regarded it as the southernmost point of Africa. This distinction goes to the more remote Cape Agulhas, about a hundred miles east as the crow flies. But it is on the rocky edge of Cape Point where one can get the feeling of being a bird in flight looking down on the foaming Indian and Atlantic oceans far below.

There is the choice of a walkway to the top or a driveway. Cape Point is actually part of the Cape of Good Hope Nature Reserve (see also ON SAFARI) with its most visible and sometimes troublesome inhabitants being a large colony of baboons.

The road back to Cape Town along the eastern shores of the peninsula leads through Simon's Town, a major naval base, and Muizenberg, a pleasant beach resort. At the latter visitors may wish to drop by the famous Rhodes Cottage. The famous and wealthy empire builder who had majestic Groote Schuur and many other mansions at his disposal, chose to spend his final agonizing days in this modest abode. It was a very hot summer and the cottage had a corrugated iron roof (since replaced with thatch).

The ailing Rhodes was propped up with pillows and a hole made through the outer wall to give him more air. The man who left his imprint all over southern Africa died on 26 March 1902 uttering the words: *"So much to do, so little done."* Kirstenbosch Botanic Gardens and Groot Constantia are favorite conclusions to this popular drive. *(Also our chapters DOWN THE GARDEN PATH and CITY SIGHTS) - and for beaches in the area RESORTS AND SPORTS).*

Stellenbosch is not only the center of a popular wine route, but almost a living museum. Famous Dorp Street is lined

Tulbagh Church

with ancient oaks and offers old world beauty with its meticulously restored Dutch, Georgian and Victorian residences. Of particular importance are 102 to 122 Dorp Street where the old Gymnasium was situated that grew into the well-known University of Stellenbosch. National leaders such as Hertzog, Smuts and Malan attended here. Today a wine museum and art gallery, Libertas Parva (also known as Klein or Small Libertas) used to be the home of the Krige family where Sybella or Isie, the wife of famous statesman Jan Smuts, spent her youth. It was built in 1780.

Further up in Dorp Street is La Gratitude, so named in 1798 by first owner the Rev. Meent Borcherds in gratitude for God's mercies. Its unique gable displays the *"all-seeing eye of God"*. Closeby Stellenbosch Hotel itself has been declared a national monument, while Die Braak (an open square in the center of town) is bordered by the old Rhenish Church, the Arsenal and Burgher House.

Paarl is less than an hour by highway from Cape Town. This town stretched out along the Paarlberg (Pearl Rock) is not only the headquarters of the famous KWV and the hub of a popular wine route. It is where Afrikaans "originated'. Today a monument at the mountain honors the birth of the world's youngest Germanic language.

Those who have additional time on their hands may wish to proceed to **Tulbagh**, famous for its meticulously restored Cape Dutch houses in a spectacular mountain setting First settled in 1699 and named after Governor Ryk Tulbagh, most of these old houses were seriously damaged in two earthquakes in 1969 and 1970. The more than thirty dwellings in Tulbagh's Kerk or Church Street are the largest concentration of national monuments in South Africa.

Afrikaner Monument - Paarl

Soon after Jan van Riebeeck settled at the Cape in 1652, his Dutch compatriots moved inland and were joined by the French Huguenots on isolated farmland. Far away from their mother countries these new citizens of Africa, the Afrikaners, developed their own version of Dutch.

Although Dutch remained the official language - Afrikaans only replaced it in 1925 - this unique version with its infusion of French, Malaysian and even African languages, was widely spoken in the mid-nineteenth century.

In 1875 a Dutch teacher of classical languages at the Paarl Gymnasium, Arnoldus Pannevis, became so enamored with this language that he decided to establish the *Genootskap van Regte Afrikaners* (the Association of True Afrikaners) to promote its usage.

Pannevis himself wrote the very first poem in Afrikaans, entitled *Ideaal* (Ideal). Today Paarl is the site for a monument dedicated to Afrikaans, consisting of several columns and a wall symbolizing the contribution of the Western world, Africa and the Malaysian people to this young language - the mother tongue today of sixty percent of South Africa's whites.

Enroute from Paarl to Tulbagh, motorists will encounter **Wellington**, rich in old architecture and the southernmost of many blockhouses erected by the British to try and prevent the Boer guerilla commandos from getting through their defence lines in the Anglo Boer War of 1899. Between Wellington and Tulbagh there is Bains Kloof Pass - scenic and slow - and for those who wish to make a side trip to picturesque Ceres, the equally enchanting Mitchell's Pass.

The state of the art 4 km Huguenot Toll Tunnel awaits those who wish to continue past Paarl along the highway over Du Toits Kloof pass to the Breede River Valley with its attractive wine estates scattered around **Worcester.** This tunnel, completed in 1988, cuts the distance by 11 km but the old road with its more panoramic views is still open to travelers with time.

On the highway beyond Worcester lies **De Doorns** at the foot of the rugged Hex River Mountains that act as the final barrier before the Karoo region starts.This range shields the semi-desert sheep-farming districts of the interior from the much needed moisture of the coastal region.

KAROO
SEE MAIN MAP - PAGES 4 & 5

Once on the plateau beyond the mountains, the road stretches long and straight towards Touws River and **Matjesfontein** which merits a visit and even an overnight by visitors traveling to Johannesburg by car or taking this route to the Klein Karoo Wine Route the Garden Route. In the 1890s Scottish railway official, James Logan, bought the farm Tweedside, which included the railway station at Matjesfontein and built an ornate Victorian-style hotel and restaurant. Passengers by train used to disembark to replen-

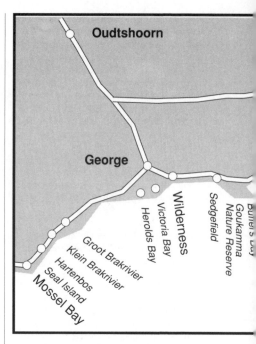

ish and rest and many stayed in to recover from all kinds of lung ailments in the clean dry Karoo air. Today the fully restored hotel is a stop along the route of the famous Blue Train.

Two hundred miles further along the N1 highway, in the heart of the Karoo, is **Beaufort West** where Dr Chris Barnard was born. Today this oasis town has an interesting museum dedicated to the famous heart surgeon.

Still in the Karoo, but much closer to Port Elizabeth than Cape Town, is **Graaff Reinet** where extensive restoration of stylish old buildings and homes draw their share of visitors off the beaten path. Founded by Governor Jacob van de Graaff and named after his wife Reinet, this town was the scene of a serious rebellion against the Dutch when inhabitants declared themselves an independent republic in 1795. The British who took over the Cape a year later brought them back in line.

146

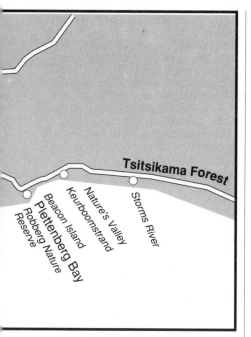

Tsitsikama Forest

Storms River
Nature's Valley
Keurboomstrand
Beacon Island
Plettenberg Bay
Robberg Nature
Reserve

GARDEN ROUTE

While the actual Garden Route starts at Mossel Bay and finishes at Storms River, most tours originate at Cape Town and terminate in Port Elizabeth. Both these two cities are major attractions themselves and have convenient air links. *(See descriptions and maps in the chapters CITY SIGHTS and RESORTS AND SPORTS).*

Here, in brief, is what visitors can expect to encounter along the Garden Route depending on how much time they have and whether they wish to detour in some parts.

One approach to Mossel Bay from Cape Town is along the N1 over the Hex River Mountains to Prince Albert Road in the Karoo where a winding mountain pass road leads down to Oudtshoorn. The more popular way is, however, to take the N2 highway past Somerset West, to Caledon and Swellendam.

Caledon is first in line after a scenic drive on Sir Lowry's Pass. It is famous for its botanic gardens. *(See DOWN THE GARDEN PATH).*

Next comes **Swellendam** in the shadows of the Clock Peaks of the Langeberg mountain range. Locals insist that they can tell the time of day from the way the shadows show on their summits. Keep in mind that this quaint little town was for a glorious three months in 1795 one of the capitals of the world. At the time this community consisting of two rows of houses decided to declare themselves independent from the Dutch rulers of the Cape. As in the case of Graaff Reinet in the Karoo, the British put an end to it when they took over control of the Cape from the Dutch. Named after Governor Hendrik Swellengrebel and his wife Helena van Damme when it was founded in 1747, much of old Swellendam still exists in authentically restored buildings.

The Garden Route starts at **Mossel Bay** where Portuguese explorer Bartholomeu Dias first set foot on South Africa soil in 1488. A museum complex is built around the spring where Dias and many successive visitors drew water. Dias named the bay Aquada de Sao Bras - the watering place of St. Blaise but in 1601 when Dutch navigator Paulus van Caerden discovered the nourishing qualities of the local mussels he named it *Mosselbaai* (Mussel Bay). The Dias Museum also comprises the famous ancient milkwood tree which became known as the Post Office Tree as passing ships left messages for each other since 1500.

From Mossel Bay onwards to Port Elizabeth, visitors have the option at several popular resorts where they can mix sightseeing with ocean bathing and fresh water swimming and other recreational activities such as golf and fishing. *(See our chapter RESORTS AND SPORTS)*

George, a few miles inland, was the first town to be established by the British after their second occupation of the Cape. Dating back from 1811 it has become one of the favorite vacation spots of the country, together with nearby Wilderness on the shore. It also has scheduled air links with major cities.

Instead of simply following the N2 Highway further north eastwards visitors usually go northwards along the R29 on a detour to **Oudtshoorn** on the other side of the spectacular Outeniqua Pass. Although the pass itself covers only a third of the 60 km to the ostrich capital (as Oudtshoorn is known) travelers usually spend extra time along the way, stopping at several vantage points to take in the beauty of the valley below, bordered by the sea.

From the 1870s until the First World War many a feather fortune was made in the Oudtshoorn district with its large ostrich population. But it did not take long for the bottom to fall out of this fickle market and today many a *volstruispaleis* (ostrich palace) are merely monuments of a bygone era to be enjoyed by tourists. Recently ostrich farming has, however, come into its own again and the big bird once again features in the local economy in more than one way. Some of them come to fame in the Ostrich Derby while giving feathers. Others end up as meat and expensive handbags and wallets. Today the total ostrich population is stabilized at one hundred thousand.

Male ostrich

After observing palaces and ostriches visitors normally continue further north to the **Kango Caves** - another 20 km of mountainous road. This magic underground includes among its hundreds of huge colorful stalactite and stalagmite formations ones named Lot's Wife and the Organ Pipes. Tours lasting two hours are conducted from December to February and during April, on the hour from 08h00 until 15h00. Along the road visitors will find one of the largest crocodile breeding farms in the country.

After George eastwards on the N2 more beach resorts are followed by **Knysna.** This attractive town with its pristine lagoon and dense forest-land started as the private domain of one George Rex, an eccentric Englishman who bought the land during the first British occupation of the Cape in 1797. Rumors started that George was the son of King George III when he turned up with the wealthy young widow Johanna, whom he married and brought over here with her four children in a coach bearing a coat of arms. After thirty five rewarding years of town building the flamboyant founder of Knysna died and was buried near the original homestead.

From Knysna past the popular Plettenberg Bay up to **Storms River** and beyond towards Humansdorp travelers will encounter a combination of beautiful beaches, thick forests and a wide variety of flowering plants. It is one of the most popular haunts for botanists, sportsmen and sightseers.

At the conclusion of the Garden Route tour an extra day or two is usually taken for further sightseeing in and around Port Elizabeth before proceeding to Johannesburg by air. There is, however, much to see in the Eastern Cape region where both the British settlers and their erstwhile foes, the Xhosa, left an interesting heritage.

EASTERN CAPE
SEE COUNTRY MAP - PAGE 4

Although Port Elizabeth is where the British settlers landed, **Grahamstown**, 130 km further to the northeast along the N2 highway, is considered by English-speaking South Africans as their spiritual home. On Gunfire Hill overlooking the town is English-speaking South Africa's equivalent of the Voortrekker Monument in Pretoria - erected by the 1820 Foundation. A National Festival of Arts is held here in the theater and conference complex every year during July. Grahamstown is not only known as Settler City. With more than forty churches for a modest population it has earned the name City of Saints as well. The 1820 Settlers Museum traces the history of British emigration to South Africa since the first British occupation of the Cape in 1895.

This town was right in the middle of the fierce Frontier Wars fought between the British and the Xhosa during the first half of the nineteenth century. Visitors will find a whole range of historic fortifications dating back to this period including the Provost and Fort Selwyn. One of the historic buildings has been converted into an entrance for Rhodes University.

On the drive towards East London *(see RESORTS AND SPORTS)*, a pleasant resort area, visitors will encounter the **Xhosa** - some still wearing their traditional garb and selling items such as clay pots and beadwork. The beadwork dates from ancient times when the Xhosa did not have a written language and conveyed messages through meticulous bead pictures. Love letters were and are still exchanged in the form of beadwork ornaments. The N2 leads through Umtata which serves as the capital of Transkei, the independent territory that may rejoin South Africa after apartheid.

Tribal headdress

The black tribes that moved into present-day South Africa several centuries ago from the central part of the continent are as varied in customs and cultures as the nations of Europe.

Travelers may remember the Venda of the northeastern Transvaal by a snake dance of bare-breasted young maidens in a ritual to the god of fertility - or the Zulu by a *sangoma* or diviner whom they saw acting as a diviner between his or her clients and their ancestors.

The young Xhosa males that they observed from the roadside in the Eastern Cape with ghost-like white painted faces may at first startle them until they learn that these are merely young men going through their initiation period to enter manhood. And they may have bought some of the interesting arts and crafts at the roadside or in city stores - wood carvings, pottery, woven baskets and rugs and intricate beadwork.

But the soul and intricate social order and beliefs of these proud tribes are only to be understood and appreciated after years of intensive study.

The round huts dotting the hills are made of mud-and-thatch. Doorways face east to protect the Xhosa from the evil spirits. (The *rondavels* or chalets in game parks are based on this age-old Xhosa hut construction).

NATAL
SEE MAP ON THIS PAGE

Natal is **Zulu** country and visitors who undertake scenic inland excursions from Durban will be able to get a taste of their tribal traditions along the way.

Incidentally, don't be fooled into believing that the prancing Zulu rickshaws along the Durban beachfront with their enormous horns-and-beadwork headdresses are true tribal specimens. They are made up for the role, pulling single-seater vehicles, Eastern style, for the entertainment of tourists. Rickshaws were incidentally introduced to Durban in the late 1800s by a sugar magnate who saw and liked it in Japan.

For those who want to get a taste of Zulu life and customs there are day trips into the Valley of a Thousand Hills and the opportunity to see Zulu dancing in a traditional village. Their beehive-shaped huts consist of thatch built around a framework of wattle poles.

Others who have more time at their disposal and are travelling by car or bus to Umfolozi, Hluhluwe or any of Natal's many other game parks, may take time along the way to get to know the Zulu in their historic homeland.

NATAL RURAL MAP

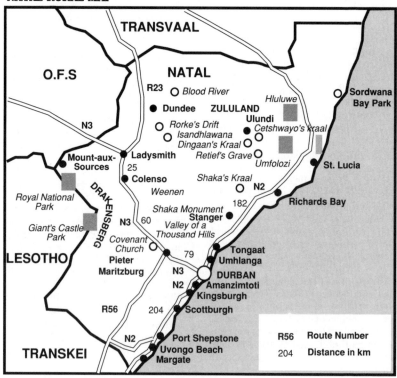

Ulundi is the present capital of the Zulu people under leadership of Mangosuthu Buthelezi.

Pietermaritzburg, situated beyond the Valley of a Thousand Hills, is where the Boers established their short-lived independence from Britain in the 1830s before they were forced once again to pack up and move. Today it is basically an English-speaking city, although the Church of the Covenant is there to remind everyone of its Afrikaner origin.

Erected in terms of the Covenant made by the Voortrekkers to build a church in honor of God if he should grant them victory over the Zulu at Blood River, it serves today as a museum. (The original burnt down in 1895 and was rebuilt in 1901). One of the most impressive buildings in town is the elaborate red brick city hall - the largest brick building in the Southern Hemisphere.

History buffs will find in the area north of Pietermaritzburg the battlefields of **Isandhlwana, Rorke's Drift** and **Blood River** where Boer and British clashed with the mighty Zulu impis or armies. The town of Weenen (Weeping) was started in 1838 by the Voortrekkers in memory of the many among their ranks who were massacred.

There are also the sites of **Shaka's, Dingane's** and **Cetshwayo's kraals** (capitals) of yesteryear and Shaka's monument at Stanger near where he was assassinated. Others who go along on this journey into the past will have ample reward in terms of scenery and wildlife. *(See our chapter HISTORIC TRAILS).*

Framing this historic hinterland are the Drakensberg mountains with their numerous resorts and the Natal beaches that have developed into one of South Africa's prime holiday regions. *(See also the chapter RESORTS AND SPORTS).*

TRANSVAAL

Close to the two major cities of Johannesburg and Pretoria there are, apart from the points of interest described in the chapter CITY SIGHTS several worthwhile short side-trips into the country. Those who seek entertainment of the Las Vegas-kind find it within two hours drive or a short trip by air

*Pietermaritzburg
City Hall Tower*

at Sun City, which is part of the independent Tswana state of Bophuthatswana. *(See also RESORTS AND SPORTS)*

Cullinan, some 25 km east of Pretoria, has become a popular add-on for visitors to the capital. This is where the Premier Diamond Mine is situated where the famous 3000 carat Cullinan diamond was found in 1905. Conducted tours of the surface workings are offered Tue-Fri. For reservations call (01213) 30050.

Sterkfontein Caves at Krugersdorp, about 20 km northwest of Johannesburg, visitors can view the site where Dr Broom found his famous missing link, Mrs. Ples. *(See HISTORIC TRAILS).* Daily tours of the caves are offered and in the adjoining Robert Broom Museum prehistoric animal and birdlife specimens are on display. The cave comprises several cathedral-shaped chambers, including Elephant Hall with its spectacular dripstone.

A cave of another kind will be encountered along the N4 highway by those who drive to Kruger or the private game parks in its orbit. **Sudwala Caves** comprises stalactites and stalagmites - brightly colored from the iron and manganese content in the limestone of the Mankelele cliffs. Visitors are given a guided tour through part of the complex. Adjoining the caves are a dinosaur park, recreational activities and accommodation.

The mountainous region north of Sudwala and Nelspruit and due west of the Kruger National Park rates as one of the most spectacular landscapes in Africa and arguably, the world. Central to this region is the **Blyde River Canyon** with **God's Window, Three Rondavels, Echo Caves** and **Mount Sheba** among its many special features.

Within a radius of 14 km of **Sabie**, situated below Mount Anderson are the **Bridal Veil, Lone Creek, Horseshoe and MacMac falls**. Originally a

gold mining camp, the town is today the center of the paper and pulp industry.

Graskop is the starting point for a popular circular journey through the Blyderiver Canyon, but it is **Pilgrim's Rest** that attracts most visitors. Named in 1873 by prospector Alec Patterson when he thought that his discovery of gold in the river would bring his long pilgrimage to a rest, the town today offers a unique glimpse of the legendary old days. Mining activities finally stopped in 1971 and the town has become a living museum. Declared a national monument, Pilgrim's Rest has 1200 residents in its frontier homesteads and the old Royal Hotel has been restored to house guests.

Further evidence of good fortune by gold seekers are the nearby Bourke's Luck Potholes. These strange rounded holes in rock were caused through the centuries by swirling waters from the Treur (Sorrow) River and were so named after Bourke discovered a good quantity of gold in the area.

BLYDE RIVER CANYON MAP

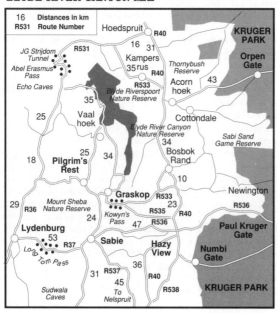

Scenic routes wind through **Abel Erasmus, Kowyn's** and **Long Tom Pass**. The latter was named after a Boer gun placement during the Anglo-Boer War. On the pass stands a replica of the famous French Le Creusot field gun, nicknamed Long Tom by the Boers. Visitors continuing north on R36 towards Hoedspruit will encounter the Abel Erasmus Pass and the JG Strijdom tunnel.

WINE COUNTRY

Franschhoek Valley - A F Trotter

South Africa's wine country is popular with both taster and tee-totaller.

The wine estates with their gracious Cape Dutch homes nestled between neat vineyards and rugged mountains, are a sightseer's delight.

Add to this picture postcard scenery some of the world's best wines and it is easy to see why the Cape winelands have become an area of great enjoyment for demanding wine connoisseurs from the old and the new world.

C ape wine country is a premier destination for tourists. To enjoy wine tasting tours and visits to the gracious estates does not require an extensive knowledge about wines. The spectacular scenery and charming white-washed Cape Dutch houses contrasting against the shadowy mountain slopes is a reward by itself. Add to that some of the world's best wines and the trip becomes a must on any connoisseur's itinerary.

EARLY BEGINNINGS

The wine industry of South Africa is as old as the country itself. Shortly after he set foot at the Cape in 1652 to establish a Dutch refreshment station, Governor Jan van Riebeeck had vines planted and wine distilled.

With the arrival of the French Huguenots in the 1680s the fledgling wine industry was given permanence and quality. In the late 1600s the colony's twentieth governor, Simon van der Stel, established his own estate, Groot Constantia, at the foot of Table Mountain. Both Van der Stel and his son Willem Adriaan encouraged wine farming by handing out tracts of land in the interior to anyone willing to develop it. Eventually

Groot Constantia

van der Stel's Constantia was purchased by Hendrik Cloete, who penetrated Europe with the quality of his product.

In the 1880s, however, the phylloxera pest, invading South Africa from the United States by way of France, almost wiped out the industry - as it did in the other important wine producing regions of the world. Recovery took twenty years as new vines were grafted with phylloxera-resistant American root stock.

COOPERATIVES

Many wine farms in South Africa are too small to have their own independent cellars. Some estates sell their grapes to wine merchants with large, well-equipped cellars such as Stellenbosch Farmer's Wineries, the Oude Meester Group, Gilbeys, Douglas Green and Union while others are organized on the basis of cooperatives where their grapes are pooled and wine made collectively. These cooperative wines are usually sold in bulk to wine distillers and merchants and only a small quantity is bottled and made available directly to the public.

There are a number of smaller wine cooperatives throughout the Cape wine region. In the Stellenbosch district alone there are no less than five.

The largest and most famous cooperative, the well-known KWV (*Ko-operatiewe Wynbouwers Vereeniging* - Cooperative Winegrowers Association) has, however, earned a name for itself as South Africa's largest quality wine producer and exporter. Its product and name is known throughout Europe and the America's and rapidly winning recognition in many other parts of the world.

ESTATES

Wine farms with sufficient capital and quality crops often operate their own fully equipped cellars, making a wide range of wines. Although they prefer to sell surplus in bulk to wine merchants who would mix them into cheaper blends, these estates take great pride in the product produced and bottled under their own name. *Estate wines* are required by law to have been made on the farm where it was grown. Only registered estates conforming to extensive, strict government regulations are entitled to use the term *Estate* on their labels.

TOURS

Some of these wine estates and most cooperatives are open to the public for tours, wine tastings and purchases. Several of them also operate their own restaurants, while others offer cheese lunches. There are also a number of interesting, some outstanding, independent restaurants in the wine regions where visitors may enjoy traditional dishes as well as continental and French country cooking.

Daily trips to the winelands are offered by tour operators from the major hotels. Visitors with their own transport can, however, make arrangements on their own. At most wine estates and cooperatives its is not necessary to call beforehand.

There are four distinct wine routes within reasonable driving distance from Cape Town: The **Stellenbosch Wine Route**, the **Paarl-Wineway**, the **Vignerons de Franschhoek Route**, and the **Breede River Valley Route**.

Recently estates and cooperatives in the more distant **Klein Karoo Region** have also started offering tourists facilities for wine tasting, cheese lunches and wine buying. Although further from Cape Town, this region is accessible to travellers on the Garden Route. *(See also RURAL ROUTES).*

Visitors who have time constraints, can still get the taste and flavor of an immaculate wine estate by including Groot Constantia on a drive around Cape Town. *(See our chapters CITY SIGHTS and RURAL ROUTES)*

**Constantia
1791 Vintage**

In 1657 South Africa's founder, Van Riebeeck of the Dutch East India Company, complained in a letter to his home office in Holland that the settlers were wasting the vines that he gave them. Instead of starting a wine industry as they were supposed to, he reported, they were planting it around houses for ornamental purposes.

This attitude changed after the arrival of the French Huguenots in 1688, who found the Cape region to be ideally suited for good wine making. Their expertise and enthusiasm laid the ground for a world-renowned wine industry.

At the end of the eighteenth century a direct descendant of Van Riebeeck's company gardener, Hendrik Cloete, was successfully marketing his Constantia wines to the rich and famous in Europe.

Wines from the Cloete Groot Constantia estate were imported by Frederick of Prussia and honorably mentioned by British author, Jane Austin. French writer Baudelaire incorporated it in one of his famous *Fleurs du Mal* and the great Napoleon, when he was exiled to St Helena and given the opportunity to select his own beverages, picked Constantia wine to go with his French champagne.

They also have the opportunity to buy most of the estate wines at liquor stores (or *bottle stores*, they are called in South Africa).

STELLENBOSCH WINE ROUTE
WINE TOUR MAP #1 ON THIS PAGE

The Stellenbosch Route was started by two prominent farmers, Frans Malan of Simonsig, and Niel Joubert, of Spier. They introduced this route in 1971 after touring the French wine country. At the center lies Stellenbosch, named after Governor Simon van der Stel, with its rich heritage in old buildings and attractive oak-lined streets. The *Public Relations Officer, Stellenbosch Wine Route, Strand Road, Stellenbosch 7600. Tel. (02231) 4310*, will assist visitors with advice and directions.

WINE TOUR MAP #1

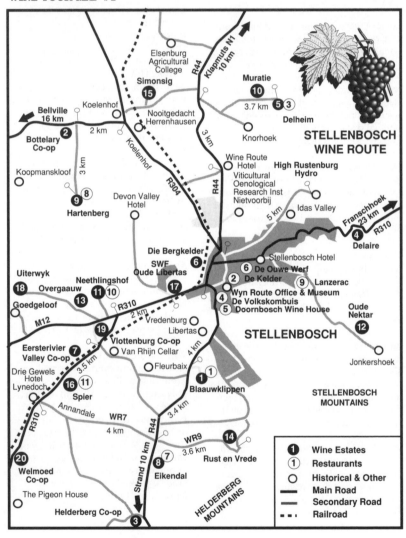

Following in alphabetical order are the wine estates and cooperatives along the route, open to the public.

1. BLAAUWKLIPPEN
P O Box 54, Stellenbosch 7600.
Tel. (02231) 90133. Fax. (02231) 98562.
Situated 4 km from Stellenbosch. One of its many owners through the years was Cecil John Rhodes who owned it for one day. He bought it at an auction in 1898 for £3,500 and sold it later that same day for £3,000. Transformed by its current owner, Graham Boonzaier, into one of the prize estates of Stellenbosch. *Wine Sales:* Mon-Fri 8h45-12h45 & 14h00-17h00. Sat: 0900-12h00. *Cellar Tours:* From 1 December-31 January, Mondays-Fridays llh00-15h00. *Estate Tours:* 1 November-31 March, Mondays-Fridays by horse drawn carriage. l0h00-12h00 & 14h00-15h45. *Cape Kitchen Products for sale* Cheese, chutney, relish and weinwurst. *Museum:* Extensive collection of Cape carriages, furniture and kitchen wares. *Coachman's Lunch:* 1 November-31 March, Mondays-Fridays 12h00-14h00.

2. BOTTELARY COOPERATIVE
PO Box 16, Koelenhof 7605.
Tel. (02231) 92204. Fax. (02231) 92205.
Established in 1946. Makes a whole range of good wines under its own label. *Sales:* Mon-Fri 08h30-17h00. Sat 08h30-13h00. *Cellar Tours:* By appointment.

3. DE HELDERBERG COOPERATIVE
PO Box 7110, Firgrove 7110.
Tel. (024) 42-2371.
Established in 1906. Only a small portion is bottled and sold under its own label. *Sales:* Mon-Fri 09h00-13h00 & 14h00-17h30. Sat 09h00-12h00. *Tours:* By appointment.

4. DELAIRE
P O Box 3058, Stellenbosch 7602.
Tel. (02231) 9156. Fax. (02231) 91270
On the Helshoogte Pass between Stellenbosch and Franschhoek. Offers breathtaking views of the Groot Drakenstein Valley to the east and Table Mountain to the west. Developed in the early eighties by wine columnist and UPI correspondent, John

Platter. *(John Platter's South African Wine Guide.) Estate Visits & Sales:* Mon-Fri 09h00-13h00 & 14h00-16h00. Sat 09h00-13h00.

5. DELHEIM
P O Box 10, Koelenhof 7605.
Tel: (02231) 92033.
Near Koelenhof in the Stellenbosch district. Came into prominence under the guidance of one of the pioneers of estate wines in the Cape, Hans Hoheisen. Serves buffet lunches and brunches, depending on the season. *Wine Tasting & Sales:* Mon-Fri 08h30-17h00. Sat 08h30-12h00. *Cellar Tours:* Monday-Friday (1 October-30 April only). *Meet the Cellar Master:* Mondays-Fridays 10h00 and 15h00. *Restaurant: Vintner's Platter:* (1 October-30 April) 12h00-14h00. *Saturday Brunch:* (1 October-30 April,) 10h30-12h00.

6. DIE BERGKELDER
P O Box 5001 Stellenbosch 7600.
Tel. (02231) 73480. Fax. (02231) 99533.
Belongs to the Oude Meester Group (Old Master) with head offices in Stellenbosch, Die Bergkelder (literally - The Mountain Cellar) serves as distributor for a number of estates, some of whom are on the wine routes, such as L'Ormarins, Uitkyk, Dewetshof and La Motte, and others such

Stellenbosch Wine Estate

as Middelvlei and Zandvliet which are not open to the public. Bergkelder also produces its own wines, including Fleur du Cap, Stellenryck, and Grunberger. *Die Bergkelder takes visitors on regular tours.*

7. EERSTERIVIER-VALLEY CO-OP
P O Box 2, Vlottenburg 7604.
Tel. (02231) 93870 Fax. (02231) 93102.
Established in 1956. Six fully certified Wines of Origin are bottled and sold under the cooperative's own label. *PAPA Cellar Tours:* By appointment.

8. EIKENDAL VINEYARDS
P O Box 226. Stellenbosch 7600.
Tel. (024) 55-1422 Fax. (024) 55-1027.
Eikendal is made up of two old farms on the slopes of the Helderberg - Longridge and Mietjiesvlei. The latter used to be called Moddergat (mudhole), commemorating

Title and Deed to a Cape Farm - 1691

the day three centuries ago when Governor Simon van der Stel's wagon got stuck on its way to a fishing trip along the coast. Today the estate belongs to a Swiss public company. *Wine Tasting & Sales:* Mon-Fri 09h00-17h00. Sat 09h00-12h00. *Lunch:* A Swiss lunch of bockwurst, ham and Swiss cheeses, available from Nov-Feb. In winter months cheese fondue is served.

9. HARTENBERG ESTATE
P O Box 69, Koelenhof 7605.
Tel. (02231) 92541. Fax. (02231) 92268.
Settled in 1692 by French immigrant L'Estreux who changed his name to the Dutch, Esterhuyzen. Vineyards fell into disrepair as new owners switched to cattle and sheep. In the 1960s father and son, Maurice and Walter Finlayson, nurtured the estate back to wine growing. *Wine Tasting & Sales:* Mon-Fri 09h00-12h30 & 13h30017h00. Sat 09h00-12h00. *Cellar Tours:* Mondays-Fridays 10h00 and 15h00. Sat 09h00-12h00. *Winemaker's Lunch:* (1 Nov-31 Mar) Mon-Fri 12h00-14h00.

10. MURATIE
P O Box 133, Koelenhof 7605.
Tel. (02231) 92330/96.
One of the very first mountain farms. The name, a corruption of the Dutch word for *ruins* (murasie), dates from about 1770, when new owners bought (and rebuilt) a burnt-down house and property originally granted to a German, Lorenz'Campher in 1685. For a short while Governor Willem Adriaan van der Stel resided here. Bought in 1907 by German painter, Georg Paul Canitz. Today his daughter runs estate. *Cellar Tours:* Thursdays by appointment. *Wine Sales:* Mon-Fri 08h30-12h00 & 14h00-17h00. Sat 08h30-12h00.

11. NEETHLINGSHOF
PO Box 104, Stellenbosch 7600.
Tel. (02231) 76832. Fax. (02231) 78171.
Known as Wolwedans (The Dance of the Wolves) when granted to Willem Lubbe in 1699. Cape Dutch homestead built by Lord Neethling, who gave the estate its current name. Recently bought by overseas entrepreneur, Hans-Joachim Schreiber, who

undertook extensive restoration and established a restaurant on estate. *Cellar Tours:* By appointment. *Restaurant:* Lord Neethling Restaurant (02231) 76905. Lunch Tue-Sun 12h00-14h30.Tea Tue-Sat 15h00-18h00. Dinner Tue-Sat 19h00-22h30.Closed Monday. Licensed for Wine and Malt. Credit cards accepted. Choice between Continental and Chinese food.

12. OUDE NEKTAR
P O Box 389, Stellenbosch 7600.
Tel. (02231) 70690. Fax. (02231) 70647.
Land was originally given to a freed slave, Jan van Ceylon, (John from Ceylon) in 1692. He named it Jan Lui (Lazy John). In 1814 the new owner's wife, Gertruide de Villiers, renamed the property Nektar. The current owner, Derrick Peck, has built a new cellar to improve and expand the winemaking capacity of Oude Nektar (Old Nectar), as it is known today.*Cellar Tours:* By appointment.*Wine Sales:* (1 Oct-30 Apr) Mon-Fri 09h30-12h30 & 14h00-16h30. Sat 09h30-12h30. (1 May-30 Sept) Wed 14h00-16h30 or by special appointment.

13. OVERGAAUW
P O Box 3, Vlottenburg 7604.
Tel. (02231) 93815.
Granted in 1682 to Hendrik Elbertsz, one of the first settlers to take advantage of the offer of free land from the Cape rulers. Overgaauw, is the maiden name of the wife of Abraham van Velden who purchased the farm in 1907. Estate has been in same family since. *Cellar Tours:* Wed. 14h30 and 16h30 by appointment. *Wine Sales:* Mon-Fri 10h00-12h00. Wed 14h00-17h00. Sat (1 Dec-31 Mar) 10h00-12h00.

14. RUST EN VREDE
P O Box 473, Stellenbosch 7600.
Tel. (02231) 93881. Fax. (02231) 93000.
Granted in 1694 to one of the Cape's first farmers, Willem van der Wereld (literally: William of the World). After passing through various hands over the centuries it was sold in a state of disrepair to Jannie Engelbrecht, expert vintner and famous South African rugby player in 1978. Today the 1780 cellar, 1825 house and 1780

Jonkershuis (Bachelor's quarters) are restored to their original state and quality wines are produced.*Cellar Tours:* By appointment. *Wine Sales & Tasting:* Mon-Fri 08h30-12h30 & 13h30-16h30 Sat (Only Dec & Jan) 09h00-12h00.

15. SIMONSIG
PO Box 6, Koelenhof 7605.
Tel. (02231) 92044. Fax. (02231) 92545.
Combination of two old estates, Nooitgedacht and De Hoop, acquired in the 1680s by blacksmith Matthys Greeff and farmer Simon de Groot, respectively. Greeff made a good living out of herbal medicines, sold his farm and moved into a big house in Cape Town. Today Simonsig (originally part of Nooitgedacht) and the adjoining De Hoop estate are run as one by its current owners, the Malans.*Cellar Tours:* Mon-Fri 10h00 & 15h00, Saturdays 10h00. *Wine Sales:* Mon-Fri 08h30-17h00. Sat 10h00.

16. SPIER
P O Box 28, Vlottenburg 7604.
Tel. (02231) 93808/9. Fax. (02231) 93514.
Named Spier by its first owner, Arnout Jansz, in 1683, after the German town, Speyer. After passing through several families the farm was settled by Andries van der Byl, who vastly expanded the vineyards and erected most of the historic buildings. The current owners, the Jouberts,

Grand entrance - Cape Dutch Style

bought the farm in the 1960s and did extensive restoration. *Cellar Tours:* On adjacent farm Goedgeloof, Mon- Fri llh00-15h00.*Wine Sales:* (Spier) Mon-Fri 08h30-13h00 & 14h00-17h00. Sat 08h30-13h00. *Spier Restaurant:* Tel. (02234) 242. Credit cards & checks accepted. Licensed for wine. Old restored slave house with traditional Cape dishes.Tue- Sun lunch. Fri & Sat dinner/supper only. *Spier Jonkerhuis/Wine House:* Tel. (02234) 512. Credit cards accepted. Offers traditional luncheon's to wine route travelers. Lunch: 12h00-14h30 daily.

17. STELLENBOSCH FARMERS WINERY

P O Box 46, Stellenbosch
Tel. (02231) 7-3400. Fax. (02231) 71355.
Stellenbosch Farmers' Winery (SFW) is a major maker and vendor of wines in South Africa. Its headquarters are situated at Oude Libertas (Old Liberty) on the outskirts of Stellenbosch. Once the property of Adam Tas, the rebellious Dutch settler who lays claim to being the first freedom fighter in this part of the world. Although it is assumed that Tas came up with the name Libertas (Libre est Tas)(Tas is Free) after he

Old Stellebosch House - A F Potter

won his battle against "corrupt" officials in Cape Town, this estate was already so named when he gained title to it by marrying the widow Grimp at the end of the seventeenth century.

SFW also owns well-known cellars such as Monis and Neder-burg Estate (see Paarl Wineway).*Cellar Visits & Tasting:* Public tours are arranged of the winery and the cellars, followed by film showings on wine and a wine tasting.*Theater:*Another attraction at Oude Libertas is an underground cellar and an amphitheater on the slopes of Papegaaisberg. (Named *parrot mountain* after the regular bird shooting competition arranged here in the seventeenth century). The theater is styled after the ancient Greek models, seats some 400 people, and was opened in 1977 with a performance by the well-known Russian pianist, Vladimir Askenazy.

18. UITERWYK

PO Box 15, Vlottenburg 7604.
Tel. (02231) 93711. Fax. (02231) 93776.
Named Uiterwyk by its original owner, Dirk Coetzee in 1682 (Outer Ward or District). Krige family purchased the estate in 1791, prospered and expanded vineyards, cellar and homestead. De Waal family have been in possession of this estate since 1864. *Wine Sales:* Mon-Fri 09h00-12h00 & 14h00-16h30, Sat 10h00-12h00.*Cellar Tours & Tasting:* By appointment.

19. VLOTTENBURG COOPERATIVE

P O Box 40, Vlottenburg 7604.
Tel. (02231) 93828/9.
Established in 1945 and sells red and white wines to the public.*Wine Sales & Cellar Tours:* Mon-Fri 08h30-12h30 & 13h30-17h00. Sat 08h30-12h00.

20. WELMOED COOPERATIVE

P O Box 23, Lynedoch 7603.
Tel. (02231) 93800. Fax. (02231) 93434.
Opened in 1941. Make wines from grapes grown in both the Stellenbosch and Paarl regions. *Wine Sales:* Mon-Fri 08h00-13h00 & 14h00-17h00. Sat 08h30-13h00.*Cellar Tours:* By appointment.

KWV Headquarters

A Gary Player Signature Course Hilton Head, South Carolina

Gary Player

DESIGN COMPANY

"The key to a great golf course is playability. You can build great golf courses without making them too tricky. That's our philosophy. Designing golf courses that will be enjoyed by golfers of all standards."

Gary Player

Please contact the relevant
Gary Player Design
Company office.

*Pier House. Strand on the Green
Chiswick, London.
W4 3NN United Kingdom
Telephone (081) 994 1444
Facsimile (081) 994 9606*

*4440 P.G. A. Boulevard – Suite 105
Palm Beach Gardens, Florida 33410 U.S.A.
Telephone (407) 624 0300
Facsimile (407) 624 0304*

*66 Rivonia Road, Chistlehurston
Sandton 2196 South Africa
P O Box 785629 Sandton 2146
Telephone (011) 883 7220
Facsimile (011) 883 7250*

RESTAURANTS
SEE WINE ROUTE MAP #1

Apart from restaurants on estates such as Spier, Neethlingshof, Blaauwclippen and Delheim, visitors have a choice between several in Stellenbosch itself, offering genuine Cape dishes and other traditional foods. Several are in historic buildings.

2. DE KELDER
63 Dorp Street, Stellenbosch..Tel: (02231) 3797. Daily.Fully licensed. Credit cards. French and traditional dishes in restored cellar (circa 1791) with a display of many period pieces in copper, silver and furniture. (*De Kelder* is the Dutch word for The Cellar)

4.DE VOLKSKOMBUIS.*Aan de Wagenweg, Stellenbosch.. Tel. (02231) 7-2121. Credit cards. Wine and malt.* In a cottage designed by Sir Herbert Baker, Cecil Rhodes' friend who also designed the Union Buildings in Pretoria. *Volkskombuis* (Country Kitchen) offers a full range of *Kaapse kos* (Cape dishes).

5. DOORNBOSCH WINE HOUSE. *Strand Road, Stellenbosch district.Tel. (02231) 7-5079. Lunch Tue-Sun 12h00.Dinner Tue-Sat 19h00. Credit cards.Licensed for wine..* In old Cape Dutch house. Offers classic French food and traditional Cape dishes. Wine cellar sells local wines from 09h00-17h00 Mon-Fri & 09h00-13h00 on Sat.

6. D'OUWE WERF.*30 Church Street, Stellenbosch.Tel: (02231) 74608. Credit cards accepted. Fully licensed.* Traditional light lunches are served in a pleasant garden at this restored country inn.

9. LANZERAC HOTEL. *Jonkershoek Road, Stellenbosch. Tel. (02231) 7-1132. Lunch & dinner. Fully licensed. Credit cards.* Situated on land originally granted to a soldier in 1692. Traditional Cape dishes and desserts served in the main dining room. Also provides dinners in its candle-lit attic and brunches outdoors

(For a complete listing of restaurants in the area see *DINING AND WINING*).

PAARL WELLINGTON WINEWAY
SEE WINE TOUR MAP #2

The Paarl Wineway is about a half-hour from Cape Town along the N1 highway. It starts at the classic headquarters of the KWV or the Winegrowers' Cooperative Society, in the attractive La Concorde section of Paarl.

As the single largest organization of its kind, KWV represents all the wine-growers of the Cape, and offers daily cellar tours, wine tastings and interesting film shows. Laborie, KWV's model wine estate further down the street, features a traditional Cape restaurant. Brochures and maps for the wine route are available from the Public Relations Department, KWV, PO Box 528, Suider-Paarl 7624. Tel. (02211) 631001. Fax. (02211) 633440.

Following in alphabetical order are the estates and cooperatives that open to the public along the Paarl Wine Route:

1. BACKSBERG ESTATE:
PO Box 1, Klapmuts 7625.
Tel. (02211) 5141. Fax. (02211) 5144.
Part of a tract of land granted in 1692 to Pieter van der Byl, one of the farmers arrested and exiled to Holland by Governor Willem Adriaan van der Stel because they complained to the authorities about alleged official corruption at the Cape. Eventually, Van der Stel and his senior officials

Paarl Parsonage

Dr Charles Kohler

Kohler of the KWV, as he was known, rescued the South African wine industry from devastation and bankruptcy at the turn of the century.

Shortly after dentist Kohler went wine farming in the Drakenstein valley in the 1890s, the bottom fell out of the barrel. First the wine price dropped to below cost as merchants played the farmers off against each other; then the dreaded phylloxera disease that devasted Europe's vineyards, infested the Cape.

In 1918, against stiff opposition from politicians, merchants and even farmers, Kohler organized the industry into a cooperative known by its Dutch name, the Kooperatiewe Wijnbouwers Vereniging (KWV) (The Cooperative Wine Growers Assocation).

The KWV stabilized the industry and became the driving force behind a flourishing export market. When he died at the age of 90, Kohler's body lay in state in the main cellar of the KWV in Paarl. A man of special vintage who saved the South African wine industry.

were recalled and Van der Byl and his fellow revolutionaries vindicated. In 1902 a Lithuanian immigrant, C L Back, purchased a piece of the original Van der Byl property, and named it Backsberg. *Wine sales:* Mon-Fri 08h00-17h30. Sat 08h00-13h00.*Cellar Tours & Tastings:* Mon-Fri 08h00-17h30. Sat 08h00-13h00.

2. BOLANDSE COOPERATIVE
P O Box 2, Huguenot 7645.
Tel. (02211) 21766. Fax (02211) 625379.
Established in 1947 and produces its wines from grapes grown in the Paarl, Wellington and Malmesbury areas.*Wine Sales:* Mon-Fri 08h30-12h30 & 13h30-17h30. Sat 09h00-12h00.*Cellar Tours:* By appointment only.

3. DE ZOETE INVAL
P O Box 591, Suider Paarl 7624
Tel. (02211) 632375. Fax. (02211) 632817.
Huguenot Hercules des Pres received this land in 1688, and named it De Zoete Inval (Dutch for *The Sweet Event*). In 1878 when he bought the farm Scottish immigrant Robert Frater tried to set up a lucrative wool-washery for the sheep farmers in the nearby Karoo. Instead, wine making become a priority.*Estate Visits & Sales:* By appointment only.

4. DRAKENSTEIN COOPERATIVE
P O Box 19, Simondium 7670.
Tel. (02211) 41051. Fax. (02211) 41055.
Established in 1906, Drakenstein Cooperative, near Simondium, is one of the oldest in existence.*Wine Sales:* Mon-Fri 08h30-117h30. Sat 08h00-13h00.*Cellar Tours:* Mon-Fri 08h30-117h30. Sat 08h00-13h00.

5. FAIRVIEW ESTATE
PO Box 583, Suider-Paarl 7624.
Tel. (02211) 632450. Fax. (02211)632591.
Major supplier of full-bodied red wines to the KWV until current owner, Cyril Back, decided in the seventies to market directly to the public. Estate also won acclaim for its French-style goat milk cheese, called Chevin.*Wine Tasting & Sales:* Mon-Fri 0830-12h30 & 13h30-18h00. Sat 08h-13h00.*Cellar Tours:* Mon-Fri 0830-12h30 & 13h30-18h00. Sat 08h-13h00.

6. KWV & LABORIE ESTATE

Main Street, Suider-Paarl 7624.
Tel. (02211) 631001. Fax. (02211) 633440
Established on 8 January 1918, the KWV
(Kooperatiewe Wijnbouwers Vereniging
or Cooperative Winegrowers Association)

is the hub of the South African wine industry. Representing more than 6000 winegrowers and processing and marketing a
large percentage of the grapes produced,
KWV has developed one of the world's
largest and most modern wineries in the

WINE TOUR MAP #2

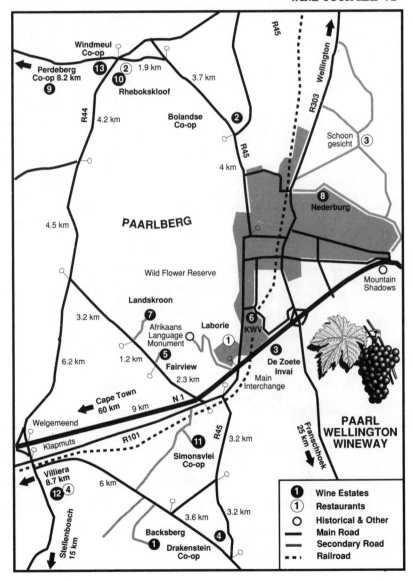

world. These wine cellars and processing facilities are open to the public. Apart from wine tastings KWV also offers interesting film shows about the industry.

KWV WINES

While the wines made from members' grapes at KWV's cellars are mainly for export and not freely available in South Africa, the Cooperative's own estate, **Laborie**, sells locally.

Purchased in 1972 by KWV to serve as a model where new experimental techniques are put to the test, Laborie was granted in 1690 to a Huguenot named Taillefert. He called it La Brie, a name that was later changed to Laborie.

KWV has restored the old buildings to their original splendor and established a restaurant which offers visitors a variety of traditional Cape dishes. Wine is for sale on the estate.

KWV wines are basically produced for export and freely available in most countries of the world where they have won numerous international awards and became household items in the homes of discerning wine drinkers. The range includes Roodeberg,Cabernet, Pinotage, Cinsaut, Shiraz, Bonne Esperance, Riesling, Steen, Chenin Blanc, Stein, Weisser Riesling, Kerner, Late Vintage, Noble Late Harvest Superior, Cape Foret, Cape Bouquet, Cape Nouveau, Petillant Blanc, Rose, Mousseaux Blanc Brut, Blanc Demi Sec, Rouge, Musante. Wines produced on the historic **Laborie estate** are sold in South Africa and include La Borie; Sparkling Blanc de Noir, Taillefert, Laborie Red, and Laborie White.

KWV Cellar Tours and Wine Tastings: Mon-Fri 09h30,11h00,14h15 and 15h45. They last one and a half hours and are conducted alternatively in Afrikaans and English. Entrance to the cellars is at Gate 5 in Kohler Street. *Wine Sales:* At Laborie wines of the area are sold. *Other facilities:* Lectures and wine courses are offered.

LABORIE RESTAURANT
Credit cards. Licensed for wine. Tel. (02211) 63-2034. Open daily for lunch (12h00-14h30) and dinner (from 19h30), except Mondays and Sunday evenings. Set in a Cape Dutch wine house, this attractive restaurant features traditional Cape dishes and deserts and a range of its own wines.

7. LANDSKROON ESTATE
P O Box 519, Suider-Paarl 7624. Tel. (02211) 631039. Fax. 632810.
Vintner-owner of Landskroon, Paul de Villiers traces his roots back to three Huguenot brothers who came to the Cape in 1689 and left an indelible mark on the wine industry. Landskroon was named by its original Dutch owner who settled on the southside of the Paarl Mountain in 1692. *Wine Tasting & Sales:* Mon-Fri 08h00-12h30 & 13h30-18h00. Sat 08h00-12h30.*Cellar Tours:* Mon-Fri 08h00-12h30 & 13h30-18h00. Sat 08h00-12h30.

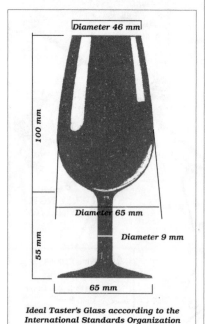

Diameter 46 mm

100 mm

Diameter 65 mm

Diameter 9 mm

55 mm

65 mm

Ideal Taster's Glass acccording to the International Standards Organization

8. NEDERBURG WINERY

P O Box 46 Huguenot 7645.
Tel. (02211) 623104. Fax. 624887.
Philip Wolvaart named the original farm after his benefactor Commissioner-General Neder-burgh of the Dutch East India Company, who made this land grant to him in 1792. The original homestead is still in use at the estate. Today Nederburg belongs to Stellenbosch Farmers Winery with head offices in Stellenbosch. *Wine Tasting & Sales:* Mon-Fri 08h30-16h30. *Cellar Tours:* By appointment only.

9. PERDEBERG CO-OPERATIVE

P O Box 214, Paarl 7621.
Tel. (02211) 838112.
Near Windmeul in the Paarl district this cooperative offers a variety of wines for sale. *Tastings & Sales:* Mon-Fri 08h00-12h30 & 14h00-17h00.

10. RHEBOKSKLOOF

P O Box 2125, Windmeul 7630.
Tel: (02211) 638386. Fax. (02211) 638504.
Granted in 1692 to Dirk van Schalkwyk. Named after Rhebok (Reebuck) that were found on the land when its original owner started farming here. The estate borders the Paarl Nature Reserve and rhebok can still be seen. *Tastings &Sales:* Mon-Fri 08h30-17h00. Sat 08h30-13h00. *Cellar & Estate Tours:* By appointment. *Rhebokskloof Restaurant:* Tel: (02231) 638606. Open daily for lunch (12h00 & 14h30) and dinner (19h30). Licensed. Credit cards accepted. Offers a variety of traditional dishes in an old homestead. Reservations advisable.

11. SIMONSVLEI CO-OPERATIVE

P O Box 584, Suider-Paarl 7624.
Tel. (02211) 633040. Fax. (02211) 631240.
A cooperative established in 1948, with a father-son wine making team. *Tastings, Tours & Sales:* Mon-Fri 08h00-17h00. Sat 08h30-13h00.

12. VILLIERA ESTATE:

P O Box 66, Koelenhof 7605.
Tel. (02232) 92002/3. Fax. (02231) 92314.
In the 1930s JWS de Villiers bought part of an existing estate and named it Villiera.

Hunter and Austrian hotel owner Helmut Ratz bought the property in the early seventies to produce wines for his European hotels as well as the local market. *Tasting & Sales:* Mon-Fri 8h30-17h00. Sat 08h30-13h00. *Cellar Tours:* By appointment. *Light lunches:* Austrian-style from 26 November until Easter on Mon-Sat 12h00-14h00.

13. WINDMEUL CO-OPERATIVE

P O Box 2013, Windmeul 7630.
Tel. (02211) 638043/100.
Processed grapes from the Paarl and Malmesbury regions since 1944. Portion bottled and marketed under its own label. *Tasting & Sales:* Mon-Fri 08h00-12h30 & 13h30-17h00.

RESTAURANTS

Apart from restaurants on wine estates such as Laborie, Rhebokskloof and Villiera, visitors also have the option of another traditional restaurant near Paarl:

Paarl Gable - A F Trotter

SCHOONGEZICHT

*Dal Josaphat Valley, Paarl.Tel. (02211) 62-3137. Teas & Lunch Wed-Mon 10h30-16h00.Dinner Fri-Sat from 19h00.Closed Tuesdays. Not licensed.Credit cards.*In the scenic Dal Josafat Valley and 5 minutes from Paarl. Offers home cooking, including traditional Cape dishes in restored farmhouse with thick walls and reed ceilings.

(See also our listing for the area in our chapter DINING AND WINING).

FRANSCHHOEK WINEWAY
SEE WINE ROUTE MAP #3

Named Vignerons de Franschhoek after a committee of local custodians formed to protect and preserve the original French Huguenot farm in the area, this route covers the scenic Franschhoek valley. A visitor's bureau in Franschhoek assists visitors from its offices at the *Oude Stallen Center in Huguenot Road, Franschhoek. Tel: (02212)3118.* Franschhoek (French Corner) has a monument and a complex of museums to bring tribute to the Huguenots to whom the wine industry at large is so deeply indebted. Around Franschhoek many farms still bear their original French names. There are no less than six called La Provence! Franschhoek valley is only 45 minutes away from Cape Town.

The following wine estates are open to the public. Some require advance notice. Most cellar tours are by appointment only.

Gable - L'Ormirins

1. BELLINGHAM WINERY
P O Box 134, Franschhoek 7690.
Tel. (02212) 31001. Fax. (0211) 641287.
The name Bellingham is believed to be a disjointed effort at Bellinchamp (the French for 'beautiful fields'). Draws its wines from a number of estates in the area, and is therefore not entitled to Wine of Origin classification. Managed by Union Wine Company. *Cellar Tours & Tastings:* Mon-Fri 10h00, 14h00 & 15h00. Sat by appointment. *Sales:* Mon-Fri 09h00-13h00 & 14h00-17h00. Sat 10h00-12h30.

2. BOSCHENDAL ESTATE
Pniel Road, Groot Drakenstein 7680.
Tel. (02211) 41031. Fax. (02211) 41413.
Bossendal was bought in 1715 by Abraham de Villiers together with the neighboring farm, Champagne, from two other Huguenots, Le Long and De la Noy, and joined them together under the name Boschendal. Estate remained with De Villiers family until turn of century when mining mogul Cecil John Rhodes purchased it. Current owner is Anglo American Corporation. *Cellar Tours, Tasting & Sales:* Mon-Fri 08h30-13h00 & 14h00-17h00. Sat 08h30-12h30. *Vineyard Tours:* Mon-Fri 11h00. Reservations essential.*Boschendal Restaurant:* Tel. (02211) 41252. Daily buffet or picnic lunches under the trees or in restored original cellar. Credit cards. Traditional Cape cuisine.

3. DIEU DONNE
P O Box 94, Franschhoek 7690.
Tel. (02212) 2493. Fax. (02212) 2355.
One of only a few properties in the valley to produce its own wine as a joint venture by a dozen wine enthusiasts. Five-gabled Cape Dutch homestead has been meticulously restored. *Tasting & Sales:* Mon-Fri 08h30-13h00. *Cellar Tours:* By appointment.

4. FRANSCHHOEK VINEYARDS
P O Box 52, Franschhoek 7690.
Tel. (02212) 2086.
Founded in 1945 on La Cotte, one of the original Huguenot farms, this is the only cooperative in the area. It obtains its grapes from 122 members, some of whom have their grapes processed and bottled sepa-

rately to entitle them to Wine of Origin classification. Other wines are bottled under cooperative label. *Tastings & Sales:* Mon-Fri 08h30-13h00 & 14h00-17h30. Sat 09h00-13h00. *Cellar Tours:* By appointment.

5. HAUTE PROVENCE
P O Box 211, Franschhoek 7690.
Tel. (02212) 3195. Fax. (02212) 3118.
Originally part of La Provence, an estate granted to French Huguenot Pierre Joubert in 1694. As with several other smaller estates in the area, also Haut Provence's grapes are vinified and bottled at the Franschhoek Vineyards Cooperative. The current owner is journalist Peter Younghusband. *Tastings :* (15 Dec- 15 Apr) Mon-Fri 14h00-16h00 & Sat 10h00-12h00. *Sales:* (15 Dec-15 Apr) Mon-Fri 14h00-16h00. Sat 10h00-12h00.

6. LA BRI VINEYARDS:
P O Box 180, Franschhoek 7690.
Tel. (02212) 2593. Fax. (02212) 3197.
Small estate at the upper side of the Franschhoek Valley where French Huguenot Jacques de Villiers first planted vines in 1694. Grapes from the estate are delivered to the Franschhoek Vineyards Cooperative where they are separately processed and bottled enabling La Bri to sell Wine of Origin wines under its own label - a method also followed by other estates in the region. *Tasting & Sales:* By appointment. Mon-Sat 10h00-17h00.

7. LA PROVENCE:
P O Box 188, Franschhoek 7690.
Tel. (02212) 2163. Fax. (02212) 2616.
Huguenot Pierre Joubert received this land in 1694 and named it La Provence after his native Provence in France. The homestead was started by one-time owner Pieter de Villiers (1756) and after his death completed by his widow, who, incidentally, married Pieter Joubert, great-grandson of the original owner. *Tasting & Sales:* Mon-Fri 08h30-12h30.

8. L'ORMARINS ESTATE
Private Bag 215, Suider-Paarl 7625.
Tel. (02211) 4-1026. Fax. (02211) 41361.
Started in 1694 by Huguenot Jean Roi and passed on to the De Villiers family who are

WINE TOUR MAP #3

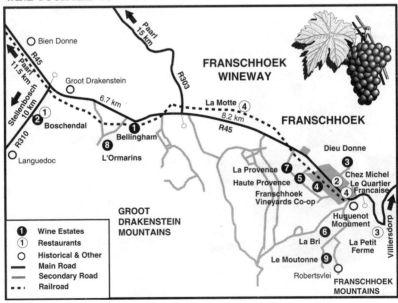

responsible for the oldest remaining building on the estate - the T-shaped homestead. The cellar dates back to 1799 and the H-shaped main residence was built in 1811. The cellar is used for storage and grapes processed and bottled by The Bergkelder in Stellenbosch. *Tours & Tastings:* Mon-Fri 09h00-16h00.

9. LE MOUTONNE
P O Box 290, Franschhoek 7690.
Tel: (02212) 2596. Fax. (02212) 2297.
This property originally belonged to French Huguenot Jacques Mouton who came to the area in 1699. After going through many ownerships it was purchased a few years ago by Ben Mouton a direct descendant of the original owner.*Tasting & Sales:* Mon-Fri 09h00-18h00. (Also *cheese lunches* in summer from 12h00-14h00).

RESTAURANTS

Apart from Boschendal, there is a choice of several exquisite restaurants in Franschhoek. The following three are among the most popular ones and reservations are definitely necessary, especially in the summer season.

Franschhoek Estate - A F Trotter

2. CHEZ MICHEL
26 Huguenot Road, Franschhoek. Tel: (02212) 2671. Feb-Nov:Lunch Wed-Mon 10h30-14h00; Dinner Mon-Wed & Sat. from 18h00. Dec-Jan: Luncheon & dinner daily. Not licensed. Credit cards. French and continental food are served French bistro style. Also Indonesian dishes.

3. LA PETIT FERME
*Franschhoek Pass Road, Franschhoek.Tel. (02212) 3016. Tue-Sun 10h30-17h00 open for teas & lunches. Closed Mondays. Licensed for wine and malt.Credit cards.*Two km beyond the Huguenot Monument on the Franschhoek Pass road leading to Villiersdorp. Genuine French country restaurant including carefully boned local trout and home-baked bread, as well as range of traditional Cape dishes.

4. LE QUARTIER FRANCAIS
16 Huguenot Rd, Franschhoek. Tel. (02212) 2248. Lunch: Wed-Sun. Dinner Wed-Sat. Licensed for wine. Credit cards. French cuisine with a touch of the Cape, utilizing fresh fish from the nearby coast and Franschhoek River salmon. Situated in a renovated 19th century cottage.

(See also our chapter DINING & WINING)

BREEDE RIVER WINE ROUTE
SEE WINE ROUTE MAP #4

This wine route covers a vast area - from Wolseley in the northwest through Rawsonville, Worcester, Robertson, Ashton, Bonnievale to Swellendam.

The Worcester Winelands Association, situated at Kleinplasie on the showgrounds on Robertson Road in Worcester, stocks wines from all its members. These can be tasted on the premises and are sold together with a range of other local products such as honey, cheese, jams, preserves and home-baked confectionary.

At most of these cellars and estates there are wine tastings and the opportunity to buy wines directly. Here are some of the interesting opportunities along the Robertson and Worcester routes in the Breede River Valley:

1. AGTERKLIPHOOGTE COOP
P O Box 267, Robertson 6705.
Tel. (02351) 2155.
About 28 kilometers from Robertson, it processes grapes from the region and bottles a portion under the Agterkliphoogte (Hill-behind-the-Rock) label.*Cellar Visits & Sales:* Mon-Fri 08h00-12h30 & 13h30-17h30.

2. ASHTON COOPERATIVE WINERY
P O Box 40, Ashton 6715.
Tel. (0234) 51135.
Opened in the sixties the co-op processes grapes for 132 members and has won acclaim as a producer of young wines.*Tasting & Sales:* Mon-Fri 08h00-17h00.

3. BERGSIG ESTATE
P O Box 15, Bergsig, Bree River 6858.
Tel. (02324) 603/721. Fax. (02324) 658.
Belongs to the Lategan family and has reputation as a wine producer that goes back to the 1930s. Although Bergsig sells most of its crop in bulk to wholesalers, some is bottled by the Breerivier Bottling Coopera-tive and sold under the estate label.*Tasting & Sales:* Mon-Fri 08h00-16h45. Sat 09h00-12h00. *Tours:* By appointment.

4. BON COURAGE
Box 589, Robertson 6705.
Tel. (02351) 4170/8.
Bon Courage was named after Goedemoed (Dutch for courage) when the Bruwer family acquired it in the 1920s.The old cellar was modernized and wines bottled on the estate since the early eighties.*Tasting & Sales:* Mon-Fri 09h00-12h00 & 14h00-17h00. *Tours:* By appointment.

5. BONNIEVALE COOPERATIVE
P O Box 206, Bonnievale 6730.
Tel. (02346) 2795.
Dates back to the sixties and processes grapes from some sixty members. Road to cellar has magnificent views of vineyards. *Tasting & Sales:* Mon-Fri 08h00-12h30 & 13h30-17h00. *Cellar Tours:* By appointment.

6. CLAIRVAUX COOPERATIVE
P O Box 179, Robertson 6705.
Tel. (02351) 3842.
Once a private cellar, this winery on the fringes of Robertson was changed into a cooperative in the early sixties serving 15 farmers.*Tasting & Sales:* Mon-Fri 09h00-12h00 & 14h00-17h00.

WINE TOUR MAP #4

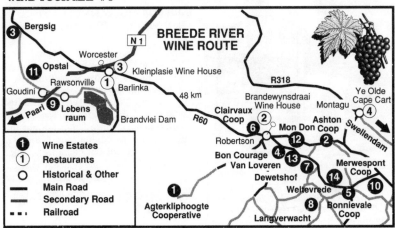

7. DE WETSHOF ESTATE

P O Box 31, Robertson 6705.
Tel. (02351) 51857.
First wine farm in the Robertson district to be given Estate status and awarded Superior classification for its wine. In the past forty years owner De Wet has been experimenting with new cultivars and new clones of established varieties. *Tours & Tastings:*By appointment.

8. LANGVERWACHT COOPERATIVE

P O Box 87, Bonnievale 6730.
Tel. (02346) 2815.
Started out as Boesmansrivier (Bushmen's River) Cooperative but changed its name to Langverwacht (Long Expected) after a name dispute with the local Boesmansrivier Cheese Cooperative.*Tasting & Sales:* Mon-Fri 08h00-12h30 & 13h00-17h00.

9. LEBENSRAUM ESTATE

P O Box 36, Rawsonville 6845.
Tel. (0231) -1137.
Until the early forties when it became an independent estate, Lebensraum was part

Seventeenth Century wine decanter and glass officially used by the Dutch East India Company's staff at the Cape.

of the farm 'Het Groote Eiland' (The Large Island). Current owner, Philip Deetlefs, represents the fifth generation for the family in this area.*Tasting & Sales:* Mon-Fri 08h30-12h00 & 13h00-17h00.

10. MERWESPONT COOPERATIVE

P O Box 68, Bonnievale 6730.
Tel. (02346) 2800.
Has for many years produced wine mainly for brandy distillation but nowadays about one-tenth of its production goes into wine, made from grapes provided by its 60 members.*Tasting & Sales:* Mon-Fri 08h00-12h30 & 13h30-17h00.

11. OPSTAL ESTATE

P O Box 27, Rawsonville 6845.
Tel. (0231) 91066.
Situated in the Slanghoek (Snake Corner) Valley, Opstal started out as a major cattle farm in the middle of the nineteenth century. Named derived from Dutch description of the homestead - *'De opstal bij de fonteine'* (The homestead at the springs). *Tasting & Sales:* 09h00-11h00 & 14h00-17h00. *Cellar Tours:* By appointment.

12. MON DON ESTATE

P O Box 360, Robertson 6705.
Tel. (02351) 4183.
Current owner Pierre Marais named his farm *Mon Don* (My Gift) when he obtained it at a nominal sum from his mother in the 1960s. Since then the vineyards have been extended.*Tasting & Sales:* Mon-Fri 09h00-12h00 &14h00-16h00. *Cellar Tours:* By appointment.

13. VAN LOVEREN ESTATE

P O Box 19, Klaasvoogds 6707.
Tel. (0234) 51505. Fax. (0234) 51336.
Imagine working on the farm called Goudmyn F (Goldmine F). The wife of Hennie Retief ,whose father bought this subdivision of the original farm, Goudmyn, in the thirties, did not like a farm called Goudmyn F (Goldmine F).She renamed it after one of her distant ancestors who arrived at the Cape in 1692, Van Loveren. *Tasting & Sales:* Mon-Fri 08h00-13h00 & 14h00-17h00. Sat 09h30-13h00.

14. WELTEVREDE ESTATE

P O Box 6, Bonnievale 6730.
Tel. (023432) 2141/6. Fax. (02346) 24600.
Current owner Lourens Jonker is the grandson of Klaas Jonker who acquired this piece of shrubland in 1902, called it *Weltevreden* (Well Satisfied). Estate is also known for its large Friesland herd, supplying milk to the largest dairy in the country near Bonnievale. *Tasting & Sales:* Mon-Fri 08h30-13h00 & 14h00-17h00. Sat 09h00-12h00.*Cellar Tours:* By appointment.

RESTAURANTS

Visitors to the area will have a number of pleasant restaurants to select from, with the following good examples of venues where ambience and food reflects the traditions of the Breede River Valley.

1. BARLINKA

Cumberland Hotel, 2 Stockenstrom Street, Worcester. Tel. (0231) 7-2641. Lunch daily 12h30-14h00. Dinner daily 18h30-24h00. Licensed. Credit cards. Stylish table settings under rough plasterwork arches. Offers wide selection of dishes.

2. BRANDEWYNSDRAAI

Voortrekker Road, Robertson. Tel. (02351) 3202. Lunch & dinner Tue-Sunday 09h00-21h00. Close Monday. Licensed for wine. Credit cards. Established by KWV, this attractive wine house offers local flavor in food and wines. The name literally means "brandywine's turn", and it offers seafood and meat dishes and traditional items such as *skaapsnek* (sheep's neck), *snoek* and *bobotie*.

3. KLEINPLASIE WINE HOUSE

*Robertson Road, Worcester. Tel. (0231) 2-0430. Daily lunches 12h30-14h30. Dinner Tue-Sat 19h00-22h00.Licensed for wine. Credit cards.*KWV has transformed historic wine house at the Worcester showgrounds into a restaurant offering traditional Cape dishes and a whole array of local wines.

(See also listings in our chapter DINING AND WINING).

KLEIN KAROO WINE ROUTE
SEE WINE ROUTE MAP #5

For those visitors who have the time to venture further into the interior, the Klein Karoo Wine Route offers interesting opportunities. This route is the brainchild of one of the prominent wine farmers of the region, Karel Nel of Boplaas. Following in alphabetical order are cellars and estates open to the public for tours, wine tasting and sales. Cellar tours are arranged by appointment only.

1. BARRYDALE COOPERATIVE

P O Box 59, Barrydale 6750.
Tel. (02971) Ask for 12/275
Started as a brandy distillery in the forties before it switched to wine making. Close to 100 farmers supply grapes. *Tasting & Sales:* Mon-Fri 09h00-12h30 & 13h30-17h00. *Cellar Tours:* By appointment.

2. BOPLAAS ESTATE

P O Box 156, Calitzdorp 6660.
Tel. (04437) 33326. Fax. (04437) 33750.
Boplaas (Upper Farm) has been in the hands of the Nel family since 1890. Situated on the fringes of Calitzdorp, it uses a modern cellar as well as a restored old one. *Tasting & Sales:* Mon-Fri 08h00-13h00 & 14h00-17h00. Sat 09h00-12h00. *Cheese Lunches:* Dec-Jan & Easter - Mon-Fri 12h00-14h00.

3. CALITZDORP COOPERATIVE

P O Box 193, Calitzdorp 6660.
Tel. (04437) 33301.
Wine making followed an abortive attempt in 1920s to export Hanepoot grapes. It Started producing wines in the forties, sells

Estate walls - Cape Dutch style

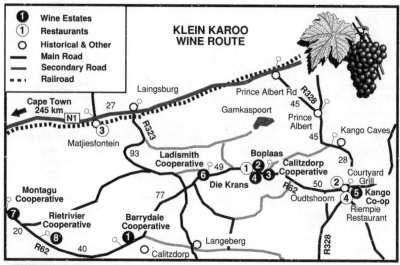

WINE TOUR MAP #5

bulk to merchants and smaller quantity bottled under its own Buffelskroon label. *Tasting & Sales:* Mon-Fri 08h00-12h15 & 13h15-17h00. Sat. 08h00-12h00.

4. DIE KRANS ESTATE
P O Box 28, Calitzdorp 6660.
Tel. (04437) 33314/64.
Belongs to same Nel family who farms on Boplaas Estate. *Die Krans* (The Rock) is situated in the Gamka River valley, close to Calitzdorp. *Tasting & Sales:* Mon-Fri 08h00-13h00 & 14h00-17h00. Sat 09h00-12h30. *Cheese Lunches:* Dec & Easter Mon-Sat 12h00-14h00 and on request for groups rest of the year. *Tours:* By appointment.

5. KANGO COOPERATIVE
P O Box 46, Oudtshoorn 6620.
Tel. (0443) 226065/6. Fax. (0443) 91038.
Situated in a region once famous for ostrich feathers. the cooperative displays a picture of the famous Rijckshof or 'ostrich palace' on its label. *Tasting & Sales:* Mon-Thu 08h30-13h00 & 14h00-17h00. Fri 08h30-13h00 & 14h00-16h00.

6. LADISMITH COOPERATIVE
P O Box 56, Ladismith 6885.
Tel. (02942) Ask for 31.

Produce wines under own label *Towerkop* (Magic Mountain) and *Swartberg* (Black Mountain). Towerkop - the highest peak in Klein Swartberg mountains. *Tasting & Sales:* Mon-Fri 08h00-13h00 & 14h00-17h00.

7. MONTAGU COOPERATIVE
P O Box 29, Montagu 6720.
Tel. (0234) 41125.
The Montagu Muscadel Farmers Cooperative expanded in the 1960s to produce dry natural wines, apart from supplying KWV with product for brandy distillation. *Tasting:* During harvest. *Sales:* Mon-Fri 08h30-12h30 & 13h30-17h00.

8. RIETRIVIER COOPERATIVE
P O Box 44, Montagu 6720.
Tel. (0234) 41705.
Makes quality rebate wines for brandy distillation and also markets table wines under its own label. *Tasting & Sales:* Mon-Fri 08h00-13h00 & 14h00-17h00.

RESTAURANTS

Apart from Die Krans and Boplaas estates where visitors are served cheese lunch during December there are a few interesting alternatives for those travellers who proceed to Oudtshoorn - home of the ostrich.

2. COURT YARD GRILL

*Queens Hotel, Oudtshoorn.Tel: (04431) 2101.Lunch 12h00-14h00. Dinner 19h00. Licensed. Credit Cards.*Restaurant in the oldest part of the restored 1809 Queens Hotel. Local dishes - including, of course, ostrich steak.

3. MATJIESFONTEIN.

Lord Milner Hotel, Matjiesfontein Village. Tel: (0020) ask for 3.Lunch & dinner.Fully licensed. Credit cards. Historic hotel, village and restaurant. Interesting stopover for travelers on N1 highway and weekend destination for Capetonians.

4. RIEMPIE RESTAURANT

Kango Protea Inn, Oudtshoorn.Tel: (04431) 6161.Licensed. Credit cards.Lunch and dinner with emphasis on *boerekos* (farmer's food), including Karoo lamb and ostrich specials.

OTHER PRODUCERS

Apart from the cellars and wine estates that are open to the public and offer wines at tastings and for sale directly to the public, there are a whole range of other good wines available. These are produced by estates and merchants that do not open their doors for the public.

In Stellenbosch, for example, **Gilbey Distillers & Vintners** has been an important vendor of wines for many years. Apart from making its own wines at Devonvale in the Devon Valley, near Stellenbosch, **Alphen** and **Bertrams**, it distributes well-known brands by other producers.

Douglas Green is another household name in South Africa. The business was started at the turn of the century by a wine farmer Piet le Roux who sold wines to customers who brought their own bottles and buckets to his convenient premises in the center of Paarl. It was renamed Douglas Green of

Old brandy still

One last item visitors often purchase at duty-free stores before returning home is a bottle of South African brandy. As one of the world's foremost producers of fine old brandy, KWV has over the past half a century made this product famous.

The first brandy was distilled at the Cape in 1672 by a humble ship's cook. Today South Africa is the world's fifth largest producer, providing pleasure to millions abroad and a livelihood for an estimated 300,000 South Africans. (Involving 6,000 wine farms and 25,000 families).

Apart from regular brandy, a unique tangerine liquor brandy is also produced under the name *Van der Hum* (What's His Name). Its tangy-sweet taste has found its way to many a palate at home and abroad.

While in the Cape travellers often call at the Van Ryn Brandy Cellars at Vlottenberg, where the whole brandy-making process can be observed, and the Oude Meester Brandy Museum in Stellenbosch, with its wide selection of brandy artifacts on display. *(See MUSEUMS in this chapter)*

Paarl when a young man with that name purchased the growing concern in the forties. Changing hands through the years and expanding its range of quality wines, Douglas Green of Paarl is no longer limited to this town. Its main bottling plant is near the Milnerton Race Course in Cape Town. Although it does its own blending and bottling, Douglas Green does not make its own wines but relies on KWV as a source.

Another merchant, **Union Wine**, started as a liquor outlet in the Karoo town of Graaff Reinet before it expanded into wine making in the Cape.

Although it is not situated on the wine routes, **Groot Constantia**, near Cape Town is a must on any wine connoisseur's itinerary. It is a short drive from Cape Town and on the scenic Peninsula route. (*Also see the chapters RURAL ROUTES and CITY SIGHTS*).

Wine Board's Seals on the neck of wine bottles

ADDITIONAL CHOICES

Apart from wines available at Constantia and the quality estates included on the wine tours, the following labels are worth considering:

Allesveloren Estate; Alto Estate; Bertrams Wines; Douglas Green; Fleur du Cap; Hamilton Russell Vineyards; Hemel-en-Aarde Wines (Hamilton Russell); Kanonkop; Meerendal Estate; Meerlust Estate; Middelvlei Estate; Oude Libertas; Stellenryck Wines (Bergkelder); Theuniskraal Estate; Twee Jonge Gezellen; Zandvliet; Zonnebloem Wines.

BUYING WINES

Part of the fun of going on wine tasting tours is buying a few bottles and reliving the experience afterwards. There are several good unlicensed restaurants in South Africa that allow patrons to bring along their own wine.

Those travellers interested in sharing these quality wines with friends and family at home, have the choice of taking a gift pack home with them or to have a consignment sent to their home address. Nowadays many estates and wineries offer these services.

KWV

As the pioneer in overseas marketing, KWV is expert in sending its wines to any doorstep around the world. In many countries, KWV has wholesalers and agents who can direct buyers to retail outlets in their specific country. *Enquiries can also be directed to KWV, P O Box 528, Suider-Paarl 7624 in South Africa. Tel. (02211) 631001. Fax. (02211) 633440.*

Other South African wine producers are also becoming more export conscious and have appointed agents in major markets abroad. (*For a list of agents and wholesalers, see the listing under KEY ADDRESSES*).

SEAL

In buying South African wines, it is important to look not only at the label but seal on the neck of the bottle. It is more than a seal of approval by the Wine & Spirit Board. It guarantees truth in labeling.Producers are required by the South African Wine & Spirit Board to provide an estimate of their production before harvesting, as well as exact wine production figures at a later date. When submitting samples of the wine for tasting, producers also have to indicate exactly how the wine will be used - whether it is to be sold as a cultivar wine, a vintage wine, a wine of origin, or a combination. After a tasting by an expert panel the wine is provisionally approved and seals provided. Seals are rationed by the Board on the basis of quantities and estimates of every specific wine.

GOLD SEAL

Although the purpose of the light-blue colored seal is to ensure accurate labeling and not to rate wines, gold seals were introduced to encourage excellence. Wines of truly outstanding quality are awarded Superior or gold seals. **There are, however, are also good wines that do not even qualify for a seal as they consist of a blend of grapes and wines produced on different estates.**

To ensure complete impartiality,the tasting panel is told only the cultivar and vintage and not informed about the source of the wine until after they have done their evaluation. *Blends* of different vintages and cultivars may also qualify for seals as long as all of it has been grown and produced within one area. While a normal classification is simply W*ine of Origin,* recipients of gold or superior seals are classified as *Wine of Origin Superior (WOS).*

BANDS ON SEALS

Buyers will find on every seal several bands that identify a specific wine on the following basis:

√   **Estate:** This imprint on the seal indicates that the wine was produced from grapes grown on the particular estate but not necessarily bottled on the estate.

√   **Origin (Blue Band):** This seal indicates that the wine was produced within one of the recognized wine regions.

√   **Cultivar (Green Band):** This means that more than 75% of the type of grape mentioned on the producers label was used in this particular wine.

√   **Vintage (Red Band):** This band indicates that more than 75% of the wine was harvested in the year indicated on the producer's label.

GRAPE TYPES

The following are the most popular white and red grape types used for wine-making in South Africa:

Producer's labels

Vintage

Origin — CONSTANTIA WYN VAN OORSPRONG SUPERIEUR

Superior

Estate Wine — GROOT CONSTANTIA LANDGOEDWYN

Cultivar — CABERNET SAUVIGNON

WHITE CULTIVARS

Bukettraube: A relative newcomer, this type is grown by a few estates to produce wines with a Muscat aroma.

Cape Riesling: At about 3.6% of all plantings, this grape represents a minor portion of the total crop. It forms, however, the basis of much of South Africa's quality dry wines. Good examples in Paarl and Stellenbosch areas.

Chardonnay: Gaining popularity in South Africa. There are many clones of this cultivar which constitutes the premier white wine in South Africa.

Chenel: This is a local hybrid between Chenin Blanc and Trebbiano that forms less than 1% of the total crop.

Chenin Blanc (Steen): This type makes up more than 30% of the all wine grapes grown in South Africa. It is used in sparkling, fruity dry, semi-sweet and fortified wines, as well as sherries.

Clairette Blanche: Used in sparkling wines, this grape ripens at the end of the season and represents about 4% of all plantings.

Colombar: Accounts for 8% of the total crops and is generally associated with brandy. Also used for blending in a dry white wine called Premier Grand Cru. Colombar wines mostly found in Robertson area.

Gewurtztraminer: Only a small fraction of the South African crop, this cultivar is used for semi-sweet wines with a spicy (gewurtz) flavor, especially in Stellenbosch and Paarl.

Hanepoot (Muscat d'Alexandrie): This is one of South Africa's oldest and most widely grown varieties. Although it is used primarily as an eating grape, it also forms basis of fortified wine called *Hanepoot*, which is produced mostly in the Klein Karoo, Paarl district, Worcester and Robertson areas.

Kerner: This variety forms a small fraction of the cultivars grown in South Africa and is used in a stern, individualistic type wine.

Palomino: This cultivar is the same used in Spain for sherry. In South Africa it is generally referred to as White French or Frans (in Afrikaans).

Rhine Riesling: This cultivar is similar in name only to Cape Riesling. Recently introduced to South Africa, it forms less than 1% of the total crop. Used to make a fragrant white wine.

Sauvignon Blanc: A relatively small percentage of the wine crop in South Africa. Used for a dry wine. Constantia is one of the prime producers.

Semillon (Green Grape): One of the original cultivars but today it forms only about 1.2% of the total crop. Although there are a few Semillon cultivar wines available, it is primarily used for blending.

RED CULTIVARS

Cabernet Savignon: In South Africa, as in France, this cultivar is very popular. It is also used in a so-called Bordeaux blend with Merlot and Cabernet Franc.

Cinsaut: A significant 6.7% of the total plantings, it is often used in blends and forms the main ingredient of several lighter reds.

Gamay: Only a few small plantings. It is used for *Nouveau* wines.

Merlot: Recently introduced and grown only by a few producers, mostly in the Stellenbosch area.

Pinotage: The first commercially successful local hybrid produced in 1925 from Pinot Noir and Hermitage (as Cinsaut was known at the time). First used in blends with Cabernet Sauvignon, today a popular cultivar wine that ages well into softness.

Pinot Noir: Transplanted from France, this cultivar is grown in small quantities. Found mainly in Paarl, Robertson and Stellenbosch areas.

Shiraz: This variety is believed to have come to South Africa from Persia via the Rhone valley. Originally used for blending with Cabernet Sauvignon, it is now offered as a popular independent cultivar by several producers in Robertson.

TYPES OF WINE

Although certified wines get more attention than the rest, they only constitute about one-tenth of all the quality wines produced in South Africa. When buying, visitors will be faced with a choice between the following types of wine:

Sparkling: In terms of an agreement with France, no South African sparkling wine may be called champagne. The most expensive on the market are the dry ones utilizing *methode champenoise*. Cultivars vary but it is more than likely that Chenin Blanc and Cape Riesling would form part of the blend.

Dry white: The most popular blends are *Blanc de Blanc* (mostly from Chenin Blanc) and *Premier Grand Cru* (made from Chenin Blanc, Riesling or Colombar). As opposed to French Premier Grand Cru, this not a quality classification but merely the name for an extra dry blend.

Semi-Sweet: Largely replaced in recent years by dry white wines, semi-sweets consist mostly of Gewurztraminer, Hanepoot (Muscat d'Alexandrie) and Rhine or Weisser Riesling grapes.

Late Harvest: The sunny climate is ideal for Late Harvest wines. A distinction is made between regular and special Late Harvest. While both have between 20-50 grams of sugar per liter all of this sweetness has to be natural in the case of Special Late Harvest. Noble Late Harvest has over 50 gm/l in residual sugar.

Blanc de Noir: These dry wines range in color from peachy to pink and are made exclusively from red grapes - including Cabernet Sauvignon and Pinotage. They are usually served during the day, chilled.

Rose: Most Roses are semi-sweet with a reasonably high sugar content, but some dry ones are on the market. Most are blends of Pinotage, Cinsaut and Cabernet, while some may contain white grapes.

Nouveau: Since its introduction in the early eighties, red Nouveau has become popular, especially in the Paarl area. This fruit red wine is mostly made from Gamay, emulating Beaujolais Nouveau, and released at a special festival in April. Served chilled, these Nouveaus are usually sold out (and drunk) within a few months after their release.

Red Wines: Most of the South African red wines in high demand are cultivar with **Cabernet Sauvignon** the largest seller. Next on the list is the locally developed Pinotage, followed by **Shiraz, Cinsaut** and **Pinot Noir.**

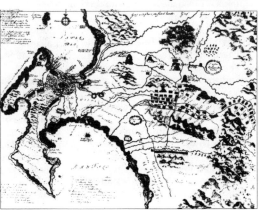

Cape winelands 1690

WINE AUCTIONS

Some foreign wine enthusiasts plan their visits to South Africa to coincide with the prime event on the South African wine calendar - the annual March auction of rare Cape wines at Nederburg, near Paarl.

Presided over by the wine auctioneer of Sothebys, London, it draws some 2,000 buyers from all over the world. Although only licensed traders and invited overseas buyers may take part in the bidding many others simply join in the festivity.

In 1983 Sotheby Parke Bernet also began conducting wine auctions in Johannesburg. At these events connoisseurs and members of the general public may offer wine for sale and the bidding is open to the public. *For details contact Sotheby Parke Bernet SA. PO Box 31010, Braamfontein 2017. Tel. (011) 339-3726.*

WINE FESTIVALS

For those who do not wish to pay top dollar for rare wines, but still wish to enjoy the bonhomie of a wine festival there are a number of young wine shows organized by KWV.

They all culminate in the South African Championship Young Wine Show, which is held annually in Cape Town. Visitors are required to buy a glass to gain admission. Buffet lunches are served.

Regional Young Wine Shows

Paarl	August
Worcester	August
Ladismith	August
Vredendal	August
Stellenbosch	September

SA Championship Young Wines

Cape Town	October

Food and Wine Festivals

Robertson	October
Stellenbosch	October

MUSEUMS

THE STELLENRYCK WINE MUSEUM
Dorp Street, Stellenbosch. Mon-Fri 09h00-12h45;14h00-17h00. Sat 10h00-13h00 & 14h00-17h00. Housed in the original cellar of the historic farm, Libertas Parva, is a collection of wine memorabilia including VOC glassware dating from the days of the Dutch East India Company, antique cellar equipment and rare copper and silver wine utensils. In the rear of the museum different types of oak maturing casks are displayed.

OUDE MEESTER BRANDY MUSEUM
Old Strand Road, Stellenbosch. Mon-Fri 09h00-12h45 & 14h00-17h00. Sat 10h00-13h00 & 14h00-17h00 Sun 14h30-17h30. Provides insights into the early history and development of brandy in the Cape. More than 1000 valuable exhibits trace the history of the distillation, maturation and blending of brandy.

VAN RYN BRANDY CELLAR AND MUSEUM
Vlottenburg near Stellenbosch. Tel. (02234) 478. Conducted tours Mon-Thu 10h30 and 14h30 -Fri 10h30. This museum dates back to 1904. Brandy is distilled in antique potstills and coopers demonstrate the art of this ancient trade. Reservations required.

RESEARCH

South Africa's Viticultural and Oenological Research Institute has its headquarters on an estate, *Nietvoorbij*, on the northern outskirts of Stellenbosch.

Besides offices, laboratories and extensive nursery facilities VORI has an experimental distillery and one of the most advanced wineries in the world.

Wine students interested in specialized information about the industry and a visit to the Research Institute should contact *VORI, at Private Bag X5026, Stellenbosch 7600. Tel. (02231) 70110.*

STAYING IN STYLE

Some travelers see hotels as a vacation destinations, while others regard them as simply overnight stops along the way.

Both types of travelers have ample opportunities in South Africa ranging from functional and modern to quaint and historical.

A star rating system helps tourists to pick the degree of luxury that they require and can afford. There are, however, also a number of exclusive (and expensive) inns that provide services well beyond five stars.

S outh Africa provides accommodation for every taste and need. Those who insist on old and classy have a good selection of historic establishments, while others who prefer the modern and brassy also have a wide choice. Budget conscious travelers are also assured of accommodation in reasonable, but still clean and efficient establishments, while campers and caravan or RV enthusiasts have many convenient, fully serviced sites at their disposal.

GRADING

In our list of hotels we used the grading system instituted by the South African Tourism Board. At the same time we have refrained from indicating rates as these change frequently and are in any event subject to discounts or special levies, depending on the season and occasion.

It is logical to assume that five star hotels are the most expensive ones. Every star means additional money in services and facilities and somehow these costs have to be passed along to the consumer.

STARS

The star system is designed to give the public an indication of the kind of services that they can expect at any

Steps at Alphen Hotel (AF Trotter)

rated establishment. There are also deluxe establishments, especially smaller inns and private lodges (including game lodges) that are not rated. This is how the South Africa Tourism Board award stars to hotels:

★ These are considered to be **good** establishments providing private bathrooms with more than half of their bedrooms and showers for the rest. One star hotels are also required to provide a twelve hour service of light refreshments and alcoholic beverages.

★★ These hotels are rated **very good** with bathrooms in 60% or more of their bedrooms and showers in the rest. They should also provide bedroom heating, radios in the room and light refreshments and alcoholic beverage, as well as reception desk service for 14 hours every day.

★★★ An **excellent** establishment with bathrooms in more than 75% of its bedrooms and showers in the remainder. They are required to provide wall-to-wall carpeting in all bedrooms, heating, three-channel radio, shaver plugs, *a la carte* meals for six hours every day, 18 hour room service, one permanent function room, 24-hour telephone service, color television in a public room, and furnishings and equipment of very good quality. (In reality color TV is provided in all rooms).

★★★★ These are establishments rated as **outstanding** with bathrooms in 90% of their bedrooms and in the remainder showers. They should also offer air conditioning and heating, shaver plugs, radios in rooms, 24 hour telephone service, television in 50% of the bedrooms and public rooms, a valet service from 07h00 until 21h00, a la carte meals for 7 hours per day, 24 hour room service for light refreshments, alcoholic beverages and light meals, two permanent conference rooms, furnishings and equipment of excellent quality, 24 hour reception desk duty, a full-time ladies hairdressing salon, transport and secretarial services.

★★★★★ Comparable with the **best** anywhere in the world. This is the standard set for hotels that aspire to five star status: At least 5% of the accommodation should be suites and the balance bedrooms with bathrooms, equipped both with bath and shower. Bedrooms should be equipped with four channel radios, television, heating and air conditioning and other amenities. Furnishing and equipment should be of outstanding quality and 24 hour room service for light meals, refreshments and alcoholic beverages provided, and full meals from 07h00 until 21h00. Valet service, 24 hour reception, full-time hairdressing salons for men and women are stipulated, and two *a la carte* restaurants, as well as conference rooms.

SYMBOLS

Hotels display their star ratings on their walls as well as on their stationery and promotional material. They also use the following symbols to indicate the extent of their services:

R	Occupancy mostly residential
T	Occupancy mostly transitory
YYY	Sells wine, spirits and beer
YY	Sells only wine and beer
Y	Sells wine and beer with meals
IH	International Status

GROUPS

Most of the **regular first-class** and **deluxe hotels** are controlled by one of the country's major hotel groups. Southern Sun, Holiday Inns, Protea Hotels and Karos Hotels have establishments in the major cities plus a few resorts hotels in smaller places. Sun International operates gambling or casino resorts in the black tribal homelands, with Sun City as its flagship.

Advertisement for one of the first boarding houses in Cape Town.

Shortly after his arrival at the Cape in 1652, founder Jan van Riebeeck authorized Annetjie de Boerin, wife of the Dutch East India Company gardener, to open an inn for the seamen and passengers of passing ships. The main condition: She had to buy all her liquor from the company store. Others followed suit and by the end of the eighteenth century competition was so stiff that representatives of the various Cape Town inns were boarding ships to line up patrons before they stepped ashore.

Inland, Boer or Afrikaner hospitality inhibited hotel growth. Strangers could always count on farmers taking them in for the night. It was only with the surge of foreign fortune seekers after the discovery of diamonds and gold at the end of the nineteenth century that hotels became a growth industry.

In recent years a number of world class de luxe hotels and gambling resorts were built and numerous quaint, exclusive old inns and residences restored to cater for a growing demand from overseas visitors.

There are also a number of establishments with **old-world charm** - hotels operated on an individual basis, especially in Cape Town where historic estates lend themselves to stylish living. Also in the Eastern Transvaal region, Natal interior, the Karoo, and remote coastal regions **country inns and lodges** are available to visitors without budget constraints looking for exquisite accommodations at a price.

Game lodges, either private ones or those run by the National Parks Board, usually feature on the itineraries of visitors who go to South Africa on safari. They vary from reasonable self-catering huts to more expensive deluxe chalets in the bush. *(See our chapter ON SAFARI for full details).*

ON BUDGET

Visitors who are operating on a budget may wish to opt for **self-catering ac-**

Dialling South African Cities from overseas:

27 +

Bloemfontein	**(51)**
Cape Town	**(21)**
Durban	**(31)**
Johannesburg	**(11)**
Kimberley	**(531)**
Port Elizabeth	**(41)**
Pretoria	**(12)**

commodation at resorts. There are a variety of time-share establishments at resort areas and furnished apartments available.

The **City Lodge Group** offers no-frill two-star accommodation at very reasonable rates in several major cities, including Johannesburg and its suburbs and Cape Town.

Their properties are popular with businessmen on extended trips and visitors on a budget. *(City Lodges, P O Box 448, Isando 1600 (011) 392-1750).*

Camping is popular and there are fully serviced sites around the country and near most of the scenic spots and popular resorts. Sites are even available within the Kruger National Park. Caravans and campers or RV's are available on a rental basis in most cities. Details and advice can be obtained from the *Caravan Club of Southern Africa, P O Box 50580, Randburg 2125. Tel. (011) 789-3202.*

Bed and breakfast is provided at a number of private homes, conveniently situated near tourist attractions and resorts. This method of travelling is preferred by many who wish to meet the locals instead of rubbing shoulders with other tourists at international-style hotels. *(Bed 'n Breakfast, P O Box 31124, Braamfontein 2017. Tel: (011) 726-6915).*

Finally, there are those who do not mind being referred to as back-packers. Among their ranks are the budget-conscious younger travellers as well as well-heeled conservation-conscious nature lovers. South Africa offers serious **hikers** a varied and interesting network of well-kept trails rich in history and wildlife, ranging from flat lands to mountains. *(See HIKING in our chapter on RESORTS AND SPORTS).*

HOTEL/INN RESORT	STARS N/R	ROOM/ SUITES	ADDRESS & ZIP	AREA CODE TELEPHONE	AREA CODE TELEFAX
GAME LODGES **SEE ON SAFARI - PAGE 27**					
MAJOR HOTEL GROUPS					
KAROS HOTELS Head Office			Box 87534 Houghton 2041	(011) 643-8052	(011) 643-4343
PROTEA HOTELS Head Office Reservations			Box 2936 Cape Town 8000 South Africa Toll Free	(021) 419-5320 (011) 484-1717 (0800) -11-9000	(021) 25-3258 (011) 484-2752
SOUTHERN SUN HOTELS **(SUN HOTELS & HOLIDAY INNS)** Head Office Reservations Overseas Offices			Box 5087 Johannesburg 2000 South Africa United Kingdom Germany, Austria (Frankfurt)	(011) 883-2200 (011) 783-5333 (0753) 85-1667 (069) 28-3278	(011) 783-2184 (011) 783-2184 (0753) 86-8197 TX: 4185856
SUN INTERNATIONAL Head Office Reservations Overseas Offices			Box 784487 Sandton 2146 South Africa United Kingdom Germany France	(011) 780-7444 (011) 783-8660 (491) 574546 (6171) 57071 (1) 42612266	(011) 780-7701 TX: 4-27427 (491) 57-6194 (6171) 54149 (1) 42868985
MAJOR CITIES					
BLOEMFONTEIN *CITY MAP # 1 - PAGE 93*					
Cecil Hotel	★★	56	Box 516 Bloemfontein 9300 Oldish comfortable hotel	(051) 48-1155	
Halevy House	★★★	22	Box 1368 Bloemfontein 9300 Central and well appointed	(051) 48-0271	(051) 26-7129
Holiday Inn	★★★	145	Box 1851 Bloemfontein 9300 Standard Holiday Inn	(051)30-1111	(051) 30-4141
Landdrost Sun	★★★★	147	Box 12015 Brandhof 9324 Good hotel near university	(051) 47-0310	(051) 30-5678
Maitland	★★	77/5	Box 221 Bloemfontein 9300 Traditional & good restaurants	(051) 48-3121	
CAPE TOWN CITY *CITY MAP #2 - PAGE 97*					
Cape Swiss Hotel	★★★	80/4	Box 21516 Cape Town 8000 On lower slopes of mountain	(021) 23-8190	(021) 26-1795
Capetonian Protea	★★★★	125	Box 6856 Roggebaai 8012 Well situated on Foreshore	(021) 21-1150	(021) 25-2215
Cape Sun	★★★★★	342/20	Box 4532 Cape Town 8000 Modern and central	(021) 23-8844	(021) 23-8875

HOTEL/INN RESORT	STARS N/R	ROOM/ SUITES	ADDRESS & ZIP	AREA CODE TELEPHONE	AREA CODE TELEFAX
CAPE TOWN CTD.					
De Waal Sun	★★★★	127/3	Box 2793 Cape Town 8000	(021) 45-1311	(021) 461-6648
			Good grounds and views		
Holiday Inn	★★★	290/2	Box 2979 Cape Town 8000	(021) 47-4060	(021) 47-8338
			Functional Holiday Inn		
Inn on the Square	★★★	170	Box 3775 Cape Town 8000	(021) 23-2040	(021) 23-3664
			On historic Greenmarket		
Metropole	★★★	39	Box 3086 Cape Town 8000	(021) 23-6363	(021) 23-6370
			Old-fashioned and warm		
Mount Nelson	★★★★★	31	Box 2608 Cape Town 8000	(021) 231000	(021) 24-7472
			Classy landmark hotel		
Park Avenue	★★★	32	Union Street Gardens 8001	(021) 24-1460	
			Convenient & comfortable		
St George's	★★★★	135/2	Box 5616 Cape Town 8000	(021) 419-0808	(021) 419-7010
			Central and modern		
Town House	★★★★	104	Box 5053 Cape Town 8000	(021) 45-7050	(021) 45-3891
			Quiet and tasteful		
Tulbagh Hotel	★★★	48/6	Tulbagh Sq Cape Town 8001	(021) 21-5140	
			Central but quiet		
CAPETOWN BEACH AREA *CITY MAP #3 - PAGE 103*					
Ambassador	★★★	64	Victoria Rd Bantry Bay 8001	(021) 439-6170	(021) 439-6336
			On cliffs overlooking sea		
Arthur's Seat	★★★	115/4	Arthur's Road Sea Point 8001	(021) 434-3344	(021) 439-9768
			Renovated hotel near sea		
Peninsula	P	112	Regent Road Sea Point 8060	(021) 462-4444	(021) 462-4593
			Recently built all-suite hotel		
President	★★★★★	127/26	Box 62 Sea Point 8060	(021) 434-1121	(021) 439-2919
			Beachfront hotel		
Ritz Protea	★★★★	216	Rhine Road Sea Point 8060	(021) 439-6010	(021) 434-0809
			Comfort near seafront		
The Bay	P	65/5	Box 21 Camps Bay 8040.	(021) 438-4444	(021) 438-4455
			Ritzy and new on Camps Bay		
Winchester	★★★	20/21	221 Beach Rd Sea Point 8001	(021) 434-2351	(021) 434-0215
			Family-style hotel near sea		
CAPE TOWN OUTSKIRTS *CITY MAP #3 - PAGE 103*					
Alphen	★★★	39	P O Box 35 Constantia 7848	(021) 794-5011	(021) 794-5710
			Famous Cape Dutch homestead		
Newlands Sun	★★★★	139/5	Main Road Newlands 7700	(021) 61-1105	(021) 641241
			Comfort in classy suburb		
The Vineyard	★★★	113	PO Box 151 Newlands 7725	(021) 64-21 07	(021) 683-3365
			18th Century Estate House		
DURBAN CITY *CITY MAP #4 - PAGE 108*					
Albany	★★★	72	252 Smith St Durban 4001	(031) 304-4381	
			Comfortable hotel in city		
Royal	★★★★★	250/18	Box 1041 Durban 4000	(031) 304-0331	(031) 307-6884
			Old, classy and classic		

HOTEL/INN RESORT	STARS N/R	ROOM/ SUITES	ADDRESS & ZIP	AREA CODE TELEPHONE	AREA CODE TELEFAX
DURBAN BEACH CITY MAP #4 - PAGE 108					
Beach Hotel	★★★	400	Box 10305 Marine Parade 4056 Large beachfront hotel	(031) 37-5511	(031) 62-2381
Blue Waters	★★★	262	Box 10201 Marine Parade4056 Well established beachfront hotel	(031) 32-4272	
Edward	★★★★	90/12	Marine Parade Durban 4000 Elegant beachfront hotel	(031) 37-3681	(031) 32-1692
Elangeni	★★★★	426/24	Snell Parade. Durban 4000 Swinging Southern Sun	(031) 37-1321	(031) 32-5527
Four Seasons	★★★	200	Box 10200 Marine Parade 4056 Comfortable beachfront hotel	(031) 37-3381	
Maharani	★★★★★	243/27	Box 10592 Marine Parade 4056 Swinging Sun with an extra touch	(031) 32-7361	(031) 62-2485
Malibu	★★★	380/8	Box 10199 Marine Parade 4056 Comfort near the beach	(031) 37-2231	(031) 62-0235
Marine Inn	★★★	336	Box 10809 Marine Parade 4056 Holiday Inn on beachfront	(031) 37-3341	(031) 62-1448
Ocean City Inn	★★★	265/3	Box 10222 Marine Parade 4056 Holiday Inn near beach	(031) 37-1211	(031) 62-0387
Tropicana	★★★★		Box 10305 Marine Parade 4056 Older, classy beachfront hotel	(031) 368-1511	(031) 37-2621
JOHANNESBURG CITY CITY MAP #5 - PAGE 115					
Braamfontein	★★★★	0/308	Box 32278 Braamfontein 2017 All-suite rotunda-shaped hotel	(011) 403-5740	(011) 403-5740
Carlton Hotel	★★★★★	663	Box 7709 Johannesburg 2000 Downtown at Carlton Center	(011) 331-8911	(011) 331-3555
Carlton Court	★★★★★		Box 7709 Johannesburg 2000 More exclusive part of Carlton	(011) 331-8911	(011) 331-3555
Devonshire	★★★★	64/2	Box 31197 Braamfontein 2017 Central and comfortable	(011) 339-8316	
Down Town Inn	★★★	224	Box 11026 Johannesburg 2000 Holiday Inn in city	(011) 333-8511	
Hillbrow Protea	★★★	121	Box 17145 Hillbrow 2038 In cosmopolitan downtown	(011) 643-4911	(011) 643-4911
Johannesburg Sun	★★★★★	666/126	Box 535 Johannesburg 2000 Ritzy downtown hotel	(011) 29-7011	(011) 29-0515
Johannesburger	★★★	385	Box 23566 Joubert Park 2044 Karos hotel near city center	(011) 725-3753	(011) 725-6309
Mariston	★★★	172/3	Box 23013 Joubert Park 2044 Comfortable near city center	(011) 725-4130	(011) 725-2921
Milpark Inn	★★★	224/2	Box 31556 Braamfontein 2017 Holiday Inn near universities	(011) 726-5100	(011) 726-8615
Park Lane	★★★	129	Box 17855 Hillbrow 2038 Modern downtown hotel	(011) 642-7425	(011) 643-4111
Protea Gardens	★★★★	214/95	Box17528 Hillbrow 2038 Garden setting near city	(011) 643-6611	(011) 484-2622
Rand International	★★★	143	Box 4235 Johannesburg 2000 Downtown hotel	(011) 29-2724	(011) 29-6815

HOTEL/INN RESORT	STARS N/R	ROOM/ SUITES	ADDRESS & ZIP	AREA CODE TELEPHONE	AREA CODE TELEFAX
JOHANNESBURG OUTSKIRTS *CITY MAP #6 - PAGE 121*					
Ascot	★★★	15	Box 95064 Randpark 2051 Small and personalized	(011) 483-1211	
Balalaika Protea	★★★	60	Box 65327 Benmore 2010 Comfortable and lively hotel	(011) 884-1400	(011) 884-1463
Gold Reef City	★★★★★	39/6	Box 61 Gold Reef City 2159 Hotel in recreated old city	(011) 496-1626	(011) 496-1626
Indaba Hotel	★★★	114	Box 67129 Bryanston 2021 Conference center and hotel	(011) 465-1400	(011) 705-1709
Rosebank Hotel	★★★	193/19	Box 52025 Saxonwold 2132 Pleasant and lively hotel	(011) 788-1820	(011) 788-4123
Holiday Inn	★★★	248	Box 781743 Sandton 2146 Vintage Holiday Inn style	(011) 783-5262	(011) 783-5289
Sandton Sun	★★★	296	Box 784902 Sandton 2196 Ritzy, stylish Southern Sun	(011) 783-8701	(011) 783-8701
Sunnyside Park	★★★	75/12	2 York Road Parktown 2193 Elegant former Milner residence	(011) 643-7226	(011) 642-0019
Airport Sun	★★★	237	Bag 5 Jan Smuts Airport 1627 Functional airport hotel	(011) 974-6911	(011) 974-8097
Holiday Inn Airport	★★★	358/4	Box 388 Kempton Park 1620 Refurbished & closest to airport	(011) 975-0112	(011) 975-5846
KIMBERLEY *CITY MAP #7 - PAGE 124*					
Colinton	★★	10	Box 400 Kimberley 8300 Small & personalized service	(0531) 3-1471	
Hanway House	★	12	Box 650 Kimberley 8300 Historic and small - drive-in pub	(0531) 2-5151	
Horseshoe Motel	★★	56	Box 67 Kimberley 8300 Comfortable and functional	(0531) 2-5267	
Kimberlite	★★	30	George St Kimberley 8300 Country style hotel - drive-in pub	(0531) 81-1967	
Kimberley Sun	★★★★	107/8	P O Box 63 Kimberley 8300 Stylish in garden setting	(0531) 3-1751	
Savoy	★★★★	43/2	P O Box 231 Kimberley 8300 Central and stylish	(0531) 2-6211	
PORT ELIZABETH *CITY MAP #8- PAGE 130*					
Algoa Protea	★★★	10	Lutman St Port Elizabeth 6001 Stylish central hotel	(041) 55-1558.	
Beach Hotel	★★★	63	Box 319 Port Elizabeth 6000 Traditional hotel on beach	(041) 53-2161	
Edward	★★	132	Box 319 Port Elizabeth 6000 Adjacent to Donkin Reserve	(041) 56-2056.	
Elizabeth Sun	★★★	210/18	Box 13100 Humewood 6013 Stylish Southern Sun hotel	(041) 52-3720.	
Holiday Inn	★★★	230/7	Marine Dr Summerstrand 6001 New beachfront hotel	(041) 52-3131	
Humewood Hotel	★★	69	Box 13023 Port Elizabeth 6013 One of older beachfront hotels	(041) 55 8961	
Hunter's Retreat	★★	7/2	Box 7044 Newton Park 6055 Smallish and intimate hotel	(041) 30-1244.	
Marine Protea	★★★	73	Box 501 Port Elizabeth 6000 On Summerstrand beachfront	(041) 53-2101	

HOTEL/INN RESORT	STARS N/R	ROOM/ SUITES	ADDRESS & ZIP	AREA CODE TELEPHONE	AREA CODE TELEFAX
PRETORIA *CITY MAPS #9 & 10 - PAGE 136, 140*					
Farm Inn	★★★	44/2	Box 71702 Die Wilgers 0041 In outskirts of Pretoria	(012) 807-0081	(012) 807-0081
Hotel Boulevard	★★★	77	Box 425 Pretoria 0001 Traditional hotel near center	(012) 326-4806	(012) 326-1366
Hotel Burgerspark	★★★★	232/6	Box 2301 Pretoria 0001 Central and busy	(012) 322-7500	(012) 322-9429
Holiday Inn	★★★	241	Box 40694 Arcadia 0007 New, central and functional	(012) 341-1571	(012) 44-7534
Manhattan Hotel	★★★	264	Scheiding St Pretoria 0002 Comfortable and convenient	(012) 322-7635	(012) 320-0721
Palms	★★★	69/4	Box 1 Silverton 0127 Several miles from Pretoria	(012) 87-1612	
Protea Hof Hotel	★★★	116	Box 2323 Pretoria 0001 Near city center	(012) 322-7570	(012) 322-9461
Victoria Hotel		8	Paul Kruger St Pretoria 0001 Restored landmark hotel	(012) 323-6052	(012) 323-0843
OTHER CITIES/TOWNS					
EAST LONDON Holiday Inn	★★★	170/2	Moore St East London 5201 Center of city	(0431) 2-7260	
Kennaway Protea	★★★	84/4	Box 583, East London 5200 Beachfront hotel	(0431) 2-5531	
GRAHAMSTOWN Cathcart Arms	★★	14	Box 143 Grahamstown 6140 Oldest licenses hotel in Cape	(0461) 2-7111	
PIETERMARITZBURG Camden	★★★	50	Box 2460 Pietermaritzburg 3200 City center and busy	(0331) 42-8921	
Karos Towers	★★★	108	P O Box 198 Pietermaritzburg 3200 City center and busy		(0331) 94-2761
GARDEN ROUTE					
ALBERTINIA Albertinia Hotel	★★		Main Street Albertinia 6795 Country Hotel	(02952) 30	(02952) 495
ARNISTON Arniston Hotel	★★★	23	Box 126 Bredasdorp 7280 Beach resort hotel	(02847) 5-9000	(02847) 5-9633
CALEDON De Overberger	★★★★		Box 7230 Caledon 7230 Victorian spa in scenic country	(0281) 4-1271	(0281) 4-1270
GEORGE Fancourt Hotel	★★★★★	30/7	Box 2266 George 6530 New on historic upmarket estate	(0441) 70-8282	(0441) 70-7605

HOTEL/INN RESORT	STARS N/R	ROOM/ SUITES	ADDRESS & ZIP	AREA CODE TELEPHONE	AREA CODE TELEFAX
GARDEN ROUTE CTD					
GREYTON					
Greyton Lodge		16	Box 50 Greyton 7233 Restored historic homestead	(02822) 9876	(02822) 9672
Post House		14	Main Road Greyton 7233 Converted 1860 Post Office	(02822) 9995	
HERMANUS					
Marine	★★	41/14	Box 9 Hermanus 7200 On beachfront	(0283) 2-1112	
KNYSNA					
Brenton-on-Sea	★★	30	Box 36 Knysna 6570 Beachfront near Knysna	(0445) 81-0081	
Knysna Protea	★★★	50/1	Box 33 Knysna 6570 Near lagoon	(0445) 2-2127	
MOSSEL BAY					
Eight Bells Inn	★★★	10/13	Box 436 Mossel Bay 6500 Horse riding tennis squash	(0444) 95-1544	
Santos Protea	★★★	58	Box 203 Mossel Bay 6500 Beachfront and comfortable	(0444) 7103	
OUDTSHOORN					
Holiday Inn	★★★	120	Box 52 Oudtshoorn 6620 Thirty km from Cango Caves	(04431) 2201	
Kango Protea	★★★	40	Box 370 Oudtshoorn 6620 Near center of town	(04431) 6161	
PLETTENBERG BAY					
Formosa Inn	★★	38	Box 121 Plettenberg Bay 6600 Chalet-type beach hotel	(04457) 3-2060	(04457) 3-3343
Plettenberg Hotel	★★★★		Box 719 Plettenberg Bay 6600 Elegant beach hotel	(04457) 32030	(04457) 32074
Beacon Island	★★★	189/8	Bag 1001 Plettenberg Bay 6600 Both time-share and regular	(04457) 3-1120	(04457) 3-1120
RIVERSDALE					
President	★★	22/1	Box 1 Riversdale 6770 Comfortable in center town	(02933) 3-2473	
Royal	★★★	12	Box 5 Riversdale 6770 Pool sauna and small	(02933) 3-2470	
SEDGEFIELD					
Lake Pleasant	★★	17	Box 2 Sedgefield 6573 Pool and tennis courts	(04455) 3-1313	
STORMS RIVER					
Tsitsikama Inn	★★		P O Storms River 6308 Historic in heart of forest	(04237) 711	(04237) 669
SWELLENDAM					
Swellengrebel	★★	51/1	Box 9 Swellendam 6740 In historic town	(0291) 41144	
WILDERNESS					
Karos Wilderness	★★★	160	Box 6 Wilderness 6560 Close to lakes and lagoon	(0441) 9-1110	

HOTEL/INN RESORT	STARS N/R	ROOM/ SUITES	ADDRESS & ZIP	AREA CODE TELEPHONE	AREA CODE TELEFAX
Holiday Inn	★★★	149	Box 26 Wilderness 6560 On beachfront	(0441) 9-1104	
RESORTS • GAMBLING					
MAFIKENG Mmabatho Sun		146/4	P O Box 600 Mafikeng 8670 Ethnic theme casino hotel	(01401)2-1142	(01401)2-1661
PORT ALFRED Fish River Sun	★★★★★	120	P O Box 323 Port Alfred 6170 Coastal casino resort golf etc	(0403)61-2101	
PORT EDWARD Wild Coast Sun		399	P O Box 23 Port Edward 4295 Coastal casino resort golf etc	(0471)512/519	
SUN CITY Kwa Maritane	★★★	.	P O Box 39 Sun City 0316 At Pilanesberg National Park	(014651)2-1820	(014651) 2-1483
Sun City Cascades	★★★★★	234/11	P O Box 7 Sun City 0316 Ritzy swimming golf etc	(014651)2-1000	(014651) 2-1483
Sun City Cabanas	★★★	284	P O Box 3 Sun City 0316 Quiet on man-made lake	(014651)2-1000	(014651) 2-1590
Sun City Hotel	★★★★★	300/40	P O Box 2 Sun City 0316 The original in this resort area	(014651)2-1000	(014651) 2-1470
RURAL TRANSVAAL					
PILGRIM'S REST Mount Sheba	★★★		Box 100 Pilgrim's Rest 1290 Time share and regular chalets	(0131532) x 17	Tx: 335638
HAZYVIEW Casa do Sol	★★★		Box 52890 Saxonwold 2132 Village resort near Kruger Park	(011) 880-2000	(011) 880-2000
Hotel Numbi	★★		Box 6 Hazyview 1242 Close Kruger Park	(0131242) x 6	Tx: 335507
Sabi River Hotel	★★★		Box 13 Hazyview 1242 Hotel & Country Club	(0131242) x 160	
MACHADODORP Bambi Protea	★★★		Box 98 Machadodorp 1170 Trout fishing enroute to Kruger	(013242) x101	Tx: 335507
MALELANE Malelane Lodge	★★★★	101/2	Box 392 Malelane 1320 Four star hotel next to Kruger	(013133) 2294	
NELSPRUIT Hotel Promenade	★★★	76	Box 4355 Nelspruit 1200 Comfortably near Kruger	(01311) 53000	(01311) 25533
Ngwane Valley Inn	★★★	42/1	Box 162 Nelspruit 1200 Close to Kruger Park	(013164) 5213	

HOTEL/INN RESORT	STARS N/R	ROOM/ SUITES	ADDRESS & ZIP	AREA CODE TELEPHONE	AREA CODE TELEFAX
RURAL TRANSVAAL CTD					
PLASTON Jatinga Lodge			Box 77 Plaston 1244 Country lodge near Kruger Park	(01311) 3-1963	(01311) 3-2364
SCHAGEN Old Joe's Kaia			Box 108 Schagen 1207 Rustic charm in Nelspruit area	(0131232) x 52	
WATERVAL BOVEN Malaga Hotel	★★★		Box 136 Waterval Boven 1195 Touch of Spain near Kruger	(013262) 431	
WHITE RIVER Cybele Lodge		9/5	Box 436 White River 1244 Mountain retreat near Kruger	(01311)50511	(01311) 32839
Hulala Lakeside	★★★		Box 1382 White River 1240 Country resort on lake	(01311) 5-1710	
Hotel Winkler	★★★		Box 12 White River 1240 Unique design on farmland	(01311) 32317	
Pine Lake Inn	★★★		Box 94 White River 1240 Golf and other sport facilities	(01311) 31186	
WINE COUNTRY					
FRANSCHHOEK Swiss Excelsior	★★	40	Box 54 Franschhoek 7690 Country hotel on wine estate	(02212) 2071/2	
MONTAGU Avalon Springs	★★★	12/29	Box 110 Montagu 6720 Situated in picturesque town	(0234) 41150	(0234) 41906
PAARL Grand Roche	P	29	Box 6038 Paarl 7620 Restored historic farmstead	(02211) 21694	(02211) 23494
Mountain Shadows		9	Box 2501 Paarl 7620 Historic manor house	(02211) 623192	(02211) 62-6796
SOMERSET WEST Lord Charles	★★★★★	188/10	Box 5151 Helderberg 7135 Upmarket in scenic country	(024) 51-2970	(024) 55-1107
STELLENBOSCH D'Ouwe Werf	★★★	26	Church St Stellenbosch 7600 Tastefully restored old mansion	(02231) 96120	(02231) 74626
Lanzerac	★★★	32/5	Box 14 Stellenbosch 7600 On old estate near town	(02231) 71132	
Stellenbosch Hotel	★★★	20	Box 500 Stellenbosch 7600 Ambience in landmark	(02231) 73644	
Wine Route Hotel	★★	47	Box 431 Stellenbosch 7600 In wine district near town	(02231) 95522	(02231) 95524
WORCESTER Cumberland	★★★	35/2	Box 8 Worcester 6850 Comfortable country hotel	(0231) 7-2641	

RESORTS & SPORTS

"Every December we're all off to South Africa to play about in the sunshine until April," wrote Rudyard Kipling to a friend many years ago.

Not everyone is as fortunate as the famous British author was to stay for months but many manage to fit in a week or two "playing about in the sunshine".

Beach resorts offer good swimming, surfing, fishing, golfing and other activities, while inland resorts have majestic mountains and lakes, hiking trails and other recreation.

South Africa ranks high in the world in sunshine days per year. Add to this unsurpassed beaches majestic mountain ranges and a rich variety of flowering plants and trees and it is not surprising that South Africans are outdoors people.

Visitors who wish to add onto their safari and sightseeing relaxing days in the sun, have a wide choice of resorts, while the sports-minded are assured of a whole range of interesting golf course, hiking trails and fishing areas.

There are also several health resorts where visitors are offered the opportunity to get into condition in unique surroundings. The most prestigious is one recently opened at Phalaborwa under the direction of the famous heart surgeon, Dr Christiaan Barnard.

BEACH RESORTS

For swimmers, surfers and sun-worshippers there are a variety of beach resorts to select from, varying from crowded ones such as the Durban or Cape Town beaches, especially during peak season, to other more secluded and remote beaches. The Indian Ocean on the Eastern Seaboard of South Africa is generally a few degrees warmer than the Atlantic ocean along the West Coast.

Surfing is good to excellent at all resorts, with the best waves in and around the area of Port Elizabeth. A few years ago a few sharks have caused some problems in the subtropical waters near Durban and prompted the authorities to install shark nets at several resorts. The remainder of the South Africa coastline has not had any significant shark presence or danger. Bathers will sometimes be cautioned against backwash caused by large waves.

Life-savers will be found at all popular beaches and visitors are cautioned not to venture far into the water at secluded ones unless accompanied by strong and experienced swimmers. They should also be careful of the African sun.

(For hotels and other accommodation at the various beach resorts see our Chapter STAYING IN STYLE and for sightseeing in major centers such as Port Elizabeth, Cape Town and Durban, read CITY SIGHTS. Restaurants are listed in WINING AND DINING).

CAPE PENINSULA
COASTAL MAP #1 - Page 193

The Cape Peninsula is not only known for its historic sights and scenic beauty. It has a number of popular beach resorts stretching from the Sea Point at the heel to Muizenberg at the bridge of its foot-shaped coastline.

Sea Point at the heel of the Peninsula, within a few minutes drive from Cape Town's center, is a well developed resort with sophisticated stores, deluxe hotels, interesting restaurants, ritzy boutiques and high-rise apartment buildings. The rocky beach does not make for good swimming and mostly used for sunbathing.

Bantry Bay, next door along the winding roadway, is a smallish, exclusive beach. Once again swimming is not its strong point, but it does offer atmosphere and even for skin-divers the possibility of crayfishing.

Clifton, next along the scenic route south, is perhaps one of the busiest stretches of sand in the Cape during peak season. There are four fashionable beaches, overlooked by stylish houses and apartment buildings nestling along the rockface above the sea. The water tends to be cold, even during early summer, but the waves are outstanding.

Camps Bay, next along the scenic route southwards, is a wide open beach facing several hotels and a desirable residential area. Popular with swimmers and surfers.

Llandudno is a smallish, exclusive beach resort 15 km further south. Situated along a sparsely populated coastline, it offers good bathing and surfing to visitors. There are no big hotels or apartment houses, but mostly residential properties. **Sandy Bay**, next door, has made a name for itself as the nude beach of the Cape. After several arguments with the authorities this form of bathing is now accepted norm for this beach.

Hout Bay is better known as a fishing community, but it also offers limited swimming along its beaches. Next along the drive to the south are **Kommetjie** and **Scarborough**, both residential areas with beaches.

After leaving Scarborough the road enters the Cape of Good Hope Nature Reserve and leads right down to the rocky cliffs of Cape Point. There are no bathing opportunities in this toe section of the Peninsula.

On the road back north towards Cape Town, visitors will encounter **The Boulders** area south of

Simon's Town with several inlets and secluded beaches between the rocks. **Fish Hoek** is a "dry" residential town (the only one in South Africa) with a pleasant beach. Further north is **St James** with a seaside hotel and popular beach favored by overseas visitors and eventually the winding road leads to **Muizenberg**. This resort is one of the busiest and most popular in peak season with its Pavilion at the center of the activity.

(For a description of the sights along the Peninsula Route see the Chapters on RURAL ROUTES and CITY SIGHTS).

COASTAL MAP #1

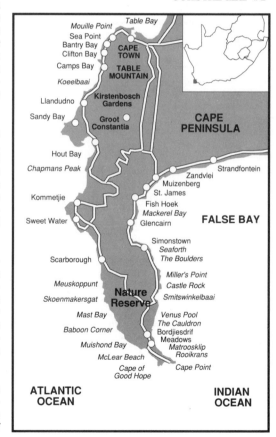

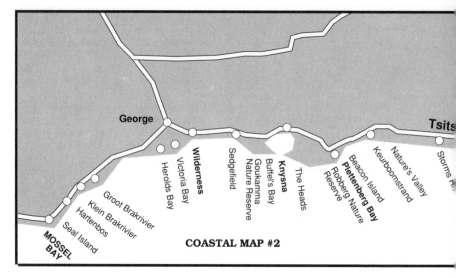

COASTAL MAP #2

EASTERN CAPE SEABOARD
COASTAL MAP #2 ABOVE

The Eastern Cape seaboard was first discovered by Portuguese explorer Bartholomeu Dias more than four hundred years ago when he planted a cross at Kwaaihoek, near Port Elizabeth. But is only recently that foreigners discovered the magnificent white stretches of sand, brilliant blue salty waters and towering waves that makes up most of this coastline along the Indian Ocean.

PERFECT WAVE

Some years ago a couple of ardent surfers set out from the United States on a world journey to try and find the "perfect wave'. Their search ended after they have tried all the famous surf waters of the world and chanced upon this long coastline. Here they found their perfect wave. The whole experience was filmed and eventually incorporated in a hit movie called *Endless Summer*.

There is no doubt any longer where the world's perfect waves are found. The beaches along the Cape eastern seaboard stretching north from Port Elizabeth to the Natal border and south towards Mossel Bay, include not only familiar ones such as Kings Beach and Humewood, but also more obscure but exotic ones such as Buffels Bay and Herold's Bay. Accommodation varies from camping sites to self-contained apartments and deluxe hotels.

PORT ELIZABETH

All three the main beaches are wide and open and provided with lifeguards. (Sharks are not a factor in these waters).

King's Beach offers a one mile stretch of pure white sand, supplemented with a fresh water pools and a tidal complex, supertube facilities, an amphitheater, waterslides and other entertainment, while **Humewood** borders recreational facilities such as an aquarium, snake park and museums. **Summerstrand** offers facilities for swimming, surfing and sailing.

South of Port Elizabeth within an hour's drive are resorts such as **Schoenmakerskop** (24 km) with interesting

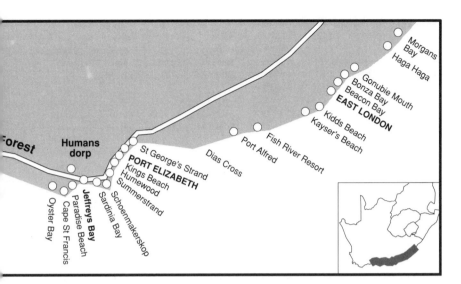

marine life and rock pools, and **Sardinia Bay**, favored by snorkelers. North within the city's orbit are **Blue Water Bay Beach**, **St. George's Strand** and the **Sundays River Resort** (44 km).

GARDEN ROUTE

The famous **Garden Route,** stretching for 400 km along one of the most spectacular coastlines in the world, has many interesting beach resorts that cater for both older and young vacationers.*(For sightseeing along the route, see RURAL ROUTES)* .

These are some of the resorts encountered along the route as visitors proceed from Mossel Bay in an northeastern direction along the route:

Mossel Bay has several attractive beaches offering opportunities for surfers, swimmers and shallow-water bathers.**Hartenbos, Kleinbrak River** and **Grootbrak River** are mostly frequented by the nearby farming community during the peak season. They all offer wide open and safe beaches. **Herold's Bay** and **Victoria Bay** are smaller, more exclusive resorts, while

Wilderness is a resort with beautiful homes and pleasant hotels. Nearby **Sedgefield** and **Buffels Bay** offer good swimming and surfing. **Plettenberg Bay** with its well-known **Beacon Island** has been developed into a major resort. **Jeffreys Bay**, about 45 minutes south by car from **Port Elizabeth**, is recognized as one of the world's most desirable surfing areas and attracts both local and international enthusiasts.

EAST LONDON

Port Alfred is situated on the outh of the Kowie River less than an hour north of Port Elizabeth. It offers a variety of activities ranging from bathing in the ocean to canoeing on the river. Nearby is the **Fish River Casino Resort**, while **East London** further east is a family resort with safe beaches. Within its orbit there are to the south, **Kidds Beach, Kayser's Beach**, **Christmas Rock** and **Chalumna Mouth** - all offering swimming and surfing. To the northeast are **Beacon Bay, Bonza Bay** and **Gonube Mouth**, about 25 km from East London.Further north are **Haga Haga** and **Morgan's Bay.**

SOUTH & WESTERN CAPE COAST
COASTAL MAP #3 ON THIS PAGE

In a southeasterly direction travelling from **Muizenberg** along the coast, the first beach encountered is **Zandvlei** and subsequently the long **Strandfontein** beach, popular with bathers and fishermen.

Next along the road is the **Strand**, a popular summer beach resort with good bathing. **Gordon's Bay** is a quaint resort with a small protected beach on the road winding towards Betty's Bay with its rocky coastline. Next in line is **Hermanus**, a well developed resort with stately houses and good hotels. Between Hermanus and Mossel Bay where the Garden Route begins, there are several small but interesting beach resorts including **Gansbaai, Pearly Beach, Struisbaai, Waenhuiskrans, Stilbaai** and **Gouritzmond.**

Driving north Cape Town visitors first encounter **Milnerton** and then **Bloubergstrand** (Blue Mountain Beach), probably the most photographed beach in the country as it offers an unobscured view of majestic Table Mountain.

Next in line is **Melkbosstrand** (Milkshrub beach) popular with the farming community as a venue for its annual New Year celebrations. This is a time for *Boeresport* (farmer's sport) on the beaches with events such as *skilpadtrek* (tortoise pull) - a kind of tug-of-war.

The big waves of **Ysterfontein** further up the western Cape coast have become popular with ardent surfers. Just north of the **Langebaan Lagoon** is a beach resort, Club Mykonos, styled after the Greek Isles, including a full range of facilities for residents of the time-share units. A smaller, exclusive development, Port Owen, is a few miles further north, near **Velddrif. Paternoste**r is a coastal village with a small beach and famous for its crayfish and perlemoen fishing.

COASTAL MAP #3

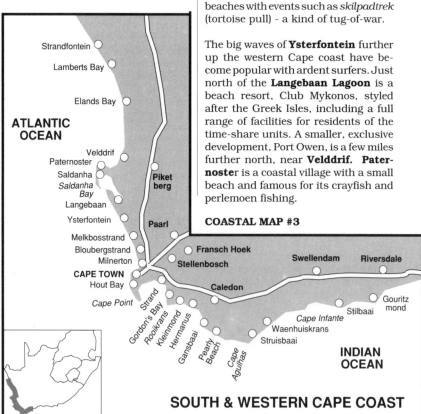

SOUTH & WESTERN CAPE COAST

Lamberts Bay with its wide beach and good fishing also happens to be the last stopover for Portuguese explorer Bartholomeu Dias before he aimed south and east in his discovery of a route around the Cape in 1487. This parochial family resort is developing into an attraction for tourists from around the country and overseas.

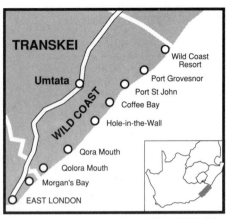

COASTAL MAP #4

WILD COAST
COASTAL MAP #4 ON THIS PAGE

This coastline runs along the eastern border of what is commonly known as Transkei, the independent state of the Xhosa and now destined to rejoin the New South Africa. This 300 km stretch of rugged wilderness and sandy white beaches along the Indian Ocean is a swimmer and surfers paradise and offers good hiking trails. It is still largely undeveloped apart from **Wild Coast Casino Resort** just south of the Natal border and a few medium-sized resorts. The most popular beaches are:

Qolora Mouth is an estuary opening up on a beach. This is the actual spot where Nongqwawuse, the young Xhosa girl claimed to have had the vision that eventually led to what became known as the National Suicide. There is a pool named after her. *(For further detail see the Chapter on HISTORIC TRAILS).* **Qora Mouth** is another small estuary with a pleasant beach, good fishing and surfing. It also provides hiking trails into the interior.

Hole-in-the-Wall graces many a calendar. The resort is named after a unique rock with waves pounding through a large hole. **Coffee Bay:** This beach against a backdrop of spectacular cliffs and mountains was named after a shipwreck incident when coffee bean cargo spilled onto the beach and

started growing in the area. It is known for its good swimming, surfing and fishing conditions.

Port St Johns: This resort is situated at the mouth of the Umzimvubu River and named after the ill-fated Portuguese ship St John that ran ashore here in 1552. The river is navigable and offers boating opportunities and fresh water swimming, apart from sea bathing from the beach.

Port Grosvenor is also named after a shipwreck. It has long been popular with divers before bathers discovered its qualities. In August 1782 the British ship, Grosvenor, struck the rocks along the shore and sank. It carried gold, jewels, coins and other precious cargo. Today the waters around this shipwreck are still the target of fortune hunters. (Although only 15 of the 123 on board drowned, the rest all perished and disappeared. There is speculation that some may have been assimilated by the native tribes in the region).

Wild Coast Resort: Situated on the Transkei-Natal border, this casino resort offers gambling, fresh and seawater swimming, angling, ski-boating, golfing and cabaret to fun and sun seekers.

NATAL BEACHES
COASTAL MAP #5 ON OPPOSITE PAGE

Between Durban's South and North Coast is the Golden Mile which provides swimming and entertainment to thousands of holiday-makers from the Transvaal and Orange Free State.

To the north of the city starting with Umhlanga are several popular beaches in a stretch of coastline commonly referred to as the North Coast. South of the city, beginning with Amanzimtoti are a whole range of beach resorts stretching as far as Port Edward. In the old days the whole area was simply known as the South Coast, but more recently the coastline has been divided rather arbitrarily into the South, Sunshine and Hisbiscus Coast.

DURBAN

The **Golden Mile** actually stretches for almost four miles from **South Beach** to **North Beach** along the city's coastline with names ranging from Brighton and Anstey's Beach to Addington and Blue Lagoon, and is probably South Africa's most heavily populated beach resort area during peak vacation periods. As one of the prime destinations for Transvaal and Orange Free State residents, it offers good bathing and surfing behind shark nets. The Golden Mile comprises a number of elegant hotels, walkways, restaurants and informal eating places, nightclubs, play parks and lawns, pavilions, piers, seawater pools, and stores - all geared to entertaining holiday makers. *(See CITY MAP #4 - Page 108).*

NORTH COAST

The coastline north of Durban has a number of popular beaches, ranging from the crowded Umhlanga Rocks to the increasingly popular, but still relatively quiet and remote Shaka's Rock.

Umhlanga Rocks offers several luxury hotels, good swimming and surfing behind shark nets. There are a variety of good stores and more than 30 restaurants. **Umdloti** has good beaches and a tidal pool, while **Tongaat** is relatively quiet with good swimming. **Ballito** is a newly developed resort with several beaches and offers swimming, surfing and fishing opportunities while **Shaka's Rock** is a quiet undeveloped beach resort.

SOUTH OF DURBAN

On the coastline south of Durban there are a number of popular beach resorts ranging from the larger more developed Amanzimtoti to the smaller more rustic Umkomaas. While the South Coast used to comprise everything south of Durban new names have sprung up for different parts of this popular coastline. Today the coast is divided into *South Coast,* immediately south of Durban, followed by the *Sunshine Coast* and the *Hibiscus Coast.*

SOUTH COAST

The beaches in and around **Amanzimtoti** are known as the South Coast. They all have shark nets, good surfing, rock and beach fishing, deluxe hotels and apartments. There is also a lagoon with boats for rental. (Shaka reportedly gave the resort its name when commenting to his troops many years ago while drinking cool water at the river mouth *Kantil amanzi a mtoti.* (So, the water is sweet).

SUNSHINE COAST

Starting with Kingsburgh and stretching as far as Hibberdene the Sunshine Coast has a variety of interesting resorts. **Kingsburgh** has several beaches with good surfing in shark-protected waters - **Doonside, Warner beach, Winkelspruit, Illovo** and **Karridene.** Warner Beach offers bathing and boating in a lagoon, while the **Winkelspruit** beaches with its tree-lined shores provides good hiking trails. **Karridene** has a lagoon and Illovo is known for its fishing and two shark-net protected bathing areas, surfing, angling and tidal pools. **Umkomaas** does not offer sea bathing but has tidal pool, while **Scottburgh** has facilities for sea bathing and surfing as well as pools

THE HIBISCUS COAST

An eighty km stretch of beaches from Hibberdene to Port Edward all provide swimming and surfing and often fishing facilities.

Hibberdene is a quiet resort with tidal pools, woodlands, wide beaches, a lagoon and an amusement park, while **Umzumbe** is a quiet resort with good swimming from several beaches. **Banana Beach** bordered by banana plantations, offers bathing and surfing. Between **Bendigo** and **Southport** there are four different beaches offering good swimming conditions.

Umtentweni is a secluded mainly residential resort with good swimming and surfing. **Port Shepstone** is a popular resort at the mouth of the Umzimkulu River offering sea and fresh water swimming and water sports. The river is navigable for several miles. **Shelly Beach** is the venue of South Africa's largest ski-boat club.

The river and lagoon at **St. Michael's-on-the-Sea** are popular with both surfers and wind-surfers, while **Uvongo** at the Vungu River Falls offers surfing and

swimming from a secluded beach. **Margate** is the focal point of the Hibiscus Coast and offers apart from swimming and surfing a whole variety of amusement parks and entertainment in restaurants and discos.

Ramsgate on the Mbezane lagoon is favored by wind-surfers and its long beach-front offers swimming and surfing.

Port Edward situated on the Umtamvuna River that separates Natal from the Cape (actually the Transkei) offers swimming and surfing.

South of the river, is the popular Wild Coast casino resort. *(See WILD COAST and GAMBLING in this CHAPTER).*

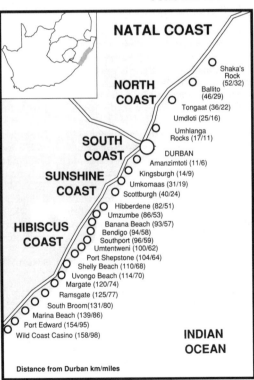

COASTAL MAP #5

NATAL COAST

NORTH COAST

○ Shaka's Rock (52/32)
○ Ballito (46/29)
○ Tongaat (36/22)
Umdloti (25/16)

SOUTH COAST

○ Umhlanga Rocks (17/11)
○ DURBAN
○ Amanzimtoti (11/6)
○ Kingsburgh (14/9)

SUNSHINE COAST

○ Umkomaas (31/19)
○ Scottburgh (40/24)

HIBISCUS COAST

○ Hibberdene (82/51)
○ Umzumbe (86/53)
○ Banana Beach (93/57)
○ Bendigo (94/58)
○ Southport (96/59)
○ Umtentweni (100/62)
○ Port Shepstone (104/64)
○ Shelly Beach (110/68)
○ Uvongo Beach (114/70)
○ Margate (120/74)
○ Ramsgate (125/77)
○ South Broom(131/80)
○ Marina Beach (139/86)
○ Port Edward (154/95)
Wild Coast Casino (158/98)

INDIAN OCEAN

Distance from Durban km/miles

FISHING

Angling is one of South Africa's most popular sports. About 250 species of freshwater fish in Southern Africa, and 1500 oceanic species have been identified along its coastline.

Trout fishing is inexpensive and mostly done in the southern mountain ranges of the western Cape, the foothills of Natal's Drakensberg Mountains and several parts of the Transvaal. Bass fishing compares favorably with international conditions.

Some of the country's game and nature reserves have dams, rivers or even a coastline - where fishing is allowed. *(For specific reserves offering fishing see ON SAFARI).*

LICENSES

Licences are not required for sea angling but there is a closed season for at least one type of fish - galjoen. Freshwater angling licences are obtainable at offices of the Receiver of Revenue and Magistrate's Courts in the various districts.

Regulations regarding size and bag limits vary from one area to another and are strictly enforced.

Most of the trout waters in the Transvaal are private and permits have to be obtained from the owners of the areas adjoining the fishing streams.

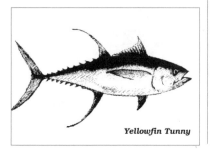
Yellowfin Tunny

CAUTION

While nobody would consider the mountain streams or inland fishing waters particularly hazardous and fishing from the beaches hardly present any mentionable dangers, rock angling in South Africa is only for the experienced and careful.

Beacons and crosses abound on the rocks between Hangklip and Gordons Bay, near Cape Town, as grim reminders of fishermen who perished while trying to land a few big ones. Anyone who wishes to go fishing in this area (and most other rocky shorelines) are well advised not to go alone. A preoccupied fisherman can easily be swept off the rocks by unexpected waves.

As elsewhere in the world visiting anglers will find the locals very amenable to spending time with them on the rocks.

SEA CATCHES

Rooikrans near Cape Point is probably one of the very few spots in the world where an angler can drop a line straight down into deep waters and get a tunny on the hook. Also Plettenberg Bay, Port Elizabeth, Durban and Mossel Bay yield these big ones.

While wind conditions in various parts of the country influence catches from the beach, high tides early in the morning or late in the afternoon are usually the best conditions for fishing at most spots.

Along the upper portion of the South African coastline stretching from East London northwards fish can be caught throughout the year, while the rest tends to be seasonal. The best yield along the Eastern Cape coastline is during summer, while the best time for fishing along western seaboard is during winter.

TYPES

Apart from trout and bass in fresh water fishing areas, the following types of fish are among the more popular species caught off the South African coastline:

Baardman	Eastern Cape, Natal
Banded Galjoen	Wild Coast & Natal
Musselcracker	Cape, Natal
Blacktail	South Cape, Natal
Galjoen	Cape, Natal
Giant Kingfish	Natal
Hottentot	West & South Cape
King Mackerel	Wild Coast, Natal
Kingklip	Cape
Queenfish	Natal
Rock Cod	Eastern Cape, Natal
Shad	Cape, Natal
Stumpnose	Natal
Tunny	Cape
Yellowtail	Cape, Natal
Zebra	Cape, Natal

For further information about trout fishing, rock and surf angling, game, deep sea and spear fishing, visitors should contact the *South African Anglers Union, 26 Douglas St, ,Horison View, Roodepoort 1725. Tel. (011) 726-5000 or the bodies specializing in the various forms of angling. (See SPORTS ORGANIZATIONS in our chapter on KEY ADDRESSES).*

GAMBLING

Several casinos cater to visitors who wish to include gambling among their pursuits while on tour in South Africa. These resorts are all situated in the black or tribal homelands as South Africa itself has steadfastly prohibited any form of gambling even down to lottery level. This may of course change as the government has invited these homelands back into a united New South Africa.

At the same time horse races are not only condoned but have grown into great social events and serve as the showgrounds of the wealthy and the playgrounds of the hopefuls.

For casino gambling visitors have a choice between the biggest and most well-known resort, Sun City in Bophuthatswana, to the newer and lesser known Fish River Casino Resort in the Ciskei. Apart from gambling these resorts all offer a variety of other pursuits ranging from golf to tennis and swimming and other water sports, either in man-made lakes or in the sea. *(For a listing of casino resorts see our Chapter STAYING IN STYLE).*

HORSE RACING

Several cities have race courses.In the Johannesburg area visitors have a choice between Turffontein, Gosforth Park and Newmarket and in Cape Town the Ascot Milnerton), Durbanville and the Kenilworth courses. The latter is famous for its annual Metropolitan Handicap where the focus is as much on the off-track fashions as the on-track races.

Durban's Greyville Race Course every year captures national attention with its July Handicap. It is probably the only race course in the world that surrounds an eighteen hole championship golf course. Although private, the Royal Durban Golf Club is open to visitors on certain conditions - as are other interesting South African courses.

GOLF

Step out on a recently built super golf course and chances are that the designer may have been Gary Player. The famous sportsman has left his imprint on the golfing landscape, not only in South Africa, but around the world.

His designs incorporate natural features instead of dominating them. This approach makes for beauty and tranquility and a test for all levels of play.

But Player is not only a man for courses, but causes. Having excelled against heavy odds, the small man with the big heart and massive record continues to be a fighter for causes.

Since 1965 when he returned his winner's purse at the US Open to the USGA for cancer research and the promotion of the game of golf, Player has been involved. His actions include the establishment of black schools and creation of opportunities for the less privileged.

Currently Gary Player Golf Academies are being established at selected resorts in South Africa, the United States, Far East and Europe. As one of the world's best shotmakers around the green, Player focuses on this area where 75% of all shots are played. His approach incorporates both the mental and physical. *The Academy has offices in Johannesburg (Tel. 011-883-7220) and New York (Tel. 212-541-5640).*

Courses in South Africa range from British-style links, where the unpredictable weather can turn easy holes into nightmares, to elevated courses on the Transvaal Highveld, where short hitters become super drivers in thin air. On some courses animal life comes into play as monkeys grab balls and disappear with them and at least one course saw fit to post a warning sign at a water hazard:*Beware of Hippos and Crocodiles.*

Cape Town sports a few links-type courses where visitors from Britain may well be thinking that they have never left home. Natal, on the other hand, is ever lush and green as subtropical regions tend to be and it shows in the manicured perfection of its golf courses. In the Transvaal winters may cause the fairways to turn brown, but winter grass ensures green greens during all seasons.

DESIGNS

Added to the charm and atmosphere of the old courses, dating back to the turn of the century, there are among the newer courses a whole crop of very attractive and demanding courses. Several of these are the creations of Gary Player who contributed so much to the game of golf not only in South Africa but elsewhere in the world. His latest is the 27-hole Fancourt Country Club near George, which has been compared to Augusta both in style and sheer beauty.

RESERVATIONS

As always, it is prudent to call the professionals at any of these course beforehand to make reservations. Some may require overseas country club references, while others don't. Some may indeed require an introduction by a local member. In any event, it is prudent for visitors who belong to country clubs to take along proof of their membership.

CARTS & CADDIES

Although the Gary Player Country Club and other resort courses have golf carts readily available, they are not widely used in South Africa. Some courses do not allow carts at all, while others limit their use to members with valid medical reasons.

Caddies are readily available and quite often very helpful not only in finding stray balls but in giving advice on all aspects of the course. Caddy fees vary from one course to another. For those who prefer to go it alone and have not taken along a light carry bag, there are pull carts.

RENTAL CLUBS

Pro shops at all the major courses have clubs for rental. *(Course distances are indicated on the cards in meters and some overseas visitors may have to practise the conversion table provided on page 238).*

DRESS & WEATHER

Mode of dress is the same as elsewhere. Depending on the season, either long or short pants are worn. It is wise to pack a windbreaker and waterproof garb and to take an umbrella along if you wish to play on any of the coastal links-type courses, where the weather can turn nasty without warning.

Barring the occasional quick thunderstorm, weather at inland courses is steady and usually consistent with forecasts.

Leave the course when storm clouds start building up as lightning can be dangerous, especially in the Johannesburg region.

Keep in mind, also, that although most private clubs have loosened up a bit, some have remained true to the old British custom of insisting on jackets in the dining rooms and certain other areas of the club house. Also, there are some who persist in allowing ladies to play only on certain days of the week.

Gary Player

Born into a South African family of modest income he became only the third man to have all four majors on his list when he won the US Open Golf Championship at Bellerive in St. Louis in 1965. (Nicklaus subsequently joined the ranks of these all-time greats).

Gary Player was one of the original thirteen golfers inducted into the World Golf Hall of Fame in 1974. His golf career has taken him some eight million miles around the world since the mid-fifties. Today he continues to add titles on the Seniors Tour to his record of more than 150 regular tournament wins in twelve different countries.

His major championships include three British Opens, one US Open, two US PGA wins and three Masters victories. Also on the list are seven Australian Opens and thirteen South African Opens.

For three years in a row (1961, 1962, 1963) he had the lowest stroke average in the world. In South Africa he was honored as the Sportsman of the Century in 1990.

He divides his time between extensive and varied business interests, golf tournaments, thoroughbred horse breeding, wife Vivien and his growing family of six children and several grandchildren.

COURSES
SEE GOLF MAP - PAGE 206

Following is a selection of some of the best known courses among the 440 registered golf clubs around the country:

JOHANNESBURG AREA

1. Bryanston Golf Club
Bryanston Drive, Bryanston 2021.
Tel: (011) 706-1361/2/3 or 706-6070/1.
Relatively open fairways and favoring big drives. Water comes into play on 12 holes. Close to Sandton and Johannesburg.

2. Crown Mines Golf Club
Booysens Reserve Rd, Johannesburg.
Tel. (011) 835-1371
Long course with water a factor on 11 holes. Greens are sown with year-round bent grass. About 6 km from city.

3. Germiston Country Club
Chapman Drive, Germiston.
Tel: (011) 827 8950/1
Established in 1898 and oldest in the Transvaal. Layout incorporates Germiston Lake. Half hour drive from Johannesburg.

4. Glendower Golf Club
Marais Road, Bedfordview, Johannesburg
Telephone (011) 453-1013
Situated in bird sanctuary with small river crossing fairways. About 20 minutes from city center.

5. Houghton Golf Club
2nd Ave, Lower Houghton, Johannesburg.
Tel: (011) 728-73371819/(011)728-3555
Site for many South African Opens and other major tournaments. Near city center, Houghton is long, testing course.

6. Johannesburg Country Club
Lincoln Street, Woodmead, Sandton.
Tel: (011) 803 3018
New course completed in 1985. Championship lay-out has already hosted several major championships, including SA Skins in 1986 and 1987.

7. Kensington Golf Club
Langerman Dr, Kensington, Johannesburg.
Telephone (011) 6164000/1.
Relatively short course with out-of-bounds fence alongside 8 holes, demanding accuracy. In the suburbs of Johannesburg.

8. Killarney Golf Club
60, 5th St, Lower Houghton, Johannesburg.
Tel: (011) 442-7411/(011) 442-8778.
Narrow course with water hazards on 11 holes and several sloping fairways. Close to city center.

9. Parkview Golf Club
Emmarentia Ave, Parkview, Johannesburg.
Tel: (011) 646 5400
For many years had as its club champion Bobby Locke. Willow trees and small river. Within easy reach of city and suburbs.

10. Randpark Golf Club
Setperkweg, Randburg.
Telephone (011) 67-5361/2.
Comprises two courses: Old Windsor Course with narrow fairways and tall trees and new Randpark Course with long and relatively open fairways. Within half hour from city center.

11. Roodepoort Country Club
Helderkruin, Roodepoort.
Tel: (011)662-1990/662-1507
New championship course opened in 1988 with water in play on 8 holes. About three-quarter hour drive from city center.

12. Royal Johannesburg Golf Club
Fairway Ave, Linksfield N, Johannesburg.
Tel: (011) 640-3021.
Comprises two courses, East and West. As venue for SA Opens and other major tournaments, East Course is more challenging than West Course. Half hour from city.

13. Wanderers Golf Club
Kent Park, Illovo, Johannesburg
Tel: (011) 447-3311
One of the oldest in South Africa and permanent venue for the SA PGA. Undulating, long and quite narrow tree-lined fairways. Near city center.

SUN CITY

14. Gary Player Country Club
Sun City, Pilanesberg, Bophuthatswana
Tel: (014651) 2100
Gary Player-designed course at casino. Site for Million Dollar Classic. Visitors have a choice of the tough championship configuration or three easier tee placements.

PRETORIA

15. Pretoria Country Club
Sydney Avenue, Waterkloof, Pretoria
Tel: (012) 46 6241
Set against the north-facing hills of capital city, water comes into play on several holes and the greens are planted with year-round grass. 15 minutes from Pretoria.

16. Wingate Park Country Club
Eastern suburbs, Pretoria.
Tel: (012) 982001
Long narrow course in a sloping wooded valley on outskirts of Pretoria. Easily accessible from Johannesburg by highway.

17. Zwartkop Country Club
Johannesburg/Pretoria Rd. Verwoerdburg.
Tel: (012) 641152/3/ (012) 642111
Named after the Zwartkop birds on property. River and trees come into play. Midway between Johannesburg and Pretoria.

PHALABORWA

18. Hans Merensky Golf Club
Molengraaf Road, Phalaborwa 1390
Tel. (01524) 5931
On Kruger Park border, carved out of rugged Lowveld terrain. Probably only course in the world warning players at water hazards against hippos and crocodiles!

NELSPRUIT

19. Nelspruit Golf Club
Wilhelm Street, Nelspruit.
Tel: (01311) 53345/22048.
Popular among visitors to game parks in the area. Extensive watering keeps this course in dry terrain green and lush.

CAPE TOWN AREA

20. Milnerton Golf Club
Bridge Road, Milnerton, Cape.
Tel: (021) 52-1097/8 (021) 52-3108.
Only genuine links in South Africa. Table Mountain forms background to championship course, squeezed between the sea and a meandering river.

21. Mowbray Golf Club
Ratenberg Road, Mowbray, Cape.
Tel: (021) 531-6491 (021) 531-4171.
Relatively short, even from the championship tees, but has a par rating of 74. Bisected by a railway line and teems with trees and strategically placed bunkers.

He is considered by experts as the best putter of all time, South African golfer Locke beat the likes of Hogan and Snead at the peak of their

Bobby Locke

careers with his magic wand on the greens. The gentlemanly figure in the plus-fours dominated the European golf scene for many years and did quite nicely during excursions to the United States.

To those in the America who blamed his awkward swing to a weak left hand, he used to say: "I accept checks with my right hand."

Four-time British Open winner, Bobby Locke was followed in the sixties by another rising star, Gary Player, who still electrifies the world golf scene.

22. Rondebosch Golf Club
Klipfontein Road, Mowbray 7700
Tel: (021) 689-9868
Links-type course set against Table Mountain offering a mix of tight driving holes and long fairways. Close to city.

23. Royal Cape Golf Club
174 Ottery Road, Wynberg.
Tel: (021) 71-6551(021) 761-6552.
Narrow fairways lined by trees and thick shrubs and undergrowth and venue for major professional tournaments. Near city.

STELLENBOSCH

24. Stellenbosch Golf Club
Strand Road, Stellenbosch 7600.
Tel: (02231) 3279/(02231) 2212
Near town against backdrop of mountains and surrounded by vineyards. Water on only 2 holes and lots of trees.

KNYSNA

25. Knysna Golf Club
Howard Street, Knysna.
Tel: (0445) 22391.
Situated along the popular Garden Route, this course nestles between rolling green hills and overlooks the Knysna Lagoon.

PORT ELIZABETH

26. Humewood Golf Club
Marine Drive, Port Elizabeth.
Tel: (041) 53-2137/8.
Links-type course separated from the beach by Marine Drive. Wide undulating long fairways and heavy rough .

27. Port Elizabeth Golf Club
Westview Drive, Port Elizabeth.
Tel: (041) 343140
Hilly course presents a stiff test on both still and windy days.

GOLF MAP

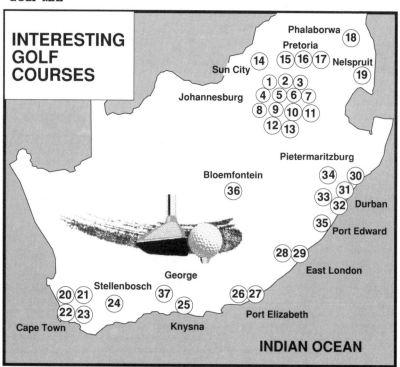

EAST LONDON

28. East London Golf Club
P.O. Box 226, East London.
Tel. (0431) 5-3350
Hosted many SA Amateur Championships since 1898. Challenging course.

29. Alexander Golf Club
Clovelly Road, Sunnyside, East London.
Tel: (0431) 46-2141
Long, open fairways favor longer hitters. Traversed by a river that comes into play on 4 holes.

DURBAN AREA

30. Durban Country Club
Walter Gilbert Road, Durban.
Tel: (031) 23-8282
Classic country course within city limits where on occasion playful monkeys may grab and disappear with a ball.

31. Huletts Country Club
P.O. Box Mount Edgecombe 4300
Tel: (031) 595331
Attractive course situated in hills about 20 minutes from Durban. Recently both course and the club house were remodelled.

32. Kloof Country Club
P O. Box 3, Kloof 3640.
Tel. 74-1328/86
Short course, but demanding. Hosted many Natal amateur golf events. About 20 minutes from Durban.

33. Royal Durban Golf Club
Mitchell Crescent, Greyville, Durban.
Telephone (031) 3091373.
Only course in the world surrounded by race track. Forms the inner core of the well-known Greyville Race Track.

PIETERMARITZBURG

34. Maritzburg Country Club
Duncan McKenzie Dr, Pietermaritzburg.
Tel: (0331) 47-1942
Sloping fairways situated in a wooded valley with water hazards on several holes.

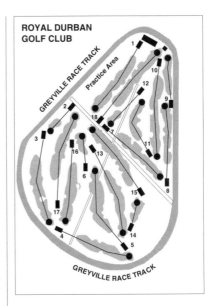

ROYAL DURBAN GOLF CLUB

PORT EDWARD

35. Wild Coast Country Club
Mzamba Beach, Port Edward 4295.
Tel (0471) 511 ext. 173.
Part of the Wild Coast gambling resort and designed by world-renowned golf course architect, Robert Trent Jones.

BLOEMFONTEIN

36. Bloemfontein Golf Club
Mazelspoort Road, Bloemfontein.
Tel: (051) 33-2907/33-2013
Changed venues several times until it Computerized irrigation and greens covered with bent grass.

GEORGE

36. Fancourt Country Club
Montagu Street George 6350
Tel. (04441) 708-8282

27-hole course designed by Gary Player as part of Fancourt Estate with antique farmstead inn and luxury condominiums. Streams, pools, towering oaks and flowers creates Augusta atmosphere.

HUNTING

So what does a piece on hunting do in this section? What does it do in a travel guide dedicated to ecotourism? In his foreword to *Wildlife Crisis*, published in conjunction with the World Wildlife, Prince Philip reveals that as a hunter in his youth he *"learnt the fundamental lesson of conservation."* This lesson, he says, is *"that if you want any game animals the following year you have to ensure a proper breeding stock and a suitable habitat."*

"Looking back now," he writes, *"it doesn't surprise me to find how many amateur naturalists came into it through shooting, stalking or fishing."*

Says the Duke of Edinborough: *"I am always amazed that so many towns-people seem to be incapable of understanding that hunting and conservation are now entirely compatible so far as conservation is concerned. They simply will not, or do not wish to recognize that in most parts of the world the leadership in conservation has come from experienced hunting sportsmen."*

CONSERVATION

In South Africa hunting and conservation have never been mutually exclusive. At times of course, indiscriminate killing has threatened certain species with extinction and in at least a few actually obliterated creatures without cause.

Cornwallis Harris

The tale of the now extinct quagga is as senseless and sad as the extermination of the passenger pigeon in the United States. Also antelope such as blesbok and bontebok would have followed the quagga into extinction if it weren't for a few thoughtful farmers who preserved a handful of these animals to serve as breeding stock.

In recent years, however, South Africa has done better than most of its peers, not only in Africa, but world-wide, in nurturing and protecting its wildlife.

Nowadays an over-abundance of animals in certain regions necessitates thinning out to prevent over-grazing, while in others a preponderance of predators over prey calls for culling.

SUPERVISION

In South Africa's game reserves this culling process is done under the strict supervision of the conservation authorities. In cases where outside hunters are invited to undertake trophy shooting the fees collected go straight into conservation. Where the game rangers do the culling themselves the sale of ivory, horns, skins, meat and other usable products also goes towards conservation and parks development.

As with those farmers who saved the bontebok and the blesbok, other enterprising folk have started game farms where they allow hunting on a strictly controlled basis. - pumping earnings back into these undertakings. This is not only good business, but makes land available to wildlife that would otherwise be utilized solely for domesticated stock.

EARLY TIMES

Before the white man arrived and settled at the Cape in 1652, Hottentot and Bushmen hunters were living in harmony with nature. Killing for food and clothing with their primitive bows and arrows and spears they never posed any serious threat to the teeming wildlife around them.

Then the Europeans started moving inland with their flint-lock guns and determination to "civilize" the land. Soon the large herds of antelope and zebra were targeted for eradication by farmers who felt that *they* were *intruding* on valuable grazing land. And predators were killed because they posed a threat to cattle and sheep. Founder Van Riebeeck saw the need to restrict hunting and his Dutch successors followed suit.

SPORTSMEN

In the 19th century when the British took control, the first sportsmen hunters started arriving in the border regions of the Eastern Cape.

Sir William Cornwallis Harris was not only one of the first but a good example of a responsible and discriminate hunter.

He was not only a hunter. He was an artist and a gentleman - and a conservationist. He wrote books which he illustrated himself.

Apart from his *Narrative of an expedition into Southern Africa*, Harris produced two other illustrated animal books. He discovered the sable antelope and sent a specimen and description to the London Zoological society.

ROOSEVELT

At the turn of the century, American President Teddy Roosevelt showed the same respect for animals while hunting in Africa. On safari in 1909 and 1910 he would only shoot for food and to collect specimens for display in American museums.

Teddy Roosevelt

In South Africa another enthusiastic hunter, President Paul Kruger set aside a large tract of land for wildlife conservation - over the objections of his farmer constituents, who saw it as a waste. The Kruger National Park today stands as a monument to a responsible hunter's farsightedness. *(See the chapter ON SAFARI).*

CONTROLS

South Africa is the only country where the entire Big Five may be hunted. (The Big Five are considered to be the most dangerous animals in Africa. They are, in alphabetical order: *Buffalo, elephant, leopard, lion and rhino).* South Africa also offers a variety antelope.

Hunting in all four provinces is tightly controlled by Nature Conservation Departments. To be issued with licenses South African professional hunters and outfitters must pass two written examinations showing sufficient knowledge of game animals, their habits, social behavior, breeding cycles; the preparation and care of trophies; the legal requirements for exporting trophies; and of the laws pertaining to hunting.

After passing these written examinations, candidates have to complete a practical test to prove a thorough knowledge of the wilds and animal behavior, tracking, firearms and first aid.

Specific standards are set for hunting camps, trophy preparation facilities, vehicles and staff. Prior to the hunt, the outfitter and his client are required to enter into a written agreement, stipulating the species and sex of game offered, fees for trophies and services provided, duration of hunt and daily rates. The local nature conservation authorities welcome enquiries and will investigate any complaints:

Cape Province:*Nature Conservation, Bag 9086, Cape Town, Tel.(021) 450217.*

Natal:*Parks Board, Box 662, Pietermaritzburg 3200, Tel. (0331) 5 1221/2.*

Orange Free State:*Conservation, Box 517, Bloemfontein ,Tel. (051) 47 0511.*

Transvaal:*Nature Conservation, Private Bag X209, Pretoria, Tel. (012) 201 2469.*

PHASA

The Professional Hunters' Association of South Africa (PHASA) is the official organ of South Africa's professional hunting fraternity. Members subscribe to the following goals set by the Association:

To conserve the game and flora To safeguard the client and particularly the non-resident client To promote the ethical conduct of hunting and to countenance only the fair chase. To maintain a high standard of professional service .

Gemsbok by Harris (Africana Museum)

The Association qualifies an animal as a properly hunted trophy when the following points apply: *It must be able to breed and feed naturally and have a sporting chance of evading the hunter.*

Professional hunters joining the Association as full members are required to furnish proof of experience and the names of satisfied clients to the Executive Committee. *The Professional Hunters' Association of South Africa, Box 770, Cremerview 2060, Tel. (011) 706-7724/5, Fax. (011) 706-1389.*

HUNTING TIPS

Trophy hunting is carried out throughout the year in South Africa, but the **peak season** is during the drier period between March and the end of October. Days are pleasant and nights tend to be cold. **Insurance** cover, if required, should be arranged before the trip. **Arms and ammunition import permits** are obtainable at the South African airport of entry. Firearms may be brought in on a temporary permit valid for the duration of the hunt. No prior clearance is required. One good rifle between the calibres of .300 and .375 is ideal and can cope with any animal up to the size of a buffalo. Rifles and shotguns may also be rented from most outfitters. Reputable taxidermists will prepare, mount and arrange export permits for **trophies.**

South Africa meets the CITES' international requirements. Before leaving on their trip hunters should obtain details on the importation of any trophies from their own authorities. **Practical clothing** for hunters are three pairs of trousers, three bush shirts, one warm jacket, socks, underwear, one balaclava and one safari hat, as well as one pair comfortable lightweight hunting boots or shoes. Medium khaki to dark green is preferable as bright colors stand out too much whilst tracking game in the bush.

OTHER SPORTS

For sport enthusiasts who do not wish to miss out on their favorite activity while on tour, or those planning a trip around different forms of outdoor and indoor recreation, there are ample opportunities in South Africa.

Tennis courts are available at hotels, resorts, clubs and many private homes. Private clubs welcome visitors. In Cape Town there are the Milnerton and Pinelands Tennis Clubs, while Port Elizabeth offers facilities at the Park Avenue Tennis Club. Also Durban's Tennis Club and the Zoo Lake Tennis Club in Johannesburg accept visitors. Some of these clubs have rackets for rent.

Squash courts are provided by some hotels and few resorts. There are also a number of commercial clubs where visitors can rent rackets and play at a modest fee. Prominent among these clubs are the Randburg Club and Hillbrow Squash Club in Johannesburg, the Goodwood Squash Center in Cape Town and the Rennies Squash Center in Durban. Also **badminton** is widely played and facilities are readily available.

Bowling is of the lawn variety and not pin bowling. A quiet, sedate and very British sport that has become extremely popular in South Africa. It is played around the country at venues ranging from hotels to resorts and private clubs. There are close to 800 clubs in existence. Guests are welcomed at most of these venues.

In a country with South Africa's long coastline, sunny skies and challenging seas, **yachting** is a natural pursuit. Off-shore racing and cruising is available at keel-boat clubs in Cape Town, Simonstown, Gordon's Bay, Hout Bay, Mossel Bay, Port Elizabeth, Durban and other coastal resorts.

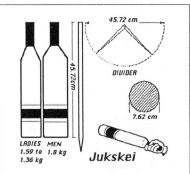

Jukskei

People play Horseshoes in the United States, Curling in Canada and Bacchi in Italy. In South Africa it's Jukskei. They're all homegrown games spontaneously developed to entertain and amuse the folks after a hard day's work.

In the 1830s Voortrekkers would remove the skeys from their wagon's ox-yoke and throw it at a pin placed in the ground some distance away. The game was called *Jukskei* (the Afrikaans for after oxen-skey).

As ox-wagons made way for motorized transport, enthusiasm for the game dwindled. In 1938 during the centenary of the Great Trek, however, the game was revived and placed on an organized footing.

Rules were formalized and equipment standardized with specially made bottle-shaped skeys.

Soon tens of thousands were competing around the country in tournaments culminating in championships at Jukskei's headquarters at Kroonstad in the Orange Free State.

Dr Chris Barnard

Situated in safari country and close to facilities ranging from golf to horse riding, the newly established Chris Barnard Health Center offers a unique experience to upmarket visitors.

This center, named after and supervised by the famous heart surgeon who performed the world's first heart transplant, is not a hydro or a hospital.It provides accommodation in tastefully designed chalets and self-contained vacation homes and includes a diagnostic division for the treatment of cardiovascular, oncological and stress-related disorders. An anti-aging program is also offered.

The complex includes an ultra-modern sport and gymnasium facility. Residents also have full access to the Hans Merensky Club with its popular golf course and squash, tennis, bowls and other facilities.

The center is close to Phalaborwa's Van Eck Airport where cars can be rented for game viewing trips into the adjoining Kruger National Park. Scenic and wildlife excursions are also arranged for its guests by the center itself. *Enquiries and reservations:Tel.(021) 24-2173. Fax. (021) 23-2331.*

Inland the largest man-made lake, Vaaldam, and other dams provide year-round sailing, windsurfing and water-skiing. Canoeing is popular.

Mass **marathon** events such as the Comrades,Two Oceans, Milo Korkie and Pretoria Marathon are favorites among overseas runners. Others are joining in cycling events.Hang Gliding, gliding and hot air ballooning are thriving in South Africa and enthusiasts will have little trouble in finding their counterparts through the respective national associations.

For foreigners who are qualified as pilots and wish to wing their way across the country independently, there are a choice of several **private aircraft** rental and charter companies.

For assistance and advice in regard to any of these sport activities and several others see the listing under SPORTS in KEY ADDRESSES.

Major events on the South African **spectator sport** calendar are rugby provincial and international games, while soccer has won considerable support, especially among black South Africans. Cricket is also a major sport. Its professional golfing the Sunshine Circuit draws top competitors from Europe and the United States.

HEALTH & FITNESS

Health and fitness centers are available in all city centers, while High Rustenburg near Stellenbosch offers a program similar to the luxury spas in Europe and North America.

Near Phalaborwa is the **Christiaan Barnard Health Center** where unique vacations are combined with expert advice and treatment under supervision of Dr Barnard.

DINING & WINING

"Everyone enjoys cooking," the saying goes,"especially when it is done by the chef of a good restaurant."

In South Africa the visitor will find no shortage of good chefs - often combined with unique settings. Types of food vary between traditional South African to Continental, French, Cajun and Japanese, and settings vary from old homesteads with period furniture to ritzy restaurants and bright bistros. There is a wide choice between a whole range of good local wines.

Those who expect a rich variety of sumptuous dishes during their travels to South Africa will not be disappointed. The food scene is as varied and interesting as the people who inhabited this country.

To take full advantage of the multitude of traditional dishes that developed in the interaction between the different European, Malay and Indian immigrants and the natives, visitors are advised to go outside the confines of their hotels. Although some hotels offer authentic traditional foods as part of their fare, the real item is usually found in specialized restaurants.

EARLY TIMES

From the very beginning of the Cape settlement in 1652, Jan van Riebeeck and his compatriots took their food seriously. Their main mission was to provide passing ships with fresh supplies and to feed the sailors. Initially they depended on meat purchased from native herdsmen and whatever produce they could save from the company gardens, under constant threat of mountain floods. But they persevered.

Van Riebeeck plate

CAPE DISHES

Soon the Malay (imported as slaves) slaved in the kitchen's to put spice into sometimes bland Dutch dishes. We are told that the crews of passing ships often invited the locals on board to return their hospitality and exchanged recipes not only for food but liquors.

Word started to spread to Europe about the fine cooking at the Cape. The new settlement earned a reputation for its unique spicy and exotic dishes.

These same Cape dishes are today offered at several restaurants in and around Cape Town - and even as far as Johannesburg.

Any menu of these traditional dishes bound to include favorites such as *bredie* (a mutton and vegetable dish), *bobotie* (spicy meat dish), *sosaties* (shishkebab look-alike with local flavor and unique taste) *(atjar* (pickles), *curried meat and fish, smoorsnoek* (smoked snoek), *yellow rice* with raisins, *melktert* (milk tart), *koeksisters* (sweet rolls), and *tipsy tart* (brandy tart).

BOEREKOS

When the locals talk about *boerekos* they are not referring to Cape dishes but a cooking style developed by the pioneer farmers as they trekked northwards in the 1830s and settled in the interior.

These hardy souls had to cope with the elements and try to keep their food edible on the move. But they liked eating hearty meals and found ways to end their toiling days with good food.

Boerebeskuit (dried farmer's rusks (biscuits) and biltong (dried strips of meat treated with salt and spices) are examples of the food that developed in the pre-refrigeration days.

Also different kind of fruit, ranging from peaches to figs, were preserved in a number of ways - cooked, bottled and dried and today forms part of many a traditional dish. *Blatjang* (chutney) and *mebos* (jelly or preserve) are unique tasting experiences in South Africa and were developed in the Cape kitchens by Malay chefs long before the Great Trek started.

OTHER INFLUENCES

Not only the Dutch and the Malays left their imprint on the eating habits of South Africans. The English brought along recipes for steam-puddings, fruit-cakes, scones, marmalade, shortbread and mince pies that found their way into country cooking. The French Huguenots perfected wine making and introduced *moskonfyt* (a runny jam made from crushed grapes), bread with sweet yeast, *oblietjies* (rolled wafers) and soetkoekies (spiced biscuits flavored with wine).

BRAAIVLEIS

A *braaivleis* or *braai* in South Africa is about as natural as having a sandwich in other parts of the world. Although many so-called steak houses offer indoor open-spit barbecues, it is still basically an outdoor event.

At the various game parks, visitors will be treated to a *braai* every night and sometimes in the afternoon as well. Meat may include venison from the area itself, but normally a braai in South Africa consists of mutton, steaks and *boerewors* (heavily spiced sausage, speckled with fat) - and often mieliepap or stywe pap is served. This is a stiff (often dryish) maize meal porridge used to retrieve the juices and sauces from the plate by hand, very much in the fashion that some would use dry bread.

RESTAURANTS

South Africa offers the visitor a wide choice of restaurants in all the major cities and popular country areas. Johannesburg alone sports more than 800 restaurants of all sorts and kinds.

Our list contains a cross-section of normally reliable restaurants, varying from **good** to **excellent** and reasonable to quite expensive. We refrained from

Leipoldt in his kitchen

He handled a kitchen knife as adroitly as a scalpel. He was not only a qualified physician, a noted botanist, an ornithologist, a journalist, historian and a famous Afrikaans poet. Louis Leipoldt was a gourmet chef and wrote several cook books still used by perfectionists in traditional and common sense good cooking.

At the turn of the century his extensive travels and studies took him all over Europe and America. In Holland he caught up with the exiled President Kruger and had the last interview with the famous Boer statesman. His duties abroad included a stint at London's famous Guy Hospital, and the position of medical attendant on the yacht of American millionaire newspaper-owner, Joseph Pulitzer.

Today many less versatile South Africans share Louis Leipoldt's love for good food and a series of restaurants named after the late poet is a constant reminder of his special contribution to the development of new variations of traditional dishes. Next to his many volumes of famous Afrikaans poetry stand creations such as *Common-Sense Dietetics (1911), Kos vir die Kenner (Food for the Expert) (1933)* and *The Belly Book (1933)*.

Classic Cape window

indicating **prices** as these change frequently without notice. For travellers on limited budgets or seeking respite from over-indulgence, there are familiar billboards and neon signs proclaiming the location of several international and local **fast-food** and take-out establishments.

CHOICE

Opinions differ on what constitutes a good restaurant because patrons happen to use different yard-sticks. In its annual rating of restaurants South Africa's *Style* magazine uses a scoring sheet devised by Peter Devereux of the *International Food and Wine Society*. Devereux weights the various aspects of restauranteurship in the following manner:

Welcome and Farewell	**10 points**
Ambience and Decor	**20 points**
Service	**20 points**
Wine List	**10 points**
Appearance of Food	**20 points**
Taste of Food	**20 points**

Even with high- scoring restaurants there is still the possibility that visitors may encounter that one off-night when the star chef is sick or there is a fight in the kitchen - or the fresh supply of produce or fish did not arrive.

Not only in South Africa, but elsewhere, restaurants may also vary overnight in character and quality as owners and/or chefs change. Some experience a trendy, glorious but short-lived Mayfly existence - full today and gone tomorrow. Even landmark restaurants are prone to problems when the kitchen hierarchy changes.

ADVICE

Our advice is simply: Use our list as a guideline, then start asking around. The locals with taste are still your best bet, even though they do have their own particular prejudices and shortcomings as judges. Use the Devereux criteria when you ask people's opinions and see what they give their recommended restaurants under each of these points.

FOOD

Our list indicates as best we could the type of food served at the various establishments. Most of these appellations need no further elaboration. Everyone is familiar with Greek, Portuguese, English, Mediterranean, Japanese, Chinese, Middle-Eastern, and French cooking, and that somewhat vaguely defined term for good food - Continental cuisine.

The large variety of ethnically oriented restaurants reflects the melting pot make-up of South Africa, with the exception of the Japanese, of whom there are only a very few living in South Africa. The emergence of quality Japanese restaurants in the major cities indicates a need to cater for an increasing number of Japanese tourists yearning for familiar food.

TRADITIONAL

In our listing of restaurants serving traditional South African dishes we did not make a distinction between *Cape dishes* and *boerekos* as most offer a mix of both. It is, however, likely that in the Cape restaurants the emphasis will be on the *Cape dishes* while the northern establishments will lean towards *boerekos*.

VENISON & FISH

Those who like venison will have a field day in South Africa where a whole range of dishes vary from springbok to kudu, ostrich. Nowadays even crocodile is available.

Visitors are bound to have locally available warthog, kudu, impala and other meats from animals culled in these game parks for ecological reasons. For the same reason some restaurants near a breeding farm in Natal now offer crocodile steaks and several establishments in the Oudtshoorn region include ostrich steaks on their menus.

As a very tasty and uniquely South African fish, Kingklip *(koningsklip)* has moved well beyond the walls of traditional restaurants to almost every menu in the country. South Africa is also renowned for its lobster tails and with rapid air links this item as well as fresh perlemoen, mussels, oysters, prawns and a variety of exotic fish species arrive on inland tables within a day after the catch.

Not readily available but a possibility at barbecues, either at public venues or private homes, is *potjiekos* (pot food). A traditional three-legged iron pot (made popular by the black tribes) is packed tight with raw vegetables, meat, fish and other nourishing items and cooked together for a length of time, preserving and mixing the flavor of all the ingredients.

DRESS

We did not try to define proper attire for every restaurant in our list. Most restaurants seem to have a lenient view of what 'properly dressed' constitutes. Although the rule of thumb is casual at most restaurants in daytime and elegantly casual in the evenings, the best advice is: Ask about the dress code when making reservations.

All the **unlicensed restaurants** listed, welcome patrons to bring along their own favorite wines and alcoholic beverages. (There is one exception - a Cape Town Malay restaurant which adheres strictly to its Muslim custom of not allowing any alcoholic beverages on the premises at all).

The absence of a liquor license gives patrons the opportunity to take along their own preferred wine and to save substantially on the cost of the meal. In most establishments no corkage is charged.

Going on a **wine** tour visitors may think of stocking up if they have unlicensed restaurants on their preferred list of places - or otherwise, they can make their selection in a nearby bottle or liquor store. See our *WINE TOUR* chapter for suggestions or ask for advice at the store.

TIPPING

Standard tipping at the restaurants on our list in the next few pages is between 10% and 15%.

Stellenbosch entrance

RESTAURANTS

TYPE OF FOOD

		EN	English	KO	Korean	PU	Pub	
AM	American	FR	French	MA	Malay	RI	Rijstafel	
BR	Brazilian	GE	German	MD	Mediterranean	SE	Seafood	
C	Continental	GR	Greek	ME	Middle Eastern	ST	Steakhouse	
CH	Chinese	HE	Health	MO	Moroccan	**T**	**Traditional**	
CJ	Cajun	I	Italian	MX	Mexican		**Cape & Other**	
CR	Creole	IN	Indian	PI	Pizzeria	VE	Vegetarian	
DE	Deli	JA	Japanese	PO	Portuguese	VN	Venison	

F:Fully Licensed • W: Wine and Beer • U: Unlicensed • N: No alcohol allowed

RESTAURANT	TELEPHONE	ADDRESS	CITY/TOWN		LUNCH	DINNER	TYPE
MAJOR CITIES							
BLOEMFONTEIN							
Beef Baron	051-47-7503	St Andrews Street	Bloemfontein	F	Mon-Sat	Mon-Sat	ST SE
Capones	051-48-0251	Kellner Street & 2nd Ave	Bloemfontein	F	Mon-Sa	Mon-Sat	IT
Carousel	051-47-4290	CR Swart Building	Bloemfontein	F	Mon-Sat	Mon-Sat	C
I'l Pescatore	051-30-4832	East Burger Street	Bloemfontein	F	Mon-Sat	Mon-Sat	C SE
Landdrost Sun	051-47-0310	Landdrost Sun	Bloemfontein	F	Mon-Sun	Mon-Sun	C
Mexican	051-30-4832	Fontein & West Burger	Bloemfontein	F	Mon-Sat	Mon-Sat	MX
Stringfellows	051-47-1331	Melville & Kellner	Bloemfontein	F	Mon-Sun	Mon-Sun	C
CAPE TOWN							
Alibi Ristorante	021-25-2497	72 Waterkant Street	Cape Town	U	Mon-Sat		IT
Anatoli	021-419-2501	24 Napier Street	Cape Town	U	Tue-Sun		ME
Andy's Bistro	021-439-2470	5 Clarens Road	Sea Point	U	Mon-Sun		CT
Ari's Souvlaki	021-439-6683	150 Main Road	Sea Point	U	Mon-Sun	Mon-Sun	GR
Beachcomber	021-438-1213	41 Victoria Street	Camps Bay	U	Mon-Sat		SE
Bellinzona	021-557-6151	1 Blaauwberg Road	Cape Town	F	Wed-Mon	Wed-Mon	C
Biesmiellah	021-23-0850	Wale Street Bo-Kaap	Cape Town	N	Mon-Sat	Mon-Sat	MA
Blues	021-438-2040	Victoria Rd	Camps Bay	F	Mon-Sun	Mon-Sun	CJ FR ME
Brass Bell	021-88-5456	Waterfront	Kalk Bay	F	Mon-Sun	Mon-Sun	SE
Buitenverwachting	021-794-3522	Buitenverwachting	Constantia	F	Tue-Fri	Tue-Sat	C
Chez Simone	021-419-1155	Thibault Square	Cape Town	F	Sun-Fri	Fri-& Sat	C
Clementines	021-797-6168	Wolfe Street	Wynberg	U		Mon-Sat	C
Delmitchies	021-434-6500	78 Main Road	Sea Point	F	Sun-Fri	Mon-Sat	SE
Dias Tavern	021-45-7547	15 Harrington Street	Cape Town	F	Mon-Sat	Mon-Sat	PU PO SE
Fisherman Cottage	021-797-6341	3 Gary Road	Plumstead	U	Tue-Fri	Tue-Sat	C T
Freda's	021-23-8653	110 Kloof Street	Gardens	F	Tue-Fri	Tue-Sat	MD C T
Gustavo's	021-438-2686	41 The Drive Geneva Dr	Camps Bay	U		Mon-Sat	PO SE
Hard Rock Cafe	021-689-1211	Main Road	Rondebosch	F		Mon-Sun	PU
Jasper's	021-461-9312	8 Breda Street	Gardens	U	Mon-Fri	Mon-Sat	C
John Jackson	021-439-8888	Peninsula Hotel	Sea Point	F		Mon-Sat	C
Kaapse Tafel	021-23-1651	90 Queen Victoria St	Gardens	U	Mon-Fri	Mon-Sat	T

Kamakura	021-434-2228	The Courtyard	Sea Point	F	Tue-Sun	Tue-Sun	JA
Kronendal	021-790-1970	Main Road	Hout Bay	F	Tue-Sun	Mon-Sat	C T
L'Entrecote Exp.	021-419-6837	St George's St	Cape Town	F	Mon-Sun	Fri & Sat	ST
La Bijou	021-439-8888	Peninsula Hotel	Sea Point	F	Mon-Sun	Mon-Sun	PU C
La Galiote	021-434-4510	Kloof Rd	Sea Point	F	Mon-Fri	Mon-Sat	FR
La Laterna	021-47-4627	60 Lower Main Road	Observatory	U		Wed-Mon	PI
La Med	021-438-5600	Victoria Road	Clifton	F	Mon-Sun	Mon-Sun	FR C
La Perla	021-434-2471	Beach Road	Sea Point	F	Mon-Sun	Mon-Sun	C SE IT
Le Chalet	021-531-1628	Ster Forest Drive	Pinelands	U	Mon-Fri	Tue-Sat	C SE
Leinster Hall	021-24-1836	7 Weltevreden St	Gardens	F	Mon-Fri	Mon-Sat	C
Maharajah	021-24-6607	230 Long Street	Cape Town	U	Mon-Fri	Mon-Sat	IN
Maria's	021-45-2096	Barnet Street	Gardens	U	Fri	Mon-Sun	GR
Napier Street	021-25-1557	34 Napier Street	Cape Town	U	Mon-Fri	Mon-Sat	C FR
Old Colonial	021-45-4909	39 Barnett Street	Gardens	F	Mon-Fri	Mon-Sat	T C SE
Ons Huisie	021-56-1553	Stadler Road	Blouberg	F	Mon-Sat	Wed-Mon	SE T
Piccolo Mondo	021-434-3960	307 Main Raod	Sea Point	F		Mon-Sat	C SE
Riempies	021-23-8844	Cape Sun Strand St	Cape Town	F	Mon-Sun	Mon-Sun	T
Rozenhof	021-24-1968	18 Kloof Street	Gardens	F	Mon-Fri	Mon-Sat	C
San Marco	021-439-2758	92 Main Road	Sea Point	F	Sun	Wed-Mon	C IT SE
Squares	021-24-0224	St George's St	Cape Town	F	Mon-Sat		CJ FR IT EN
Stones	021-439-6747	The Courtyard	Sea Point	U	Mon-Sat	Mon-Sun	C SE
Taiwan City	021-461-1414	Plein & Darling Sts	Cape Town	F	Mon-Sun	Mon-Sun	CH
The Ferryman's	021-419-7748	Cape Town Docks	Cape Town	F	Mon-Sat	Mon-Sat	PU
The Restaurant	021-438-4444	The Bay Hotel	Camps Bay	F	Mon-Sat	Mon-Sat	C T
The Tent	021-45-3840	21 Derry Road	Vredehoek	U		Mon-Sun	ME
The Wharfside Grill	021-790-2130	Mariner's Wharf	Hout Bay	F	Mon-Sun	Mon-Sun	SE
Topolino	021-461-8787	17 Derry Street	Vredehoek	F		Tue-Sun	PI SE
Truffles	021-72-6161	161 Main Road	Heathfield	F	Tue-Sat	Tue-Sat	C
Upper Crust	021-419-1940	Long Street	Cape Town	F	Mon-Fri		C
Vineyard Hotel	021-64-2107	150 Colinton Road	Newlands	F		Mon-Sat	C SE

DURBAN

Aldo's	031-37-0900	15 Gillespie Street	Durban	U	Mon-Sat	Mon-Sat	MD
Api Taki	031-305-4451	320 West Street	Durban	F	Mon-Sat	Mon-Sat	RI CH
Aura-Mar	031-37-6037	40 Mona Road	Durban	U	Mon-Sun	Mon-Sun	PO MD SE
British Sporting	031-309-4017	16 Stamford Hill Rd	Durban	F	Mon-Sat	Mon-Sat	IN ME
Cattleman	031-37-0382	139 Marine Parade	Durban	F	Mon-Sun	Mon-Sun	ST
Colony	031-368-2789	Oceanic Sol Harris Cr	Durban	F	Mon-Sun	Mon-Sun	C VN
Coimbra	031-32-7876	130 Gillespie Street	Durban	F	Tue-Sun	Tue-Sun	PO SE
Elarish	031-466-2086	Grovesnor Center	Bluff	F	Mon-Sat	Mon-Sat	IN
Greek Taverna	031-21-5433	213 Musgrove Road	Durban	U	Mon-Fri	Mon-Fri	GR
La Dolce Vita	031-301-3347	460 Smith St	Durban	F	Mon-Sat	Mon-Sat	IT
Le Montmartre	031-32-6548	West & Aliwal St	Durban	F	Mon-Fri	Mon-Fri	FR
Le Troquet	031-86-5388	860 Old Main Road	Durban	F	Mon-Fri	Mon-Fri	FR
Leipoldt's	031-304-6644	The Workshop	Durban	F	Sun-Frii	Sun-Fri	T
Les Saisons	031-32-7361	Maharani Hotel	Durban	F		Mon-Sat	C
Michael's Cuisine	031-763-3429	15 Waterfall Center	Durban	F	Tue-Sat	Tue-Sat	C SE
Nataraja	031-305-3143	The Workshop	Durban	F	Mon-Sun	Mon-Sun	IN ME
O Cacador	031-37-7214	546 Point Road	Durban	F	Mon-sat	Mon-Sat	MD SE
Papadum	031-32-7361	Maharani Hotel	Durban	F	Mon-Sun	Mon-Sun	IN
Paros	031-21-0115	297 Moore Rd	Durban	U	Tue-Sun	Tue-Sun	GR
Playhouse Legends	031-304-3297	The Natal Playhouse	Durban	F	Mon-Fri	Mon-Sat	C
Punchinello's	031-37-1321	Elangeni Hotel	Durban	F		Mon-Sat	C

Razzmatazz	031-903-4131	21 Beach Rd	Amanzimtoti	F	Mon-Fri	Mon-Sat	VE
RJ's	031-304-8685	36 Gardiner Street	Durban	F	Mon-Sun	Mon-Sun	ST
Roma Revolving	031-37-6707	John Ross House	Durban	F	Tue-Sun	Tue-Sun	IT
Royal Grill	031-304-0331	Royal Hotel	Durban	F	Sun-Fri	Mon-Sat	C
Royal Steakroom	031-304-0331	Royal Hotel	Durban	F	Mon-Sun	Mon-Sun	ST PU
Saagries	031-32-7922	47 West Street	Durban	F	Mon-Sun	Mon-Sun	IN
Scalini	031-32-2804	237 Marine Parade	Durban	F	Tue-Sun	Tue-Sun	IT
Sir Benjamin's	031-37-3341	Parade Holiday Inn	Durban	F		Mon-Sat	C
Squire's Loft	031-303-1110	295 Florida Road	Durban	F	Mon-Sun	Mon-Sun	ST VE
St Geran	031-304-7509	31 Aliwal Street	Durban	F	Mon-Fri	Mon-Fri	CR SE
Stax	031-32-5291	237 Marine Parade	Durban	F	Mon-Sun	Mon-Sun	ST PU
Steers	031-32-2991	14 Brickhill Rd	Durban	F	Mon-Sun	Mon-Sun	ST SE
Sukihama	031-37-1321	Elangeni Hotel	Durban	F	Mon-Sun	Mon-Sun	JA
The Orient	031-37-2083	191 Marine Parade	Durban	F	Mon-Sun	Mon-Sat	CH KO
The Cabin	031-561-2211	Beverly Hills Hotel	Umhlanga	F	Mon-Sun	Mon-Sun	SE
Tong Lok	031-37-0736	562 Point Road	Durban	F	Mon-Sun	Mon-Sun	CH
Ulundi	031-304-0331	The Royal Hotel	Durban	F	Mon-sat	Mon-Sat	IN
Villa D'Este	031-37-0264	29 Gillespie Street	Durban	F	Tue-Sun	Tue-Sun	IT SE
Wolfgang's	031-23-2861	136 Florida Road	Durban	U	Mon-Fri	Mon-Sat	FR

JOHANNESBURG

Anton van Wouw	011-402-7916	111 Sivewright Ave	Doornfontein	F	Mon-Fri	Mon-Sat	T
Arcangelo's	011-29-4990	Jeppe Street	Johannesburg	F	Mon-Fri		AM IT
Baccarat	011-880-1835	Admirals Court	Rosebank	F	Mon-Sat	Mon-Sat	C
Belem Infante	011-435-1004	Belem Building	Regents Park	F	Mon-Sat	Mon-Sat	PO
Bougainvilia	011-788-4883	Cradock Ave	Rosebank	F	Mon-Fri	Mon-Sat	C
Butler's	011-403-5740	Braamfontein Hotel	Braamfontein	F	Mon-Fri	Mon-Sat	C
Cachaca	011-483-2439	Grant & William Rd	Norwood	F	Tue-Sun	Tue-Sun	BR
Caramba Prawn	011-887-0455	Louis Botha Ave	Johannesburg	F	Mon-Fri	Mon-Sat	SE
Carvers	011-678-5417	51 Mountainview Ave	Randburg	F	Tue-Fri	Tue-Sat	C T
Casa Portugesa	011-883-6140	Maud Street	Sandown	U	Mon-Sat	Mon-Sat	PO SE
Casalinga	011-957-2612	Muldersdrif Rd	Honeydew	F	Wed-Sat	Wed-Sat	IT
Chanel et Renoir	011-618-3130	69 Browning Street	Fairview	F	Tue-Fri	Tue-Sat	FR
Chaplins	011-726-2507	85 4th Avenue	Melville	F	Mon-Fri	Mon-Sat	C
Chapters	011-783-8701	Sandton Sun Hotel	Sandton	F	Mon-Fri	Mon-Sat	C
Chardonnay's	011-786-1618	Old Pretoria Rd	Wynberg	F	Mon-Fri	Mon-Sat	C
Chez Rachel	011-648-4114	32 Fortesque Street	Yeoville	U	Mon-Sun	Mon-Sun	MO ME
Club Room	011-331-8911	Carlton Court	Johannesburg	F	Mon-Sun	Mon-Sun	C
Coco de Mer	011-974-5127	43 Barbizon Rd	Croydon	F	Mon-Fri	Mon-Sat	SE
Colonial Restaurant	011-788-1337	34a Cradock Avenue	Rosebank	F	Mon-Sat	Mon-Sat	P
Daruma	011-447-2260	Corlett & Athol Rd	Melrose North	F	Tue-Sat	Tue-Sun	JA
Deale's Wine Bar	011-838-5441	27 Diagonal St	Johannesburg	F	Mon-Fri	Mon-Fri	PU
Delfini	011-648-3500	42 Hunter Street	Yeoville	W	Tue-Sun	Tue-Sun	GR
Denton's	011-331-3827	125 Fox Street	Johannesburg	F	Mon-Fri	No dinner	C
Dickens Inn	011-787-7219	Craig Park Center	Craighall	F	Mon-Fri	Mon-Sat	EN
Die Koffiehuis	011-888-1779	32 Seventh Street	Linden	U	Mon-Fri	Fri & Sat	T Dinos
011-622-3007	Bedford Center	Bedfordview	F		Mon-Sat	Mon-Fri	C
Dragon Tower	011-725-1727	95 Twist Street	Hillbrow	W	Wed-Mon	Wed-Mon	CH
Elaine's	011-648-0801	9a Rockey Street	Yeoville	U	Mon-Sun	Mon-Sun	IN
Fat Franks	011-339-7057	Biccard Street	Johannesburg	F	Mon-Sat	Mon-Sat	CJ
Fisherman's Grotto	011-834-6211	14a Plein Street	Johannesburg	F	Mon-Fri	Mon-Sat	SE
Founders Grill	011-672-4216	4 Gordon Road	Florida North	F	Mon-Fri	Mon-Sat	ST SE
Franco's Trattoria	011-646-5449	54 Tyrone Ave	Parkview	U	Tue-Sun	Tue-Sun	IT

Name	Phone	Address	Area		Days	Days	Code
Frank's	011-883-5810	Grayston Center	Sandown	F	Mon-Fri	Mon-Sat	IT
Freddie's	011-726-1908	Main Road	Melville	F	Mon-Fri	Mon-Sat	C T
Freddie's	011-783-7418	136 11th Street	Parkmore	U	Mon-Fri	Mon-Sat	C T
Frog	011-987-2304	376a Jan Smuts Ave	Craighall	F	Mon-Fri	Mon-Sat	C
Front Page	011-726-1917	10 Main Road	Melville	F	Mon-Sat	Mon-Sat	S
Front Page	011-788-8400	Rosebank Mall	Rosebank	F	Mon-Sat	Mon-Sat	ST T PU
Garbo's	011-642-0614	Claim Street	Hillbrow	F	Tue-Sun	Tue-Sun	C
Gartrile Son & Co	011-29-0485	81 De Villiers Street	Johannesburg	F	Mon-Fri	Mon-Sat	EN T
Gatrile's Sandton	011-883-7398	5 Esterhuizen Street	Sandown	F	Mon-Fri	Mon-Sat	EN T
Gillooly's Rest	011-53-2825	Gillooly's Farm	Bedfordview	F	Mon-Sat	Mon-Sat	C T
Golden Capital	011-834-6886	7 Commissioner Str	Johannesburg	U	Mon-Sun	Mon-Sun	CH
Gramadoelas	011-725-1795	31 Bok Street	Johannesburg	F	Tue-Fri	Tue-Sun	T
Grayston	011-783-5262	Sandton Holiday Inn	Sandton	F	Mon-Fri	Mon-Sat	C
Grill Mediterranean	011-880-3143	192 Oxford Road	Illovo	U	Tue-Sun	Tue-Sun	MD
Happy Palace	011-724-5831	36 Twist Street	Johannesburg	F	Mon-Sat	Mon-Sat	JA
Hard Rock Cafe	011-447-2583	204 Oxford Road	Illovo	W	Mon-Sun	Mon-Sun	PU ST
Harridans	011-838-6729	Market Theater	Johannesburg	F	Tue-Fri	Tue-Sat	C
Horatio's	011-726-2247	10 Seventh Street	Melville	F	Mon-Fri	Mon-Sat	SE
Idle Winds	012-669-0165	Hartbeespoort Dam Rd	Doornrandjie	F	Tue-Fri	Tue-Sat	C T
Il Grifone	011-642-3420	St David's Place	Parktown	F	Mon-Fri	Mon-Sat	IT
Ile de France	011-482-8215	Bompas Road	Dunkeld	F	Sun-Fri	Mon-Sun	FR
Kaiserhof	011-837-4012	133 High Street	Brixton	W	Mon-Fri	Mon-Sun	GE PU
Kapitan's	011-834-8048	11a Kort Street	Johannesburg	F	Mon-Sat		IN
Koala Blu	011-482-2477	9 Seventh Street	Melville	U	Daily	Daily	VE HE
La Bocca	011-787-0450	Hill Street Mall	Randburg	W	Mon-Sun	Mon-Sun	IT
La Lampara	011-728-471	50 Grant Ave	Norwood	U	Tue-Sun	Tue-Sun	IT
La Mama's	011-787-2701	Geneva & Eileen St	Randburg	F	Mon-Sun	Mon-Sun	IT
La Margaux	011-788-5264	3 Rivonia Road	Illovo	F	Mon-Fri	Mon-Sat	C
La Palhoyta	011-337-6377	59 Troye Street	Johannesburg	F	Mon-Sun	Mon-Sun	PO
La Torre	011-614-5757	42 Bezuidenhout St	Troyeville	F	Mon-Sat	Mon-Sat	IT
Le Chablis	011-884-1000	Sandown Center	Sandown	F	Mon-Sat	Mon-Sat	C
Le Creole	011-726-4104	11 Main Street	Melville	U	Mon-Fri	Mon-Sun	FR CR T
Leipoldt's	011-339-2765	94 Juta Street	Braamfontein	F	Sun-Fri	Mon-Sat	T
Leo	011-802-6838	Braides & Klevin Dr	Sandton	F	Tue-Sun	Tue-Sun	IT
Les Marquis	011-783-8947	12 Fredman Drive	Sandown	F	Mon-Fri	Mon-Sat	C
Lien Wah	011-788-1820	Tyrwhitt Ave	Rosebank	F	Mon-Sun	Mon-Sun	CH
Linger Longer	011-339-7814	94 Juta Street	Braamfontein	F	Mon-Fri	Mon-Sat	C T
Lobster Hole	011-887-0458	73 Corlett Drive	Birnam	F	Sun-Fri	Sun-Sat	SE
Lord Prawn	011-783-9214	125 11th Street	Parkmore	F	Sun-Fri	Sun-Sat	SE
Luchi's Place	011-403-1404	De Korte & Station	Braamfontein	U	Mon-Fri	Mon-Sun	IT
Lupo's	011-880-4850	281 Jan Smuts Ave	Dunkeld	U	Tue-Sun	Tue-Sun	IT
Ma Cuisine	011-880-1946	7th & 3rd Ave	Parktown	F	Mon-Fri	Mon-Sat	FR C
Mama's Place	011-648-7201	2a Rockey Street	Yeoville	F	Wed-Mon	Wed-Mon	IT
Marialda	011-23-4415	108 Kerk Street	Johannesburg	W	Mon-Sat	Mon-Sat	PO
Meo Patacca	011-880-2442	20 Chaplin Road	Illovo	F	Tue-Sun	Tue-Sun	IT
Ming's Place	011-337-7175	100 Plein Street	Johannesburg	F	Mon-Sat	Mon-sat	CH
Moosehead	011-880-6551	Rosebank Mall	Rosebank	F	Mon-Fri	Mon-Sat	MX CJ
Mykonos	011-447-3205	347 Jan Smuts Ave	Craighall	F	Mon-Sun	Mon-Sun	GR
Nino da Genova	011-726-3801	4a Seventh Street	Melville	W	Tue-Sun	Tue-Sun	IT
O'Galito	011-440-4281	37 Darwin Avenue	Savoy Estate	F	Tue-Sun	Tue-Sun	PO SE
Oasis	011-788-4115	Hyde Park Square	Hyde Park	F	Mon-Sat	Mon-Sat	SE C
Old Batavia	011-789-1726	Selkirk & Blairgowrie	Randburg	F	Tue-Fri	Tue-Sun	RI
Osteria Giovanni	011-783-3503	60 Rivonia Road	Sandhurst	U	Tue-Sun	Tue-Sun	IT
Paesa Pizzeria	011-680-4838	126 Harry Street	Robertsham	F	Tue-Sun	Tue-Sun	IT

Name	Phone	Address	Area		Open	Open	
Pappas Restaurant	011-705-1521	Kingfisher Dr	Fourways	W	Mon-Sun	Mon-Sun	GR
Pappas Restaurant	011-804-3480	Southway & Raymond	Kelvin	W	Mon-Sun	Mon-Sun	GR
Parreirinha	011-435-3809	Sixth Street	La Rochelle	F	Mon-Sat	Mon-Sat	PO
Passero Bistro	011-786-0157	71 Corlett Drive	Birnam	U	Mon-Sun	Mon-Sun	PU
Pasta Parlour	011-442-7372	Tyrwhitt Ave	Rosebank	F	Mon-Sat	Mon-Sat	IT
PD's	011-788-4865	Illovo Center Rudd Rd	Illovo	F	Mon-Sat	Mon-Sat	C IT
Pearl Garden	011-803-1781	24 Ninth Avenue	Rivonia	F	Tue-Fri	Tue-Sat	CH
Perfumed Garden	011-724-6316	43 King George's St	Johannesburg	F	Sun-Fri	Mon-Sun	ME
Porta Romana	011-880-4320	Third & Seventh Ave	Parktown N	F	Mon-Sun	Mon-Sun	IT
Risky Business	011-726-8142	11b Seventh Street	Melville	U	Mon-Sat	Mon-Sun	IN
Roma Trattoria	011-726-3404	25 Fourth Ave	Melville	W	Tue-Sat	Tue-Sun	IT
Sai Woo Parkwood	011-447-2924	126 Jan Smuts Avenue	Parkwood	F	Wed-Sun	Tue-Sun	CH
Sant'Anna	011-884-5008	Sandton City	Sandton	F	Mon-Sat	Mon-Sat	IT
Sausalito	011-783-3305	Linden & Ann Rds	Sandown	U	Sun-Fri	Sun-Mon	AM C
Seawave Inn	011-615-3708	16 Sovereign Street	Bedfordview	F	Sun-Fri	Sun-Sat	SE
Seoul House	011-789-2818	396 Jan Smuts Ave	Craighall Park	W	Tue-Sun	Tue-Sun	KO
Sfuzy's	011-726-5803	Milpark Empire Road	Auckland Park	F	Mon-Fri	Mon-Sat	SE C
Sizzling Gourmet	011-614-1311	Kitchener Ave	Kensington	W	Mon-Sun	Mon-Sun	GR
Squire's Loft	011-884-5038	Grayston & Katherine St	Sandown	F	Mon-Sun	Mon-Sun	ST
St James	011-29-7011	Johannesburg Sun	Johannesburg	F	Mon-Sat	Mon-Sat	C
Suki Hama	011-29-7011	Johannesburg Sun	Johannesburg	F	Sun-Fri	Mon-Sun	JA
Trien	011-482-2366	79 Third Avenue	Melville	U		Mon-Sun	T
Tastevin	011-643-7226	Sunnyside Park Hotel	Parktown	F	Tue-Fri	Tue-Fri	C
The Baytree	011-782-7219	Hans Strydom Dr	Linden	F	Tue-Fri	Tue-Sat	FR
The Crown	011-835-1181	Gold Reef City	Johannesburg	F	Mon-Sun	Mon-Sat	C VN
The Fiddler	011-803-2611	Rivonia Main Rd	Rivonia	F	Mon-Fri	Mon-Sat	C
The French Nook	011-786-8810	71 Corlett Drive	Birnam	W	Mon-Fri	Mon-Sat	FR
The Hangar	011-805-3715	131 Walton Rd	Midrand	F	Mon-Sun	Tue-Sat	C
The Herbert Baker	011-726-6253	5 Winchester Rd	Parktown	F	Sun-Fri	Mon-Sat	C
The Partridge	011-316-3155	Old Kempton Park Rd	Olifantsfontein	F	Mon-Fri	Mon-Sat	FR T VN
The Prospect Room	011-643-7226	Sunnyside Hotel	Parktown	F	Mon-Fri	Mon-Sat	C
The Red Chamber	011-788-5536	The Mews	Rosebank	F	Mon-Sun	Mon-Sun	CH
The Ritz	011-880-2470	17 Third Avenue	Parktown N	F	Mon-Sat	Mon-Sun	C GR
The Tent	011-803-7025	Rivonia Square	Rivonia	W	Tue-Sun	Tue-Sun	ME
The Three Ships	011-331-8911	Carlton Hotel	Johannesburg	F	Tue-Fri	Tue-Sun	C
The Valley Inn	011-886-1667	Riverview Shopping Ctr	Craighall Park	F	Mon-Fri	Mon-Sat	C GE
The White House	011-883-7090	56 Wierda Rd	Sandton	F	Mon-Sat	Mon-Sat	C
The Wine Cafe	011-482-1872	3 Stanley Avenue	Richmond	F	Mon-Fri	Mon-Sat	DE
Theo's	011-447-2979	31 Tyrwhitt Ave	Rosebank	F	Mon-Sat	Mon-Sat	GR
Thermann's	011-728-2771	214 Louis Botha Ave	Orange Grove	U	Mon-Fri	Mon-Sat	FR T
Touchdown	011-402-8105	Ellis Park Stadium	Johannesburg	F	Mon-Fri		C
Traders	011-787-1351	Republic Rd & Kent Ave	Randburg	F	Mon-Fri	Mon-Sat	MX CJ
Trattoria Fiorentina	011-339-3410	Noswai Hall Bertha Street	Braamfontein	W	Mon-Fri	Mon-Fri	IT
Turn 'n Tender	011-339-2565	81 De Korte Street	Braamfontein	F	Mon-Sat	Mon-Sat	ST
Vergilius Norwood	011-728-2048	38 Grant Avenue	Norwood	F	Sun-Fri	Mon-Sat	SE
Villa Borghese	011-23-1793	95 De Villiers Street	Johannesburg	F	Mon-Sun	Mon-Sun	IT
Yang Tse	011-725-2767	24 Edith Cavell Street	Hillbrow	U	Tue-Sun	Tue-Sun	CH
Zoo Lake	011-646-8807	Zoo Lake Gardens	Johannesburg	F	Tue-Sun	Tue-Sat	C
KIMBERLEY							
Carrington's	(0531) 31751	Kimberley Sun	Kimberley	F		Mon-Sat	C VN
Mario's Pasta	(0531) 29283	Sanlam Center	Kimberley	W	Mon-Sun	Mon-Sun	IT
Safari Steak House	(0531) 24621	2 Market Square	Kimberley	U	Mon-Fri	Mon-Sat	ST
Tiffany's	(0531) 26211	Savoy Hotel	Kimberley	F	Mon-Sun	Mon-Sun	IT

PORT ELIZABETH

Bella Napoli	041-55-3819	6 Hartman Street	Port Elizabeth	U	Mon-Sun	Mon-Sun	IT T EN
Boodles	041-53-3131	Holiday Inn	Port Elizabeth	F	Mon-Fri	Mon-Sat	C SE
El Cid	041-55-5664	93 Parliament Street	Port Elizabeth	W	Mon-Fri	Mon-Sun	ST SE
It's Country	041-52-3835	16 Evatt Street	Port Elizabeth	U	Mon-Sun	Wed-Mon	C T EN
La Fontaine	041-55-9029	Rink Street	Port Elizabeth	F	Mon-Sun	Mon-Sun	IT
Margot's	041-52-3352	32 Evatt Street	Port Elizabeth	U	Mon-Fri	Mon-Sat	FR
Nelson's Arm	041-55-9049	3 Trinder Square	Port Elizabeth	W	Mon-Fri	Mon-Sat	SE
Ranch Steak House	041-55-9684	Russel & Rose Sts	Port Elizabeth	W	Mon-Sun	Mon-Sun	ST
Saucy Mermaid	041-55-1558	Algoa Protea Hotel	Port Elizabeth	F	Mon-Sun	Mon-Sun	C SE
Sir Rufane Donkin	041-55-5534	5 George Street	Port Elizabeth	W	Mon-Fri	Mon-Sat	EN T SE
The Bell	041-53-2161	Beach Hotel Marine Dr	Port Elizabeth	F	Mon-Fri	Mon-Sat	C EN
The Coachman	041-52-2511	Lawrence Street	Port Elizabeth	W	Sun-Fri	Nob-Sun	ST SE
Tivoli	041-35-2096	Pamela Arcade 2nd Ave	Port Elizabeth	U	Mon-Sat	Mon-Sat	IT

PRETORIA

Allegro	022-322-1665	State Theater Church St	Pretoria	F	Mon-Fri	Mon-Sat	C T
Ambassadeur	012-322-7500	Burgerspark Hotel	Pretoria	F	Mon-Fri	Mon-Sat	C
Chez Patrice	012-708-916	Soutpansberg & Wells	Riviera	F	Tue-Fri	Tue-Sat	FR
Ella's at Toulouse	012-341-7511	Fountains Valley	Groenkloof	F	Mon-Fri	Mon-Sat	FR
Delarey's	012-344-4040	529 Jordaan Street	Pretoria	F	Mon-Fri	Mon-Sat	T
Goldfields	012-322-1665	State Theater Church St	Pretoria	F	Mon-Fri	Mon-Sat	C
La Perla	012-322-2759	Skinner Street	Pretoria	F	Mon-Fri	Mon-Sat	C
La Madeleine	012-44-6076	258 Esselen Sunnyside	Pretoria	F	Tue-Fri	Tue-Sun	FR T
Lombardy	012-87-1284	Tweefontein Farm	Pretoria East	F	Tue-Sat	Tue-Sat	C
Oude Kaap	012-322-7570	Protea Hof Hotel	Pretoria	F	Mon-Sat	Mon-Sat	C T
Pasqual's	012-46-4367	103 Club Street	Waterkloof Ht	F	Mon-Sat	Mon-Sat	C T
Stadt Hamburg	012-83-3273	Brae St Willow Brae	De Wilgers	F	Mon-Sat	Mon-Sat	C GE
Viktor's	012-326-8282	Church Street	Arcadia	F	Mon-Fri	Mon-Sat	C

OTHER CITIES

EAST LONDON

Collette	0431-25531	Kennaway Hotel	East London	F	Mon-Sun	Mon-Sun	C ST SE
Guido's	0431-56501	Peace Street	East London	U	Tue-Fri	Tue-Sun	IT
Le Petit	0431-35-3685	54 Beach Road	Nahoon	W	Mon-Fri	Mon-Sat	C FR
Movenpick	0431-21840	Orient Beach	East London	F	Sun-Fri	Mon-Sat	C FR

PIETERMARITZBURG

La Provence	0331-42-4579	180 Loop Street	Maritzburg	F	Mon-Fri	Mon-Fri	C

RURAL

MUIZENBERG

Gaylords	021-5470	65 Main Road	Muizenberg	U	Wed-Sun	Wed-Sun	IN
Shrimptons	021-88-5225	19 Alexander Rd	Muizenberg	U	Mon-Sun	Mon-Sun	C SE

GARDEN ROUTE

HERMANUS

The Burgundy	(0283) 22800	Market Square	Hermanus	F	Tue-Sun	Wed-Sat	FR SE

KNYSNA

De Meulengracht	(0445) 22127	51 Main Street	Knysna	F	Mon-Sun	Mon-Sun	T

MOSSEL BAY

Camelot	(04441) 2035	Marsh Street	Mossel Bay	F	Mon-Sat	Mon-Sat	SE

SWELLENDAM

Zanddrift	(0291) 42550	Swellengrebel St	Swellendam	U	Mon-Sun	Mon-Sat	T

WINE ROUTE

FRANSCHHOEK

Boschendal	02211-41252	Boschendal Estate	Drakenstein	W	Mon-Sun		T
La Petit Ferme	02212-3016	Franschhoek Pass	Franschhoek	F	Tue-Sun		FR T
Le Quartier Francais	02212-2248	Main Road	Franschhoek	F	Mon-Sun	Wed-Sat	FR T

PAARL

Laborie	(02211)632034	Taillefert`Street	Paarl	W	Mon-Sun	Tue-Sat	T
Rhebokskloof	02211-638606	Rhebokskloof Estate	Paarl	F	Mon-Sun	Fri&Sat	T
The Harlequin	021-92-1993	281 Voortrekker Street	Parow	F	Mon-Sat	Mon-Sat	IT SE
Wagon Wheels	02211-25265	57 Lady Grey Street	Paarl	W	Tue-Fri	Tue-Fri	ST SE

SOMERSET WEST

Chez Michel	024-516069	41 Victoria Street	Somerset West	U	Tue-Fri	Tue-Sat	C T
Ou Pastorie	024-22120	41 Lourens Street	Somerset West	F	Tue-Sun	Tue-Sat	C T

STELLENBOSCH

Lord Neethling	02231-76905	Neethlingshof Estate	Stellenbosch	F	Tue-Sun	Tue-Sat	CH T C
Mamma Roma	02231-6064	Stelmark Center	Stellenbosch	F	Mon-Sun	Mon-Sun	C IT
De Volkskombuis	02231-72121	Old Strand Road	Stellenbosch	F	Mon-Sat	Mon-Sat	T
Doornbosch	02231-6163	Old Strand Road	Stellenbosch	F	Tue-Sun	Tue-Sat	T C
Le Pommier	02231-91269	Helshoogte Pass	Stellenbosch	F	Tue-Sun	Tue-Sat	T
Ralph's	02231-3532	3 Andringa Street	Stellenbosch	U	Sun-Fri	Mon-Sat	C

TULBAGH

Paddagang	0236-300242	23 Church Street	Tulbagh	F	Mon-Sun		T

RESORTS

SUN CITY

Peninsula	014651-2100	Cascades Pilanesberg	Sun City	F	No lunch	Mon-Sat	C
The Silver Forest	014651-2100	Sun City Pilanesberg	Sun City	F	No Lunch	Mon-Sat	C
Raffles	014651-21000	Sun City Hotel	Sun City	F	Mon-Sun	Mon-Sun	C

OTHER OPINIONS

During his ten year tenure from 1652 until 1662, South Africa's founder, Jan van Riebeeck, wrote extensive diaries about life at the southern tip of the African continent. His interesting observations have since been published. Honors for first expert writer about South Africa therefore go to him.

But after Van Riebeeck came Conan Doyle, Churchill, Kipling, Mark Twain, Rider Haggard, Buckley, Michener and many more.

I t can be argued that never has so much been written by so many about so few.

Although it ranks twentieth in the world as far as land goes, South Africa is not a big country when it comes to population. At latest count the total stood at 34 million.

Not many people but certainly a great variety of blacks, browns, whites, cultures, customs and creeds. Interesting people and talented.

South Africa has in its past and present world-renowned scientists like Dr Chris Barnard and Sir Basil Schonland who reached the top of the ladder in medicine and nucleur science; statesmen like Jan Smuts who wrote the preamble to the UN Charter, and Albert Luthuli, the stately black leader who received the Nobel Peace Prize; sportsmen with the stature of a Gary Player, and entertainers ranging from singer Miriam Makeba to the dancer Juliet Prowse.

Will Rogers

Rider Haggard

CREATION

The story is told of the Lord giving instructions to one of his angels during Creation.

"To whom," asked the angel, *"shall we give diamonds?"* *"South Africa, Zaire and Botswana,"* came the answer.

"And gold?" the angel asked. *"To*
South Africa, Russia and Canada,"* came the reply from Heaven.

"What about chrome, Lord?" *"We give it to South Africa and Zimbabwe."*

"But Lord," protested the angel, *"why do we give everything to South Africa?"*

"Wait," said the Lord, *"until you have seen what kind of people I am going to give it."*

DRAMA

Rich in potential, ridden with problems. That is South Africa. It makes for a drama (sometimes tragedy) as it strives towards greater unity, harmony and equality amidst a wealth in minerals, scenery and wildlife.

Although much has been written about South Africa's wildlife and beauty, it is this intriguing interaction between cultures, colors and credos that brought so many prominent pundits to its shores.

FOREIGNERS

Over the years this country and its people have been the focus of foreign notables such as Rudyard Kipling, Rider Haggard, Winston Churchill, Arthur Conan Doyle, Mark Twain, Will Rogers, Allen Drury, James Michener and many more.

A little book about the Boers, written by nine-year old American schoolboy, Allen Dulles, and proudly published by his parents, has become a treasured Africana item - after Dulles went on to become head of the CIA.

The very same British master of intrigue, Sir Arthur Conan Doyle, who created the likes of Sherlock Holmes and his Dear Mr Watson, wrote a hefty book in 1902 called *The Great Boer War.*

The accounts by Winston Churchill, *From London to Ladysmith to Pretoria* and *My Early Life*, are biographical. He got to know the Boers not only as an observer but as his captors after he fell in their hands as a prisoner of war. While in the front line, British poet and writer Rudyard Kipling contributed many verses about the war and the Boers and spent time in Cape Town writing and relaxing.

More recently two outstanding books about the Boer War appeared in Britain - one by South African author Rayne Kruger entitled *Goodbye Dolly Gray* and the other more recent one by British author Thomas Pakenham, *The Boer War*.

Following the Equator resulted from American Mark Twain's extensive lecture tour of South Africa at the turn of the century, while fellow countryman and humorist, Will Rogers started his career as a rope artist in Johannesburg and wrote extensively about the country and its people. These interesting observations were later incorporated in several of his biographies, including one by his wife Betty.

At the turn of the century Rider Haggard of *King Solomon's Mines* fame wrote several historical novels about South Africa including *The Witch's Head* (about the Zulu) and *Swallow* (about the Great Trek). A more recent historic novel, *The Covenant* by James Michener, is often read by many foreigners before embarking on their trip to South Africa. *The Washing of the Spears*, by American author Donald Morris, is a gripping story of the rise and fall of the Zulu nation, first published in 1976.

In recent years *apartheid* took center stage and much of the writing from abroad focused on this unfortunate topic. Among those who wrote books were Allen Drury (*A Very Strange Society*) and Father Trevor Huddleston with *Naught For Your Comfort*, while Englishmen Paul Johnson (Modern Times) and Malcolm Muggeridge and Americans ranging from William Buckley to Carl Rowan and hosts of other contemporary commentators joined the debate in writings and appearances.

SOUTH AFRICANS

South Africa has of course also produced its own crop of widely acclaimed writers - writing about themselves and their own country.

Although there have been other South African novels before hers, Olive Schreiner's *Story of an African Farm* is considered to be the first notable fiction to have come from this country. Written under the pseudonym Ralph Iron, this little novel became an instant success in Britain after its appearance in 1883. She never repeated her success but pioneered the way for a whole string of distinguished South African novelists since.

Although Sarah Gertrude Millin has published a few collections of short stories, her legacy is that of historian. Not the academic type, but one who had the knack to get to the heart of the matter with a few bold brilliant strokes. Her biographies of Jan Smuts

Olive Schreiner

Sarah Getrude Millin

and Cecil Rhodes are classics as are *The South Africans* and *The Measure of My Days*.

Widely published abroad, Stuart Cloete wrote many gripping stories about the Great Trek and the Boers, ranging from *Turning Wheels* to *Rags of Glory*. Currently Wilbur Smith is continuing the tradition from Cape Town with novels tracing the South African story right up to the present.

But it is Alan Paton's story about the black man's plight, *Cry,the Beloved Country*, that made the greatest impact overseas in recent years. Following in his footsteps, Doris Lessing and Nadine Gordimer also used this theme in several celebrated novels. In 1991 Gordimer became the first South African and only the second woman ever to receive the Nobel Prize for Literature. Among the poets and playwrights who made their mark abroad are Roy Campbell, Guy Butler and the contemporary Athol Fugard who electrified overseas stages with *Blood Knot* and other productions.

CJ Langenhoven

PJ Philander

AFRIKAANS

Much has been written about South Africa in Afrikaans, the young language derived from Dutch that is spoken by the majority of the country's whites and most of its Colored people. Still easily understood and enjoyed by the Dutch, some of these poems, plays, novels and other Afrikaans writings have become available to the rest of the world in translated form.

Poets Jan Celliers and A G Visser who agonized so eloquently about the plight of the Afrikaner after the Boer War paved the way for Louis Leipoldt, NP van Wyk Louw and Dirk Opperman. As an historic novelist Frans Venter, whose books have been translated in many languages, followed in the footsteps of men like DF Malherbe and J van Melle. Currently widely read abroad, novelists Andre Brink and Coetzee and poet Breyten Breytenbach are part of a genre of Afrikaans protest writing pioneered by personalities such as Etienne Leroux and Jan Rabie.

To the flip-side of the Doris Lessing and Nadine Gordimer, are Afrikaans writers Elsa Joubert with *Poppie Nongena* and Dalene Matthee with novels such as *Fiela's Child*, depicting the predicament of race in South Africa. As Afrikaans speakers, the Coloreds have produced their own stable of serious poets and writers, including PJ Philander and Adam Small.

HUMOR

Not all is serious in South Africa. C J Langenhoven who lived wrote and even found time for politics during the earlier part of this century, is best described as South Africa's Mark Twain and Will Rogers, rolled into one.

While Langenhoven uttered and recorded his quips and stories in Afrikaans, another Afrikaner Charles Bosman entertained the English-speaking world in their own mother tongue with a wide range of humorous writings.

Now deceased, both Bosman and Langenhoven would approve of the ability among South Africans today to laugh at their own shortcomings and idiosyncrasies as evidenced by the popularity of Pieter Dirk Uys and his ilk and the constant supply of new self-deprecating jokes.

BLACK WRITERS

As in the case with Afrikaans writers, meaningful black writers in South Africa who write in their native tongue have to rely on translated versions to reach a wider audience.

Written languages in Xhosa, Zulu, Venda and the other South African tribes are the result of the efforts of British, American and European missionaries in the nineteenth century. It is therefore logical that in everyone of these languages the first book to appear in the newly written form was the Bible.

Since then a number of notable authors in their mother tongue have emerged among the various tribes. Over the years several classics from the past have been translated into English and other European languages, including Thomas Molofo's *Tshaka* that appeared in South Sotho and B W Vilakazi's *Noma Nini* and Xhosa writer JJR Jolobe's *Umyezo*.

The modern trend among many black writers is to write in English, making their works much more readily accessible to the outside world. Their ranks naturally include Mazisi Kunene, Lewis Nkosi and Alex la Guma, some of whom became internationally known as protest writers in the apartheid years.

These modern writers were following in the footsteps of Sol Plaatje, an accomplished black writer who became the first secretary of the African National Congress in 1913. He was christened Solomon Tshekisho by his Tswana parents but adopted his father's nickname as his own last name. He spoke eight languages and wrote in several, including English. His works range

from translations of Shakespearian plays into Tswana to original novels and political books.

WILDLIFE

South Africa's natural beauty and wildlife have been the focus of attention long before people and their problems became a preoccupation of the world's writers. *Travels In The Interior of South Africa*, published in two volumes in the 1820s and written and illustrated by the British naturalist William Burchell, remains among the best ever written about South African fauna, flora and travel. Thomas Baines who came to South Africa in 1842 and stayed until his death in 1875 left a legacy of paintings and diaries that were published in various forms. Baines also started out with David Livingstone on one of his famous journeys but was, so it turned out, unjustly accused and dismissed for theft.

Although he came to South Africa in 1841 as a missionary, David Livingstone would later earn world-wide acclaim as an explorer. He did not only earn the enmity of Baines but of many of his fellow missionaries. There is "no more Christian affection between them and me," wrote Livingstone, "than between my riding ox and his grandmother." Nevertheless, among Livingstone's writings is *"A Popular Account of Missionary Travels and Researches in South Africa"*, printed in 1875. Traveling to South

Sol Plaatje

Stuart Cloete

Africa in the 1830s to recover from fever contracted in India and to hunt and sketch animals, William Cornwallis Harris produced his famous *Narrative of an Expedition into Southern Africa* in 1838. Richly illustrated, this classic has since been republished and entertains not only hunters, but naturalists and travel book readers.

Afrikaans author, Eugene Marais, gained world-wide recognition with his writings in Afrikaans about various forms of wildlife. Subsequently translated titles such as the *Soul of the Ant* and *My Friends the Baboons* became popular with readers around the world. Marais , who was a bit of a political activist, would at one stage incur the wrath of President Kruger for his political views.

The best animal story in South African English literature was written by another activist, Percy FitzPatrick, who also ran afoul of Transvaal President Paul Kruger. FitzPatrick was one of the men who tried to overthrow the Boer government in 1896 and spent two years in prison for high treason before he wrote the classic *Jock of the Bushveld* - a dog story that is popular until this day with both the young and old.

Percy FitzPatrick

Laurens van der Post

Not only as a novelist, but a naturalist and a humanist, Sir Laurens van der Post has made an important contribution to literature in South Africa. His *Venture to the Interior*, published in 1952, counts among the finest descriptive writings about South Africa.

WHERE?

The question will be asked: Where do I get these books?

Some of the recent ones should be available at the neighborhood library, while others can be obtained while in South Africa.

Several of the very old volumes have been reprinted recently in commemorative editions by South African publishing houses and those that are out of print may sometimes be obtained from one of several Africana dealers. There are at least one in every city dealing in these out-of-print and antique books about South Africa.

Africana, for those who do not know, simply means old African or South African objects in print, paintings and illustrations.

Both Fitzpatrick's *Jock of the Bushveld* and the writings of Cornwallis Harris have recently, for example, been reproduced in attractive bindings - replete with their original drawings.

LIST

Our list is just a short guideline. Visitors who take the time to visit a few of the well-appointed bookstores while in South Africa will find a much wider choice dealing with every aspect of local life, both fact and fiction. Topics range from cooking to conservation, wines to wind-surfing, politics to poetry, travel to trading and husbandry to hunting.

Happy hunting.

FURTHER READING

CULTURES

Bergh, J S	**TRIBES AND KINGDOMS** Illustrated story of black tribes	**D Nelson, Cape Town 1987**
Brooke Simons, Phillida	**CAPE DUTCH HOUSES** Guide to Cape Dutch houses and estates	**C Struik, Cape Town 1987**
De Vosdarl, C	**CAPE DUTCH HOUSES AND FARMS** Account of origin of Cape Dutch styles	**Balkema, Cape Town 1971**
Elliott, Aubrey	**The Magic World of the Xhosa** Intriguing story of Xhosa customs	**Collins, London 1975**
Trotter, A F	**THE OLD CAPE COLONY** Artistic impressions of the old Cape	**Maskew Miller, Cape 1902**

COOKING

Rood, Betsie	**101 SOUTH AFRICAN RECIPES** Easy to follow traditional food recipes	**Tafelberg 1977 Cape Town**

HISTORY

Conan Doyle, Arthur	**THE GREAT BOER WAR** Masterwork about Boer War	**Philips, London 1902**
De Villiers, Les	**SOUTH AFRICA DRAWN IN COLOR** Book about Smuts and color question	**Gordon, Johannesburg**
Hunt & Bryer	**THE 1820 SETTLERS** Illustrated history of British settlers	**D Nelson, Cape Town 1987**
Michener, James	**THE COVENANT** Historical novel about South Africa	**Random House,, NY 1980**
Morris, Donald	**THE WASHING OF THE SPEARS** Rise and Fall of Zulu nation	**J Cape, London 1972**
Pakenham, Thomas	**THE BOER WAR** History of Anglo-Boer War	**Weidenfeld, London 1979**
Van Zyl & Grutter	**THE STORY OF SOUTH AFRICA** Good concise guide to SA history	**H & R, Cape Town 1981**
Venter, C	**THE GREAT TREK** Illustrated history of the Great Trek	**D Nelson, Cape Town 1985**

BUSINESS

De Villiers, Les	**DOING BUSINESS WITH** **SOUTHERN AFRICA**	**Business Books Intl** **New Canaan CT 1991**

GENERAL

Hawthorne, Peter	**THE TRANSPLANTED HEART** Journalists ccount of first transplant	**R McNally,New York 1968**

FURTHER READING CTD

SPORT & RECREATION

Olivier, Willie & Sandra	THE GUIIDE TO HIKING TRAILS Guide to hiking in South Africa	Southern, Pretoria 1988
Player, Gary	TO BE THE BEST Good insights in Player's South Africa	Sidgwick ,London 1991
Wynne-Jones, Aubrey	HUNTING Guide to hunting in South Africa	Southern, Pretoria1980

WILDLIFE

Cillie, B	MAMMALS OF SOUTHERN AFRICA Extensive guide for game viewers	Frandsen, Sandton 1987
Cornwallis Harris, W	WILD SPORTS OFSOUTHERN AFRICA New edition of old classic	C Struik, Cape Town 1987
Maclean, G L	ROBERTS BIRDS OF SOUTH AFRICA Comprehensive guide for bird-watchers	Bird Fund, Cape Town
Newman, K B	NEWMAN'S BIRDS OF S AFRICA Useful guide for bird-watchers	Macmillan, 1983
O'Hagen, Tim	SOUTHERN AFRICAN WILDLIFE Readers Digest guide to wildlife	Cape Town 1989
Palgrave, K C	TREES OF SOUTHERN AFRICA Guide for botanists and florists	C Struik Cape Town 1977
Vogts, M	SOUTH AFRICA'S PROTEACEAE Guide to famous indigneous flowers	C Struik Cape Town 1982

WINES

De Jongh, S J	ENCYCLOPAEDIA OF SA WINE Useful guide to wine making	McGraw Hill, Isando 1976
Hughes, David	COMPLETE BOOK OF SA WINE Comprehensive and richly illustrated	C Struik, Cape Town 1988
Hughes, David	WINE BUYER'S GUIDE Guidelines for wine buying	C Struik, Cape Town
Platter, John	SOUTH AFRICAN WINE GUIDE Useful pocket guide	Platter,Somerset West

Conservation Magazines
African Wildlife (Wildlife Society of Southern Africa)
Custos (National Parks Board)
Lammergeyer (Natal Parks Board)

KEY ADRESSES

BUS/COACH TOURS

	TELEPHONE	TELEFAX
Connex		
Johannesburg	**(011) 774 4205**	**011-23-0271**
Durban	(031) 307-3773	
Cape Town	(021) 218-2191	
Bloemfontein	(051) 47-6352	
Port Elizabeth	(041) 6-8243	
Los Angeles	**800-727-7207**	**818-507-5802**
London	**071-287-1133**	**071-287-1134**
Hylton Ross Cape Town	(021)438-1500	438-2919
Rand Coach Tours Johannesburg	(011) 339-1658	403-1383
Sealink Cape Town	(021) 25-4480	419-7072
Springbok Atlas		
Johannesburg	(011) 493-3780	493-3770
Durban	(031) 304-7938	305-6470
Cape Town	(021) 417-6545	47-3835

CAR RENTAL

Associated Car Rental		
323 Voortrekker Road Goodwood 7460	(021)591-8228	(021)591-5270
88 Beit Street Doornfontein Johannesburg2020	(011) 402-0733	(011) 402-0757
Adelphi Rent-A-Car 94 Main Road Sea Point 8001	(021) 439-6144	(021) 439-5093
Avis		
Head Office P O Box 221 Isando 1600	(011) 974-2571	(011) 974-1030
Toll-Free Reservations Domestic	0809-41-3333	
Toll-Free Reservations International	0800-03-4444	
Avis Chauffeur Drive		
P O Box 1233 Parklands Johannesburg 2121	788-5435	(011) 788-5489
P O Box 64 Constantia Cape Town 7848	689-5971	(011) 689-2144
Budget		
Head Office P O Box 1777 Kempton Park 1620	(011) 392-3907	(011) 392-3-15
Toll-Free Reservations	080 001-6622	
Cape Car Hire 240 Main Rd Diep River Cape Town 7945	(021) 72-5354	(021) 72-0383
Dolphin Car Hire 114 Main Rd Sea Point Cape Town 8001	(021) 439-9696/7	(021) 439-9697
Ed's Car Hire 23 Buitensingel St Cape Town 8001	(021) 23-6924	(021) 23-6609
Europcar		
P O Box 16736 Johannesburg 2000	(011) 402-6328	(011) 404-1808
371 Main Rd Cape Town 8001	(021) 439-1144	(021) 439-4031
20 Hunter Street Durban 4001	(031) 368-3572/5	(031) 368-3511
Goodwood Car Rental 11 Voortrekker Rd Goodwood 7460	(021) 591-0155	(021) 591-0597
Holiday Car Rental 17 Prince St Cape Town 8001	(021) 45-3229	(021) 45-3229
Imperial		
Head Office P O Box 260177 Excom Johannesburg 2023	(011) 337-4380	(011) 29-8054
Reservations Toll Free	0800—110157	
Key Car Rental Head Office P O Box 585 Pinetown Durban 3600	(031) 72-7202	(031) 701-5880
Panther Car Hire 45 Main Road Sea Point Cape Town 8001	(021) 439-3177	(021) 439-6309
Pride Car Hire 371 Main Rd Sea Point Cape Town 8001	(021) 439-1144	(021) 439-4031
Rolls Royce Hiring P O Box 464 Cape Town 7848	(021) 794-3932	(021) 794-7218
Royal Car Rental P O Box 261148 Excom Johannesburg 2023	(011) 331-8411	(011) 331-3680
Supermove Car Hire P O Box 444 Parow 7500	(021) 592-1684	(021) 591-8371
Swift Car Hire Jan Smuts Airport Johannesburg	(011) 397-1787	
Tempest Car Hire 55 West St Kempton Park Johannesburg 620	(011) 394-5510	(011) 975-0024
Thrifty Rent-A-Car Newton & Spanner Johannesburg 394-4418	(011) 970-2780	

CAMPERS/MOTORHOMES (RV)

Campers Corner P O Box 48191 Roosevelt Park Jhb 2129	(011) 789-2327	(011) 787-6900
Capricorn Campers P O Box 1530 Somerset West 7130	(024) 55-2331	(024) 55-4062
CI Leisure Rentals P O Box 137 Pinetown Durban 3600	(031) 701-2203	(031) 701-2200
Knysna Camper Hire P O Box 1222 Knysna 6570	(0445) 22-444	(0445) 82-5887
Leisuremobiles P O Box 3722 Johannesburg 2000	(011) 888-1562	(011) 888-1794

CITY PUBLICITY ASSOCIATIONS

Bloemfontein Publicity Association Box 639	(051) 405-8490
Cape Town CAPTOUR	(021) 25-3320
Durban Publicity Association Church Square	(031) 304-4934
Johannesburg Publicity Association 84 President	(011) 29-4961
Kimberley Tourist Information City Hall	(0531) 80-6264
Port Elizabeth Publicity Association Market Square	(041) 52-1315
Pretoria Information Bureau Munitoria	(012) 21-2461

HOTELS
(See STAYING IN STYLE - Page 179)

RESTAURANTS
(See DINING AND WINING - Page 213)

SOUTH AFRICAN AIRWAYS

South Africa Rotunda Air Terminal Johannesburg	(011) 774-4197
Argentina 794 Avenida Sante Fe Buenos Aires	311-8184/5/6
Botswana Old Lobatsi Rd Gaborone	(0192) 37-2397
Belgium Rue Ravenstein 601000 Brussels	(02512) 313617
Brazil Av Rio Branco 245 Rio de Janeiro	262-6002
Denmark Vesterbragade 6C1620 Copenhagen	01.14 30 31
France 12 Rue de la PaisParis	(1) 42.61.57.87
Germany Bleicherstrasse 60-626000 Frankfurt 1	069-960-2253
Greece 12-14 Karageorgi Servias St Athens	
Hong Kong 702 New World Office Salisbury RdKowloon	3-722-5768
Israel 1 Ben Yehuda St Tel Aviv	65-1844
Italy Via Barberini 2900187 Rome	(06) 601-864
Ivory Coast Immeuble Alpha 2000Abidjan DI BP 1528	33-2952
Japan Akasaka 1-1-2 Mato Akasaka Mianto-Ku, Tokyo	(03) 470-1901
Malawi Victoria Ave Blantyre	76-0311
Mozambique Fonte Azul Praca 25 De Junho Maputo	3-3730
Namibia List Bldg Kaiser Muller St Windhoek	61-298-2386
Portugal Rua Joaqium Antonio De Aqutar1000 Lisbon	536 102/7
Spain Gran Via de Los 634 Barcelona	
Switzerland Talacker 218001 Zurich	(01) 211-51-30
Taiwan Bank Towers 205 Tun Hua North Rd Taipei 10692	(02) 713-6363
United Kingdom 251/259 Regent St Oxford CircusLondon	01.437-9624
United States 900 Third AvenueNew York NY 10022	800-722-4768
Zimbabwe Lintas House Salisbury Township Harare	73-8922/9

SOUTH AFRICAN TOURISM BOARD (SATOUR)

Head Office Private Bag X164 Pretoria 0001	(012) 347-0600	(012) 45-4768
Austria Stefan-Zweig-Platz 11A-1170 Vienna	(222) 4704 5110	(222)47045114
France 98 Avenue de Villiers 75017 Paris France	(1) 4227-4020	(1) 4267-8015

SATOUR CTD

Germany Postfach 101940 Frankfurt 6000	(69) 2-0656	(69) 28-0950
Israel 14th Floor, Century Towers PO Box 3388, Tel Aviv	(3) 527-2950	(3) 527-1958
Italy Via M. Gonzaga 3 Milan 20123	(2) 869-3847	(2) 869-3508
Japan 2 Moto Akasaka Minato-ku Tokyo 107	(3) 3 478 7601	(3) 3 478 7605
Netherlands 7E Locatellkade 1 1076 AZ Amsterdam	(20) 664 6201	(20) 662 9761
Switzerland Seestrasse 42 CH 8802 Kilchberg Zurich	(1) 715 1815	(1) 715 1889
Taiwan Bank Tower Building 205 Ilm Hau North Road Taipei	(2) 717 4238	(2) 717 1146
United Kingdom No 5 & 6 Alt Grove London SW19 4DZ	(81) 944 6646	(81) 944 6705
USA 747 Third Avenue, 20th Floor New York, N.Y. 10017	(212) 838 8841	(212) 826 6928
USA 9841 Airport Blvd Suite 1524 Los Angeles CA 90045	(213) 6418444	(213) 641 5812
Zimbabwe Mercury House P O Box 1343 Harare	(4) 70 7766/7	(4) 70 7767

SOUTH AFRICAN DIPLOMATIC MISSIONS

Argentina 1058 *Buenos Aires* Ave Marcelo T. de Alvear	(1) 311-8991	(1) 111475
Australia *Sydney* N.S.W. 2001 (Consulate) 8 Light House	(2) 233-8188	(2) 23-16851
Austria *Vienna* A 1190 Sandgasse 33	(222) 32-6493	(222)32-7584
Belgium 1040 *Brussels* Rue de la Loi 26	(2) 230-68-45	(2)2301336
Bolivia *La Paz* Calle 22 7810 Calacoto	79-2101	SALEC BV 327U
Brazil 22270 *Rio de Janeiro* Rua Volutarios da Patria	(21) 266-6246	(21)2862649
Canada *Ottawa* KIM IM8 I5 Sussex Drive	(613) 744-0330	(613)7448287
Montreal H3B 4S3 Quebec Suite 2615 I Place Ville Marie	(514) 878-9217	(514)8783973
Toronto MSX IE3 Ontario Exchange Tower Suite 2515	(416) 364-0314	(416)3638974
Chile *Santiago* Philips 16-Piso 3°	(2) 33-6394	Tx: 340676
China (Republic) *Taipei* Bank Tower Tun Hwa	(2) 715-3250/4	(2)7123214
Denmark DK-1011 *Copenhagen* Montergade 1	(1) 14-6644	(1) 93-5017
Finland 00160 *Helsinki* 16 Rahapajankatu	(0) 65-8288	(0) 65-5884
France 75007 *Paris* 59 Quai d'Orsay	(1) 4555-9237	(1)4551-8812
Germany 5300 *Bonn* Auf der Hostert 3	(228) 82010	(228) 352579
Hamburg 2000 13 Harvestchuderweg 37	(40) 41-2961	(40) 4106901
Munich D-8000 2 Sendlinger-Tor-Platz 5	(89) 2605081	(89)2603459
Frankfurt am Main 6000 I 37-39 Ulmenstrasse	(69) 723741	(69)7241099
Greece *Athens* 115-26 124 Kifissias Avenue & Latridou St	(1) 6922-125	(1)6930572
Hong Kong Sunning Plaza 10 Hysan Ave.Causeway Bay	(5) 773279	(5)8904137
Israel *Tel Aviv* 64734 Yakhin House 2 Kaplin Street	(3) 25-6147	(3)265532
Italy 00198 *Rome* Via Tanaro 14	(6) 844 3246,	(6)8443408
Milan 20121 Vicolo San Giovanni Sul Muro 8	(2) 809036	(2)866402
Japan *Tokyo* 102 414 7-9 Hirakawa-cho 2-ch Chiyoda-ku	(3)265-3366	(3)2376458
Malawi *Lilongwe* 3 (Embassy) Mpico Building City Centre	730-888	734-205
Monaco *Monte Carlo* Palais Armida I Boulevard de Suisse	(93) 30-8244	
Netherlands *The Hague* Wassenaarseweg 40	92-45-01	70-458226
Norway *Oslo* Myrveien 2 1342	(2) 535816	(2)590890
Paraguay *Asuncion* (Embassy) Casilla de Correo 1832	(21) 44-331	(21)445768
Portugal *Lisbon* Avenida Luis Bivar 10 1097	(1) 53-5713	(1)545216
Spain *Madrid* 6 (Embassy) Edificio Lista Calle de Claudio	1) 227-3153	(1)593-1384
Barcelona Gran Via de les Corts Catalanes 634-6°C	(3) 318-0797	
Sweden 115 23 *Stockholm* Linnegatan 76	(8) 24-3950	(8) 607136
Switzerland *Berne* 3005 I Jungfraustrasse (31) 44-20-11	(31)4442064	
Geneva 1204 65 Rue du Rhone	(22) 35-7801	(22)357973
Zurich 3027 221 Seestrasse CH-8700	(1)19110840	
United Kingdom *London* WC 2N SDP Trafalgar Sq	(1) 930-4488	(1)8391419
Birmingham B3 2HS 135 Edmund Street	(21) 2367471	Tx:338764 SGSB
Glasgow G2 IBX 69 West George Street	(41) 221-3114	(41) 2217413
USA *Washington* DC 20008 3051 Massachusetts Ave NW	(202) 232-4400	(202) 2651607
New York NY 10016 333 East 38th Street	(212) 213-4880	(212)213-0102
Chicago IL 60611 200 South Michigan Avenue	(312) 939-7929	(312) 9397481
Beverley Hills CA 90211 50 North La Cienega Boulevard	(213) 657-9200	(213) 6579215
Houston TX 77056 1980 Post Oak Boulevard	(713) 850-0150	(713) 8508738
Uruguay *Montevideo* Edificio Artigas Casilla de Correo	961-209	2962319
Zimbabwe *Harare* Temple Bar House Baker Avenue	70-7901/6	703559

SOUTH AFRICAN WINE AGENTS ABROAD

Gift packs up to 12 bottles to various parts of the world:

KWV Gift International 643 Grand Parade Cape Town	(021) 461-5969	(021) 461-0100
SFW International Division Box 46 Stellenbosch 7600	(02231) 73400	
Gilbeys Deeds Marketing Box 137 Stellenbosc 7600		
Bergkelder Gift Service Box 184 Stellenbosch 7600	(02231) 73480	

Wine Agents Abroad:

Austria

KWV Scaffer & Co Keplerstrasse 114 Graz 8020	(0316) 915660	(0316)91135090
Bergkelder Mounier & Co Scheringgasse 4 Vienna 1140	(0222) 975553	(0222)971634

Belgium

KWV Galtraco Lange Nieustraat 31/1 Antwerp 2000	(03)2260251	(03)2252678
SFW Dierckxsens Van Luppenstraat 24 Antwerp 2018	(03)2305444	(03)2186434
Gilbeys De Leeuw 685 Ninove Steenweg Brussels 1080	(02)5226888	
Union Wine Vlaamse Kaai 11, B-2000 Antwerp	(032)162910	(032)376026

France

KWV Fingrapp 19 Rue d'Enfer Roye-Sur-Matz 60310	(0444) 25233	(0444) 26703
SFW William Pitters Rue Banlin Lormont 33310	6405005	6868401
Bergkelder Jutexim 176 Jean-Jaures Pavillons-Sous-Bois	(01)48487563	

Germany

KWV - Eggers & Franke Toferbohmstrasse 8 Bremen 1	(0421)3053110	
SFW Weinwelt Mack & Schule Neuenstrasse 45 Owen/Teck	(07021) 570134	(07021) 83243
Bergkelder VC Schlumberger KG Postfach 1128 Meckenheim	(02225) 88090	(02225) 880951
Union Wine HM Witt & Co Heerenstrasse 7 Bremen 33	(0421) 253641	(0421) 253642

Hong Kong

KWV Sims Trading Co 1-11 Au Piu Wan St Shatin		
SFW Techorient 90 Sung Wong Toi Rd Kowloon	3657019	3631437

Israel

KWV Beit Hamashke 3 Beit Hapoalim St Rehovot	(09972)8469257	(09972)8470333

Netherlands

KWV Wijn Expeditiekantoor Nieuwstraat 3 Heesch 5384	(04125) 4141	
SFW & Union Wine Lenselink Loswal 2A Hilversum	(035) 42952	(035) 233078
Bergkelder Kaapkelder Hoofstraat 140 Apeldoorn	(055) 215389	(055) 219850
Gilbeys VanderPlas Import Hollands End 79 Ankeveen	(035) 64076	

Japan

KWV Kokubu & Co1-1 Nihonbashi Chuo-Ku Tokyo	(03) 2764141	
SFW Royal Liquor 8-16 Hiroo 5 Chome Shibuya-Ku Tokyo	(03) 4400621	(03) 4465628
Union Wine 203 Matsuishi Bldg Hiroo Shibuya-ku Tokyo	(033) 4405501	(033) 4405502

Taiwan

KWV Gummy Corp 199 Chung King North Rd Taipei	(02) 7310618	
Bergkelder Well Join Industry Box 67279 Taipei	(02) 7310618	

SPORT ORGANIZATIONS
(See also the chapter RESORTS AND SPORTS)

National Organizations
Archery 32 Delaware Ave Northlands Durban-North 4051
Badminton SA Union 20 Aletta Ave Isando 1610   (011) 609-6801

SPORT ORGANIZATIONS CTD

Bowling P O Box 47177 Parklands 2121	(011) 788-0005
Canoeing SA Federation Box 5 McGregor 6708	(02353) 733
Cricket SA Union Box 55009 Northlands Johannesburg 1620	
Cycling P O Box 28 Bloemfontein 9300	(051) 74685
Equestrian SA Federation Box 69414 Bryanston 2021	
Fishing SA Anglers Union 26 Douglas St Roodepoort 1725	(011) 726-5000
Fishing, Deep Sea SA Ass. Box 723 Bedfordview 2008	(011) 53-1847
Fishing, Game SA Skiboat Ass. Box 4191 Cape Town 8000	(021) 21-3611
Fishing, Rock & Surf SA Ass. 28 Silverleaf Ave Wynberg 7800	(021) 219-2629
Fishing, Trout	
Cape Nature Conservation Box 9086 Cape Town 8000	(021) 45-0227
Natal Fish Preservation Box 662 Pietermaritzburg 3200	(0331) 5-1221
Transvaal Nature Conservation Private Bag X209 Pretoria 0001	(012) 201-2361
Golf SA Golf Union Box 1537 Cape Town 8000	(021) 46-7585
Golf SA Ladies Golf Union Box 135 Vereeniging 1930	
Gliding, Hang Gliding & Hot Air Ballooning	
Aero Club of SA Box 9 Johannesburg 2000	(011) 783-8840
Hiking Federation of SA P O Box 17247 Groenkloof Pretoria 0027	(012) 46-7562
Horse Racing Jockey Club of SA Box 74439 Turfontein 2140	
Marathon SA Road Runners Ass. Box 6463 Roggebaai 8012	(021) 21-6500
Jukskei SA Board Box 297 Pretoria 0001	
Mountaineering Club of SA 97 Hatfield St Cape Town	(021) 45-3412
Rugby SA Board Box 99 Newlands 7725	
Scuba Diving SA Underwater Union Box 201 Rondebosch 7700	(021) 69-8531
Squash Rackets Ass. of SA Box 783033 Sandton 2146	(011) 883-4390
Table Tennis SA Union Box 5461 Durban 4000	
Tennis SA Union Box 2211 Johannesburg 2000	(011) 402-3580
Waterski SA Association Box 68834 Bryanston 2021	(011) 440-6421
Windsurfing SA Ass. Private Bag X16 Auckland Park 2006	(011) 726-7076
Yachting Cruising Ass. of SA Box 5036 Cape Town 8000	(021) 41-1056
Yachting SA Racing Ass 82 1st Ave Dunvegan Edenvale 1610	(011) 783-4443

WILDLIFE ORGANIZATIONS

National Parks Board	
Head Office P O Box 787 Pretoria 0001	(012) 343-1991
Southwestern Cape P O Box 7400 Roggebaai 8012	(021) 419-5365
Southern Cape P O Box 774 George 6350	(0441) 74-6924
Cape	
Nature Conservation Private Bag X9086 Cape Town 8000	(021) 210-2269
Nature Conservation Private Bag X1126 Port Elizabeth 6000	(041) 55-7388
Natal	
Natal Parks Board Box 662 Pietermaritzburg 3200	(0331) 47-1961
Wildlife Society 100 Brand Road Durban 4001	(031) 21-3126
Kwazulu Bureau of Natural Resources Ulundi 3838	(0020) Ask for 3
Orange Free State	
Nature Conservation Box 577 Bloemfontein 9300	(051) 405-5245
Transvaal	
Nature Conservation Private Bag X209 Pretoria 0001	(012) 323-3403

WINE ESTATES
(See WINE COUNTRY - Page 153)

METRIC CONVERSION

TO CHANGE	TO	MULTIPLY BY
acres	hectares	.4047
bushels (U.S.)	hectoliters	.3524
centimeters	inches	.3937
cubic feet	cubic meters	.0283
cubic meters	cubic feet	35.3145
cubic meters	cubic yards	1.3079
cubic yards	cubic meters	.7646
feet	meters	.3048
gallons (U.S.)	liters	3.7853
grains	grams	.0648
grams	grains	15.4324
hectares	acres	2.4710
hectoliters	bushels (U.S.)	2.8378
inches	millimeters	25.4000
inches	centimeters	2.5400
kilograms	pounds	2.2046
kilometers	miles	.6214
liters	gallons (U.S.)	.2642
liters	pints (dry)	1.8162
liters	pints (liquid)	2.1134
liters	quarts (dry)	.9081
liters	quarts (liquid)	1.0567
meters	feet	3.2808
meters	yards	1.0936
metric tons	tons (long)	.9842
metric tons	tons (short)	1.1023
miles	kilometers	1.6093
millimeters	inches	.0394
pints (dry)	liters	.5506
pints (liquid)	liters	.4732
pounds avdp	kilograms	.4536
square feet	square meters	.0929
square meters	square feet	10.7639
square meters	square yards	1.1960
square yards	square meters	.8361
tons (long)	metric tons	1.0160
tons (short)	metric tons	.9072
yards	meters	.9144
Celcius	Fahrenheit	x9 +5 +32°
Fahrenheit	Celcius	-32° x5 +9

Cross-Winds

 Slippery Road

 Tunnel

 Height Restriction

 Width for One Vehicle

 Unguarded Level Crossing

 Traffic Signals Ahead

 Temporary Emergency or Police Light

 Children

 School Patrol Ahead

 Pedestrians

 Pedestrians Crossing

 Cyclists

 Stop/Go Control Ahead

 Trucks Crossing

 Road Workers

 Grader at Work

 Motor Gate To Left

 Gate

 Sheep

 Wild Animals

 Horses

 Cattle

 One Track

 Two Tracks

 Three Tracks

 Cross Roads

 T-Junction

 Side Road Junction

 Staggered Junctions

 Skewed Junction

 Sharp Junction

 Road Narrows from both sides

 Road Narrows From One side

 Two-Way Traffic

 End of Dual Highway

 Dual Highway Starts

 Y-Junction

 Traffic Circle

 Gentle Curve To Right

 Sharp Curve to Right

 Hairpin Bend

 Winding Road

Steep Descent

Steep Ascent

 Jetty Edge or River Bank

Dip or Drift

Uneven Road

Loose Gravel and stoneS

Falling Rocks

239

Index

A

B

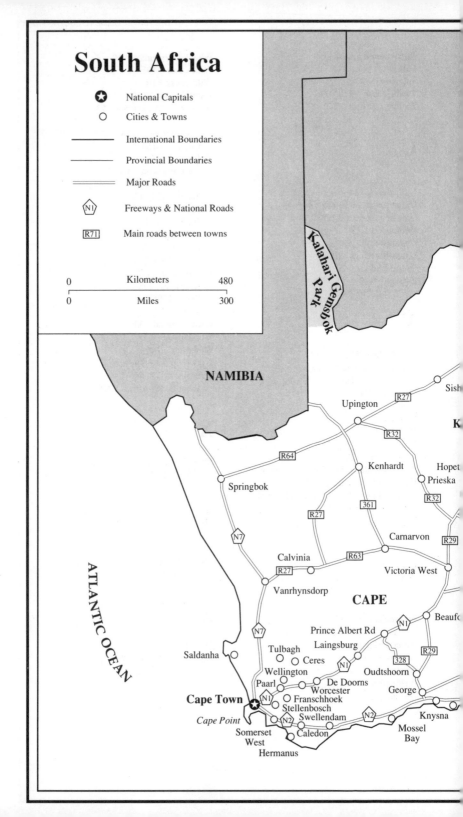

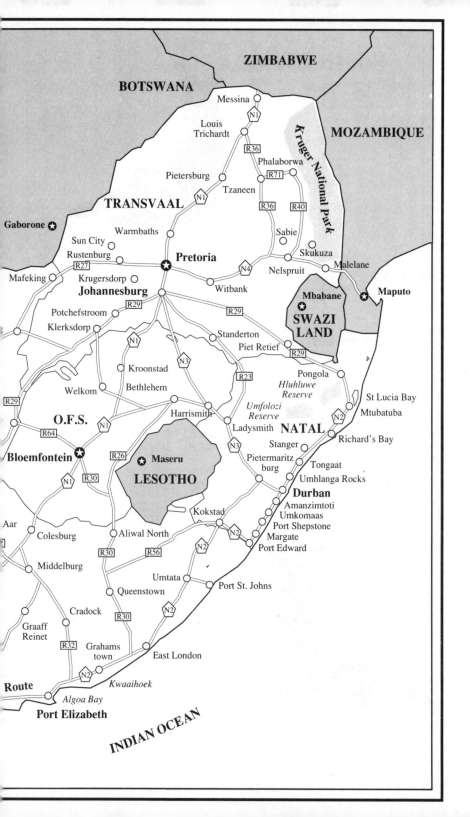

CREDITS

Illustrations on pages 153, 144, 157, 160, 161, 165, 168, 171, 180, 216 and 217 reproduced with the kind permission of Maskew Miller of Cape Town, who published THE OLD CAPE COLONY by A F Trotter.

The drawing of Sir Herbert Baker on page 139 is based on a painting in the possession of the Bank of England.

We acknowledge with thanks the courteous and efficient assistance from the South African Library in Cape Town and the Africana Library in Johannesburg. Several of our drawings are based on historic originals of paintings, water colors and sketches in their possession.

Photos: Cape Argus

Photos: Cape Argus